The Holy Trinity

The Holy Trinity

Hans Urs Von Balthasar and His Sources

Katy Leamy

☞PICKWICK *Publications* · Eugene, Oregon

THE HOLY TRINITY
Hans Urs Von Balthasar and His Sources

Pickwick Publications
An Imprint of Wipf and Stock Publishers
199 W. 8th Ave., Suite 3
Eugene, OR 97401

www.wipfandstock.com

ISBN 13: 978-1-62564-730-6

Cataloging-in-Publication data:

Leamy, Katy.

The holy trinity : Hans Urs Von Balthasar and his sources / Katy Leamy.

vi + 174 p. ; 23 cm.—Includes bibliographical references and index.

ISBN 13: 978-1-62564-730-6

1. Balthasar, Hans Urs von, 1905–1988. 2. Trinity. 3. Trinity—History of doctrines. I. Title.

BT111.3 .L42 2015

Manufactured in the U.S.A.   04/08/2015

Contents

Introduction

In "A Résumé of My Thought," Balthasar summarizes the whole of his work as an exploration of relation between infinite and finite, between God and humanity:

> The Christian response [to the question of why Yahweh, why Allah, created a world of which he did not have need in order to be God] is contained in these two fundamental dogmas: that of the Trinity and that of the Incarnation. In the Trinitarian dogma God is one, good, true, and beautiful because he is essentially Love, and Love supposes the one, the other, and their unity. And if it is necessary to suppose the Other, the Word, the Son, in God, then the otherness of the creation is not a fall, a disgrace, but an image of God, even as it is not God.[1]

Balthasar believes that the Christian response to the fundamental questions about infinite and finite being, about God and creation, cannot be correctly articulated or addressed outside of the context of relation. In the quote above, each of the transcendentals is considered, not purely as a mode of being, but as an aspect of the activity of relation. The question of creation extends the mystery of relation to the possibility of relation between infinite and finite. Ultimately, Balthasar locates the response to these questions in the triune life as it is revealed in the incarnation.

If the whole of Balthasar's thought is an exploration of the nature of infinite and finite being in terms of relation, then a thorough exploration of the notion of relation, particularly the triune relation, is essential for interpreting Balthasar's work. Vital to Balthasar's own articulation of the dogmas of the incarnation and the Trinity is the kenotic Trinitarian theology of Sergei Bulgakov. The ways in which Balthasar both incorporates and

---

1. Balthasar, "Résumé."

modifies Bulgakov's Trinitarian theology provide an insight into his over-arching theological agenda. This book points to the ways in which Sergei Bulgakov, a twentieth-century Russian Orthodox theologian, is an impor-tant resource for Balthasar, directly and indirectly influencing key doctrinal points as well as the overall shape and direction of his theological project.

To this end, I explore how Balthasar employs and adapts the thought of Sergei Bulgakov with the Trinitarian theology of Thomas Aquinas to form a kenotic Trinitarian theology that is based on the notion of person-hood as a relation of self-donating love. It is a Trinitarian theology that is descriptive of both the divine life as relation and human nature made in the image of God. The structure of this Trinitarian theology leaves a sphere for genuine human and divine freedom and agency that can be characterized as a real drama. When we look at Balthasar's Trinitarian theology in light of Bulgakov, and particularly as a re-reading of Bulgakov in light of a Thomis-tic Trinitarian theology, we are not only able to more clearly understand the implications of Balthasar's own Trinitarian theology, but also to highlight the beauty and relevance of Bulgakov's Trinitarian contribution. Finally, this reading of Balthasar's Trinitarian theology, read in light of a Thomistic adjustment of Bulgakov, provides an excellent point of integration for an ethics that takes into account not only individual virtues and perfection, but also the social/relational context of human personhood. This ethics is based in a concept of human nature bearing the *imago trinitatis*, and fulfill-ing that nature through sacramental participation and ethical extension of Christ's self-offering love.

The implications of Balthasar's particular kenotic Trinitarian theol-ogy are most clearly seen in a sacramental ethical paradigm. In his work *Symbol and Sacrament*, Louis Marie Chauvet describes the ethical life of the church as an embodied extension of her sacramental identity as the body of Christ. However, Chauvet's concern is primarily to emphasize the nature of the cross as a revelatory act of the triune God that requires a continued participatory enactment by the church in the world.[2] Chauvet points to theologians such as Balthasar and Moltmann as examples of a Trinitarian theology of the cross that "cannot be disconnected from its fulfillment *in us*. The *Logos* of the cross demands that we give a body in our selves, through a travail of morning, to the divine meontology . . . Consequently, the God

---

2. He points to Karl Barth's theology of the cross as an example of an insufficiently Trinitarian notion of God. Because of this "he is obliged to limit the Church's 'instru-mental' role: it is no more than a *passive* tool in God's hands." Chauvet, *Symbol and Sacrament*, 541.

'above us' cannot be spoken of in a Christian way except on the basis of the God 'among us.'"[3] Chauvet's point here is essential: that the Christian understanding of God must come from God's self-revelation on the cross and that this God continues to be present through the church's embodied participation in the paschal mystery through her eucharistic and ethical self offering. However, if the church's self-offering is a participation in the Son's self-offering to the Father, the practical implications and expectations for what that looks like are intimately connected to the inner-Trinitarian dynamic in the paschal event. For this reason, a sacramental ethical system is inherently directed by the particular Trinitarian theology that grounds it. Thus, we can expect rather different anthropological and ethical implications from a Moltmanian Trinitarian theology than of a Balthasarian Trinitarian theology. As we will see, a sacramental ethical theology that proceeds from Balthasar's kenotic Trinitarian theology is particularly suited to address the concerns of the poor and oppressed, or "sinned-against."

OUTLINE OF THE ARGUMENT

Chapter 1

I will first demonstrate Balthasar's dependence on Bulgakov's kenotic Trinitarian theology. Balthasar acknowledges his dependence on Bulgakov's Trinitarian theology, but rejects Bulgakov's concept of Sophia. Both of the ways in which Balthasar follows and rejects Bulgakov have major theological importance for Balthasar's Christology, Trinitarian theology, and anthropology. Bulgakov's kenotic Trinitarian theology provides the basic structure for one of the central theses in Balthasar's corpus: the paradox that suffering and glory are interchangeable when describing the act of self-abandoning love that is the divine ousia.

Bulgakov, like Balthasar, does not shy away from the claim that the passion of the Son—his suffering, his death, and descent into hell— is revelatory of the very life or essence of the triune God. Bulgakov also maintains divine impassibility as well as creaturely contingency. However, the heart of Bulgakov's theological work lies in his belief that Christ reveals the inner-triune relation in his suffering and death, as well as the extent to which tragedy and suffering can be taken up and transformed in the communion of self-offering love. Thus, there is no creaturely reality that is not

3. Ibid., 534.

beckoned by its very essence into the perichoretic joy of God's life as God's self-revelation to the creature in the creature. The Son has rendered death into eternal life by "trampling down death by death," and the destiny of the cosmos to become the new creation is already visible and transformative.

However, Balthasar also has a major concern with Bulgakov's theology; he believes that Bulgakov's sophianic setting of this Trinitarian theology fundamentally distorts the Creator/creature relation. Bulgakov's sophiological paradigm arises from the need to posit both a distance as well as unity between God and creation. Bulgakov seeks to do this in a distinctly Trinitarian manner. One of the major influences on this project is Bulgakov's reading of Thomas Aquinas. In his interpretation of Aquinas it is not the triune persons who are the basis for unity and distinction between Creator and creatures, but rather an artificial distinction between the powers of the divine nature. Bulgakov sees this distinction as the basis for many of the errors in Western theology, and posits Sophia—or the living but non-hypostatic, kenotic love between the divine persons—as the basis for unity and difference between God and creation. Sophia allows Bulgakov to base the unity and difference in the relation of kenotic love hypostatized by the triune persons and extended in Christ to creation.

As we look at how Balthasar adopts and adapts Bulgakov's theology, we will see how his agenda is shaped by this fundamental premise—that questions about God and creation, unity and difference, are ultimately questions about persons in relation. Balthasar follows Bulgakov saying that: If Christ is to be a genuine revelation of both God and humanity, and enable human participation in the divine relation, then human beings and all of creation must be genuinely distinct from God. If humanity is to partake of the good that is the transformation of death into life, human beings and God must have an analogous freedom, an analogous "personhood," that makes relation and thus participation possible. However, as we will see in chapter two, the sophianic setting of Bulgakov's Trinitarian thesis at times obscures the relational "distance" between God and creation that Balthasar wishes to preserve.

Chapter 2

In the second chapter I focus on the Trinitarian theology of Thomas Aquinas which allows Balthasar to employ and interpret Bulgakov's Trinitarian theology apart from sophiology. Thomas provides Balthasar with a way to describe both the transcendence and immanence of God vis-á vis creation with the concept of relation and the opposition of relation.[4] This gives him a definition of personhood that contains within it both perfect unity and infinite difference based upon the very activity of kenosis. Human personhood is an analogous relation based in participation in the activity that constitutes the divine persons. Balthasar is able to separate Bulgakov's Trinitarian theology from its sophiological context using the concepts of personhood as relation and analogy enabling participation. Balthasar's decision to do so reveals a deep concern for both divine and human freedom in the economy of salvation, a consequence which is particularly evident with his theology of the descent into hell.

Chapter 3

In chapter 3 I show how Balthasar brings together the Trinitarian theologies of Bulgakov and Aquinas with the thesis that absolute love as it is enacted in the eternal triune relation of self-offering *is* the divine essence.[5] Balthasar believes that Sophia compromises the very thing that makes it possible to say that suffering = glory = ousia, namely the absolute kenotic abandonment of the persons constituting the relation that is the divine essence. Thomas's Trinitarian theology, where the divine essence is relation, serves as a corrective foundation for Bulgakov's insight. With this Trinitarian theology, Balthasar is able to exegete the paschal mystery in such a way that Christ's suffering, death, and descent into hell are a revelation of the immanent triune life. However, Balthasar is able to do this without slipping into the theologically and anthropologically dangerous claims, either that Christ's suffering is constitutive of the divine life (in a Moltmanian sense), or (as Moltmann describes Barth's theology of the cross) that a "'trans-Christological reserve' in the last analysis [allows him] to avoid a total identification of the hidden God with the revealed God."[6] Instead,

---

4. Though Balthasar himself does not consistently articulate his notion of participation and analogy in Thomistic terms, it is clear that he is informed by Thomas on these points. See *Final Act*, 60–65, 305, 386–89.

5. "'Love is thus more comprehensive than being itself; it is the "transcendental" par excellence that comprehends the reality of being, of truth, and of goodness'" (*Truth of God*, 176–77 quoting Siewerth, *Metaphysik der Kindheit*, 63).

6. Chauvet, *Symbol and Sacrament*, 541.

Balthasar claims that the depths of the self-abandoning love that eternally constitutes the divine essence as relation.

Chapter 4

The proving ground for Balthasar's Trinitarian claim, that the relation that constitutes the divine life is kenotic love, lies in his theology of Christ's descent into hell. For this reason it is essential on this point to understand how Balthasar adopts and adapts Bulgakov's Trinitarian theology in order to fully grasp the meaning and implications of Balthasar's theology of the descent. At the beginning of his work *Mysterium Paschale*, Balthasar introduces Bulgakov's Trinitarian theology as the starting point for his theology of the descent into hell. This chapter will examine the ways in which Balthasar's theology both depends upon and differs from Bulgakov's with respect to Christology and the descent into hell. Two important differences arise: First, the nature of both divine and human personhood. Second, the nature of human freedom and sin, including what is necessary to overcome it. In particular, this comparison reveals the importance, for Balthasar, of Christ assuming the reality of human sin, both individual and social. By bracketing Sophia, Balthasar is able to retain a space for genuine human freedom and all of its consequences.

Balthasar sees Christ's descent into hell as a Trinitarian act, a revelation of the eternal immanent kenosis that constitutes the divine relation. Both Bulgakov's and Balthasar's kenotic Trinitarian theologies get played out in the descent. Here we see how the descent is a revelation of the immanent triune life and a recapitulation of human nature, the event in which every creaturely "No" to God is taken up within the Son's "Yes" to the Father. Balthasar's bracketing of Sophia shows his concern for a genuine human agency characterized by participation. It also reveals the nature of divine goodness and the telos of human beings as a creaturely participation in that good. A comparison of Bulgakov and Balthasar on this subject adds to the conversation by, first, showing how completely Balthasar's notion of freedom—creaturely or divine—flows from the inner triune life. We must understand personhood and freedom primarily through God's self-revelation in Christ. Through this lens human freedom is revealed to be a participation in the absolute obedience and surrender that constitutes the Son's relation to the Father. This is the starting point for the sacramental ethics that I will discuss in the final chapter.

Chapter 5

In the fifth chapter I begin to apply Balthasar's Trinitarian theology as the basis for a sacramental ethics. This is not an arbitrary application, but rather the natural extension of Balthasar's Trinitarian theology where Christ reveals both divinity and humanity in his self-offering to the Father, and that human personhood is founded and perfected by participation in the kenotic love that constitutes divine relation. However, my appropriation of Balthasar entails an appropriation of his sources as well. To clarify concepts like suffering as glory, or participation, I need to refer back to some of Balthasar's own sources, Bulgakov and Aquinas. Throughout this chapter I integrate the perspectives of these theologians in order to establish a Trinitarian basis for a sacramental ethic that entails solidarity with the most vulnerable in society as part of the human telos as persons in relation.

To this end I ask the question: How do humans participate in the suffering that is glory? I address the issue of why this concept of the divine life and human participation in it is vital for both individual and social virtue. If Christ's self-offering on the cross is taken to be revelatory of the divine life *ad intra*, then in some way this must also be revelatory of the good as the criterion of flourishing for human nature. Both personal and social human flourishing must be evaluated in light of the fact that God's glory and power are revealed in the suffering and helplessness of the Son. The events of Christ's passion, however, are not only a revelation of what personhood entails, they are the ongoing basis for human participation in the relation of the divine life. I argue that for a form of ethical reflection that flows from sacramental participation in the triune life as an appropriation through our own enactment of Christ's sacrifice of the relation that is the triune life. This vision of the good for human life provides a way for addressing concrete suffering and evil in history. It requires an "incorporation" into Christ's sacrifice through sacramental participation and the appropriation of the sacramental identity through self-offering in concrete actions.

Sergei Bulgakov's Trinitarian theology is a central component of Balthasar's Trinitarian theology, which is vital to his entire theological project. Therefore, a comparison of the two authors is very important for Balthasar scholarship as a whole. In my conclusion I will revisit some of the insights such a comparison can provide for understanding both Balthasar's theology and his overall project; in particular, how the notion of persons and relations informs the relationship between kenotic Trinitarian theology, Christology, and divine and human freedom. The act that constitutes divine personhood is an eternal act of self-emptying love in relation. This act is perfectly revealed in Christ with his self-offering in the paschal event, and is appropriated by human persons to the degree that they participate in the same act of self-offering to God and one another. Christ's self-offering redefines our notion of "the good" for human nature as a relation of kenotic love where suffering and helplessness are transformed into glory and freedom. As we unpack these connections it becomes clear that Balthasar employs Bulgakov's insight in what is, arguably, the central doctrine for his theological project. Both similarities and differences provide vital insights into Balthasar's theology of the divine life, human freedom, and salvation history.

Why does this matter? I spend the majority of this dissertation arguing that Balthasar relies on both Bulgakov and Thomas Aquinas to shape his Trinitarian theology. This matters because Balthasar's work is thoroughly, inextricably Trinitarian. The thesis that Balthasar appropriates from Bulgakov, that the kenotic relation of love is the divine essence and that Christ's suffering and death reveals the immanent triune life, is, I would argue, central to his entire corpus. However, I cannot provide a detailed commentary on all of Balthasar's work in this dissertation. What I do provide is an analysis of Balthasar's theology of the descent into hell in light of my thesis about his dependence upon Aquinas and Bulgakov that clarifies how the descent relates to his Trinitarian theology as well as anthropology.

I think the payoff comes when we evaluate the notion of "the good" that arises from Balthasar's Trinitarian theology and explore the implications and mechanisms for concrete human interaction that come out of it. I would argue that Balthasar's theology is generally an underutilized resource for more practical studies like liberation theology or medical ethics. This Trinitarian theology isn't just a kind of moral model for imitation. Balthasar's Trinitarian theology asserts that God is a relation of self-abandoning love and that God has made himself available to us through our own nature as persons and our own ability to offer ourselves, to participate in Christ's self-offering to the Father through our own self-offering in love. What is more, this is the very good that constitutes human happiness. Self-abandoning love is not just the activity that constitutes the divine nature as relation. This self-offering is the proper activity for human nature as well. As we appropriate Christ's own self-offering in love, we partake of the "adoption of Sons" that is our share in the life of God, and in that activity is a joy that transforms suffering, fostering a power in helplessness, a wisdom in not knowing, riches in poverty, and eternal life in death.

The practical import of Christ's self-offering that makes brothers and sisters out of torturers and the oppressed is the possibility, or rather necessity, that we can experience our humanity as only in offering ourselves in and with the Son. There is a great need for this kind of theological anthropology that understands solidarity, not as a supererogatory act, but as the very fulfillment of our human nature. This organic connection between human happiness and solidarity is necessary when

> We see that notions of the common good become fragmented and a new subjectivity emerges, all too universal, of persons defining their communities' teachings not according to the traditions but according to their insulating imaginations. For this reason the call to solidarity and the promotion of justice is extraordinarily urgent today.[7]

This is the theological foundation for the social principle of solidarity, of seeing myself as Christ's sister, and seeing my sister in the marginalized and oppressed.

The Trinitarian theology that Balthasar develops by appropriating Bulgakov in a Thomistic light is able to form the organic connection between self-offering and self-fulfillment by positing human personhood as an image of the divine personhood where a total self-abandonment to the other constitutes the divine unity and eternal joy. Thus, a deeper insight into the sources of Balthasar's Trinitarian theology and its implications for his work is not only useful for Balthasar scholarship, but can serve as a resource for understanding ourselves as human persons and our path to fulfillment.

7. Keenan, "Impasse and Solidarity."

1

How Do You Solve a Problem like Sophia?

INTRODUCTION

At several key junctures Balthasar turns to "Bulgakov's Trinitarian insight" to set up theological trajectories (the descent into hell) as well as resolve theological dilemmas (divine impassibility and immanent kenosis). This chapter will give an overview of Bulgakov's theology with respect to both his "Trinitarian insight" as well as his complicated system of "sophiology." My thesis is that Bulgakov's sophiology is a function of his Trinitarian theology. Sophia allows Bulgakov to maintain divine impassibility and simplicity while positing the most intimate relation between the triune life and the Trinitarian foundation of creation.

In order to understand why Balthasar decides to place one of Bulgakov's central theses at the heart of his own theology, while simultaneously dismissing his overall system, we need to take a closer look at the way that Bulgakov's sophiology and Trinitarian theology are related. This chapter will focus on the overall background and structure of Bulgakov's Trinitarian theology in relation to his sophiology, which sets up a discussion of Balthasar's appropriation and adjustment of Bulgakov via Aquinas in the following chapter. This chapter will proceed as follows: 1) I will first glance at three important sources for Bulgakov: the Russian sophiological tradition, nineteenth- and twentieth-century kenotic theology, and Thomas Aquinas. Although the first two provide much of the overall content and structure for his thought, it is Bulgakov's interaction with Thomas Aquinas that I will focus on here. Within Bulgakov's objections to Aquinas we find the *raison d'être* for a sophiological rendering of Trinitarian theology. Furthermore, Aquinas is a consistent dialogue partner in Balthasar's appropriation of Bulgakov, and so a detailed understanding of how Bulgakov situates himself with respect to Aquinas is essential for my overall project. 2) In the second section of this chapter I present Bulgakov's Trinitarian insight. For Bulgakov, the divine life is a relation of kenotic love.[1] This love is a kind of suffering or pathos which itself constitutes relationality. Further, the triune relation is eternal and simple, and the one relation that is the divine life constitutes the three divine persons in their uniqueness. 3) Next, before turning to Bulgakov's sophiology as it functions in specific contexts I will review four theological theses that Bulgakov thinks are not adequately addressed in a Thomistic paradigm. Bulgakov believes that only a sophiological reading of the three doctrines I cover in section four can adequately conform to these four theses. 4) Accordingly, in the fourth section of this chapter I provide a summary of Bulgakov's sophiological rendering of three key doctrines. First, I look at Bulgakov's Trinitarian theology, both the idea of the kenosis of the persons as well as the relationship of the persons to Sophia in her divine and creaturely aspects. Second, I focus on Bulgakov's idea of the "eternal humanity" of the Son as the paradigm for the relationship between God and creation, as well as the basis for the incarnation. In turn, the eternal humanity of the Son sets up a third dimension of sophiology, namely, the relationship between humanity and the church, or salvation history.

The conclusion of this chapter points to the fact that, for Bulgakov, it is the Trinity, not Sophia, which is the theological focal point of his theology. Sophia cannot be the central figure in his thought because she is always the revelation or communication between persons. She is the life of the persons themselves engaged in the act of communication. Sophia is the manifestation of the triune life, or the glory of God, which constitutes the foundation of creaturely being as an image of the triune relation.

1. Bulgakov maintains that the divine nature or substance *is* the activity of absolute kenosis, or self-donation to an "other," an activity that implies both identity and difference. The term "relation" provides the necessary flexibility to refer both to what is one in God as well as the three divine persons. I continue to develop the implications of this term in the first two chapters.

BACKGROUND

The Intersection of Russian Sophiology with the Kenotic Theology Movements

Bulgakov's sophiology remained a work in progress throughout his life. His intellectual evolution from naïve Christianity to Marxism, and then from a philosophical theism to Russian Orthodoxy was accompanied by an evolving notion of the traditional Russian concept of Sophia, the wisdom of God. Near the end of his life Bulgakov was accused of heresy. Some believed his sophiology had taken priority over and distorted the traditional teachings of the church. In his work *Sophia, The Wisdom of God* Bulgakov presents the most mature account of his sophiology as a response to these accusations. In his introduction to this work, Bulgakov offers a historical background to Russian sophiology, which, although it is not the most thorough account of the sophiological tradition, does highlight the particular figures and ideas within the tradition who influenced his own understanding of Sophia.[2]

Bulgakov explains that the Russian preoccupation with Sophia can be traced back to the origin of Christianity in Russia. When emissaries were sent out by Prince Vladimir of Kiev in 989 to investigate various religions, it was the liturgical expression of worship in the Cathedral of Sophia in Constantinople that captured the Russian religious imagination. The report of the emissaries that "We did not know whether we were on heaven or on earth" is an apt expression of the Russian sophiological impulse.[3] Sophia is the presence of God on earth, in the world, through the cosmos. She is the gathered-togetherness, or *sobernost*, of all things that is the expression of divinity, or in some strands of the tradition, is divinity itself.[4] In particular,

2. In 1935 the Moscow Patriarchy and the Church in Exile based in Yugoslavia censured Bulgakov for making of Sophia a "fourth hypostasis" in God. He was later cleared of the charges of heresy. Nichols, *Wisdom from Above*, 9.

3. Bulgakov describes the cathedral enthusiastically in the following quote from his "Autobiographical Notes" in *Sophia*, xiv, 1–4. "Truly, the temple of St. Sophia is the artistic, tangible proof and manifestation of St. Sophia—of the sophianic nature of the world and the cosmic nature of Sophia. It is neither heaven nor earth, but the vault of heaven above the earth. We perceive here neither God nor man, but divinity, the divine veil thrown over the world. How true was our ancestors' feeling in this temple, how right they were in saying they did not know whether they were in heaven or on earth! Indeed, they were neither in heaven nor on earth, they were in St. Sophia—between the two."

4. A footnote by the translator, Boris Jakim, defines *sobernost*: "Derived from the Russian *sobirat*, 'to gather,' and related to *sobor*, 'council,' it is usually used to describe the

Bulgakov highlights three facets of the sophiological tradition that feature prominently in his work: first, the unity of humanity as an image of something divine or eternal; second, the unity of humanity with the cosmos as a whole; and third, the whole of creation as both a revelation of God and the presence of God in and for a contingent other. Bulgakov believes that these three concepts as expressed sophiologically not only give a Russian cultural application to Christianity, but in fact are presented in scripture, at times assumed by the church fathers, and are the precise concepts necessary to resolve many modern theological dilemmas. He goes further and comments, not only is sophiology a theoretical resolution to theological problems, it gives a practical basis for the "theandric" activity that is the mission of the church, the conversion of the world to Christ in whom we "live and move and have our being."

Bulgakov's adoption of these particular emphases within sophiology, and the conclusion that Christ is the source and goal of all creation can primarily be traced to the influence of Vladimir Soloviev (1853–1900). Bulgakov gives Soloviev the title of the "first Russian sophiologist,"[5] and adds

---

divinely inspired fellowship of believers in the church, their 'catholicity.' Here, Bulgakov extends this concept to the entire universe." Bulgakov, *Lamb of God*, 104. Although Jakim here is describing the creaturely *sobernost*, this presupposes and implies a *sobernost* that exists within the divine life. The creaturely *sobernost* is a participation in the divine *sobernost*. The idea of all humanity or *sobernost* is a vital component of Russian spiritual life, and it is this idea that is at work here. Nicholl, in *The Triumphs of the Spirit in Russia*, 165, explains *sobernost* in terms of liturgical experience: It "refers to the feeling one experiences in the cathedral, or the church, when the Liturgy brings all the worshippers into a common unity so that each of them feels to belong to everyone else there and to the organic whole that they form." This book is a general introduction to the spiritual culture informing the major twentieth-century Russian theologians.

5. Ibid., 9. Bulgakov does not embrace Soloviev uncritically. He cautions that within Soloviev's work "we can detect elements derived from the ancient Gnostic systems, together with the obvious influence of Western sophiology in the writings of Boehme and others. All this is further complicated by his own poetic mysticism." Nevertheless, the critical achievement in Soloviev's system is a pivotal influence for Bulgakov. Balthasar, too, sees in Soloviev a helpful appropriation of German idealism that "in place of the Protestant 'dialectic,' which relentlessly transcends all things to find its term in the absolute Spirit, the basic conceptual model in Soloviev's thought is the catholic '*integration*' of all partial points of view and forms of actualization into an organic totality that annuls and uplifts all things in a manner that preserves that which is transcended far more successfully than in Hegel" (Balthasar, *Studies in Theological Style: Lay Styles*, 283–84). For Soloviev, the resurrection of the body—achieved by the Son's *kenotic* triumph on the cross—is the term of progress. The result of kenosis is reintegration or reunion that retains the integrity of the cosmos. "In Christianity, Plato's ideal world is transformed into the living, active Kingdom of God, which does not operate 'over against' the material

"I regard Soloviev as having been my philosophical 'guide to Christ.'"[6] The central point in Soloviev that both Bulgakov and Balthasar develop is that

> In God's *kenosis* (which perfects the whole process of creation by transcending it from within), human *kenosis* is freely given space in God so that the human consciousness may give itself over absolutely to the divine. In this act, man is freed from all sinful isolation for him who is total unity . . . This twofold kenosis is the essence of the person of the God-Man no less than of his work, his death on the cross, and it is at the same time absolute glory in twofold form—the self-glorification of God in his creation as much as the glorification in God of the whole man, the man who, in the voluntary death of love, is victorious over all the disastrous contingencies of the material world and so has achieved for himself and for all humanity and the cosmos the resurrection of the body.[7]

The identification of kenosis, glory, and the nature of God is central for Bulgakov (and Balthasar). Bulgakov develops Soloviev's thesis in a Trinitarian framework as an interpretive lens for the Christian tradition. Sophia—as kenosis/glory that is both the divine nature as well as the foundation and end for the cosmos—enables him to hold together Greek metaphysical principles and German idealism to re-interpret traditional Christian formulations such as Chalcedon in a way that is both consistent with traditional Orthodoxy as well as relevant in the modern philosophical context.

The kenotic theology movement in the nineteenth and twentieth centuries attempted to incorporate Hegelian philosophy as an interpretation of the kenotic hymn in Philippians 2. The incarnation is God's self-emptying into an "other" for the sake of God's own self-completion. Bulgakov mentions several versions of this basic formula: those of Thomasius, Gess, Dorner, which he calls "one sided,"[8] and the Anglo-American line of the tradition which he argues has been so corrupted by liberalism and

---

being of the factual reality of this world with indifference, but rather endeavors to make this world the vessel and the vehicle of absolute being . . . the harmony of the ideal world, the inner unity of all things, reveals itself in Christianity through the power of the divine-human personhood of Christ as its living reality" (ibid., 287).

6. Bulgakov, *Sophia*, 10.

7. Balthasar, *Studies in Theological Style: Lay Styles*, 324 citing "The Spiritual Foundations of Life" (1882–84) from *God, Man and the Church*, trans. D. Attwater (London: J. Clarke, 1938) 99–101.

8. Bulgakov, *Lamb of God*, 220.

rationalism that it can be "lumped in with modernism."[9] The basic premise that all of these accounts hold in common is a kind of necessity for God to "develop or complete himself," a necessity that results in pantheism.[10] In contrast, Bulgakov argues that in true kenotic theology, the "other" must be more than a development or completion within divinity itself. The divine and creaturely cannot be collapsed into one another without destroying the possibility of genuine relation. Bulgakov explains that God needs the world, not to complete God's own nature, but "for the world itself."[11] This necessity can only be categorized as

> The necessity of love, which cannot not love, and which manifests and realizes in itself the identity and indistinguishability of freedom and necessity. For love is free by its nature, but it is not arbitrary in its freedom. It is determined by its inner structure . . . God is a relative concept that already includes a relation to the world.[12]

Thus, we see that Bulgakov wants to maintain truly distinct divine and creaturely natures in order to preserve the possibility for a genuine relation between them, as well as the genuine kenosis, or self-emptying into an "other," that happens in the incarnation. However, he argues that the doctrine of the incarnation as it is formulated at Chalcedon does not provide a sufficient framework to discuss the mystery of kenosis. He states the problem thus:

> What does this kenosis really mean, and in what sense is it possible? What postulates must it satisfy to be more than just a monophysitic mixing of the natures by absorption? In becoming man, God does not stop being God; even after descending from heaven, He remains in heaven. Likewise, man does not stop being man after he receives God into himself. In voluntary self-humiliation, God renounces something, abandons something, in order to become accessible to man, in order to make possible the approach to man. And man, in opening himself up to receive God, transfigures himself, but this occurs without the human essence being abolished, without the possibilities implanted in this essence being destroyed. What is needed is a mediation, an ontological bridge to effect this union—a ladder on which this ascent-descent can be accomplished. The conventional opinion is that there can be no

9. Ibid.

10. Ibid., 120.

11. Ibid.

12. Ibid., 120–21.

> mediation between God and the creature: *tertium non datur*. But in reality there *is* such a mediation between God and the creature: *tertium datur,* and this *tertium* is Sophia, the true Wisdom of God, eternal and creaturely.[13]

Sophia, or the divine nature as eternal kenotic act, provides Bulgakov with a framework to discuss both the identity and difference within God as triune, as well as between Creator and creature. Bulgakov believes that only a sophianic rendering of the Creator/creature difference can preserve the fullness of divine reality in relation to the fullness of creaturely reality while simultaneously providing a basis for their union.

Bulgakov situates his sophianic interpretation of central Christian doctrines solidly within the church tradition. Although he is proposing a kind of "new" reading of the triune life, the incarnation, and the church, he consistently strives to show that Sophia is not an innovation, but rather a coherent and faithful resolution to the metaphysical difficulties posed to Christianity as a result of its heritage in Platonic and Aristotelian philosophy. Bulgakov sees these difficulties epitomized in the work of Thomas Aquinas.

Bulgakov's Reading of Thomas Aquinas

Bulgakov's sophiological setting of the Trinitarian insight, and Balthasar's decision to bracket sophiology as a misleading concept need to be read against the backdrop of Thomas Aquinas's discussion of God both as God relates to God's self and as God relates to creation. In particular, Bulgakov focuses on Thomas's distinction between the divine nature as directed *ad intra* and the divine nature as directed *ad extra*. Bulgakov posits Sophia as a "solution" to the problem of identity and difference within the Creator/creature relationship as Thomas presents it. Because Thomas is a foundational dialogue partner for both Bulgakov and Balthasar, I take a good amount of space in the current chapter and the next to explain both of their positions as they are responses to and adaptations of the Thomistic tradition.

In the third work of his major trilogy, *Bride of the Lamb*, Bulgakov traces the theme of Creator/creature difference first through the pre-Christian philosophers, then into Christian articulations of faith, and finally culminating in Thomas Aquinas. He notes the struggle to maintain a real

13. Ibid., 220.

distinction between God and the world that does not end up in some form of dualism. This struggle intensifies with the Christian need to describe, not only the difference between God and the world, but the significance of God *becoming* part of the world in the incarnation of the Son. Bulgakov believes that the doctrines of the Trinity and the incarnation, as well as the conclusion that the church in the world retains a kind of dual nature as both creaturely and at once eternal/divine, all require some kind of bridging concept—a mediator between God and the world. Bulgakov points out that in Thomas Aquinas, and generally in the West, this mediatory role has been articulated in terms of the incarnation of the Son. However, Bulgakov argues that underlying the Chalcedonian formula that the Son unites human and divine natures in himself without separation or confusion is the same metaphysical difficulty present in Aristotle and Plato: there is no clear articulation of what exactly constitutes the identity and difference between God and the world. Aquinas's discussion of "nature," both in God and analogously in the world, does not overcome this difficulty, but rather exacerbates it by positing an inherent "alienness" between divine and creaturely nature. Bulgakov interprets this alienness between divine and human natures as simultaneously a kind of break, or dualism, which would require some kind of independent ground for creaturely being apart from God, or/and a kind of pantheistic univocality, which establishes the "creaturely difference" only in the "defective" manner in which individual creatures manifest the divine essence.[14] For Bulgakov, there can be no alienness or difference between God and the creature that is not simultaneously the basis for unity. The concept of "analogy" always requires a further "bridging" concept that must be drawn, not from an abstract notion of "nature," but from nature understood as a shared life and self-revelation. Bulgakov recasts the Thomistic understanding of the Creator/creature difference first by extracting the concept of nature from an essence/nature as being/act kind of paradigm, and then by removing the distinction between divine act *ad extra* and *ad intra*. With these "anthropomorphic" distinctions gone, Bulgakov is able to posit a Trinitarian metaphysics with Sophia as a "common" nature between God and creation that maintains both the absolute

---

14. In the next chapter, I demonstrate how Balthasar clarifies this "alienness." In fact, he uses Bulgakov's own Trinitarian theology to demonstrate that this alienness is the creaturely embodiment of Thomas's notion of the opposition of relations in the triune life. Thus it forms the basis for both unity and difference, both in God's own life and between creatures and their Creator.

contingency of creation and the simplicity of the triune act that is the life of God.

Bulgakov's notions of both personhood and the divine/creaturely nature arise out of his desire to maintain an absolute simplicity in the essence and activity of God, as well as establish the primacy of the revealed doctrine of the Trinity over a kind of natural or Aristotelian rendering of the Creator/creature relationship. He believes that Western theology in particular, as exemplified by Thomas Aquinas, has imported the pagan notion of an impersonal divine being into the Christian understanding of the triune God. He objects to Thomas's distinction between divine activity *ad intra* and *ad extra*, first, because it bases the distinction of persons within the divine nature as well as the nature of human persons on a logical distinction between intellect and will rather than on the simple act of self-donation; and second, because the God whose immanent activity is generative of the triune life cannot be simple if God's economic life is fundamentally different.

The problem with Aquinas's account, according to Bulgakov, is an artificial distinction between the activity and the essence of God. There are three difficulties within this distinction. First, the basis for the diversity of persons within God arises from a further distinction in divine activity between the faculties of intellect and will, which applies only to the immanent divine life, whereas with respect to the economic life of the Trinity, Thomas considers divine activity only simply. Bulgakov believes this faulty distinction obscures the personal nature of the divine life or essence both *ad intra* and *ad extra*, and implies that the image of God found in creation is limited to abstract qualities rather than a personal image. Second, the incarnation of the Son remains incoherent within this framework because there is a fundamental alienness introduced between God and creation, between God's life *ad intra* and *ad extra*, so that Christ's teaching and acts are not in fact a real revelation of who God is; rather, the glory of God is only revealed in the ways that Christ's humanity and suffering do not necessarily conceal it. Finally, Bulgakov believes this dichotomy between God and creation, between Christ's divine and human natures, introduces an arbitrariness into both God and humanity. Aquinas argues for a "necessary" causality vis-à-vis creation as it proceeds from the divine intellect or ideas, in contrast to a "free" causality vis-à-vis creation as it proceeds from the divine will. Bulgakov sees this distinction as inserting a fundamental discrepancy between God's will and intellect—a problem which is further complicated when these powers are understood as the basis for the processions of the Son and the Holy Spirit. If divine freedom requires a kind of non-correspondence between the Creator as he is for himself and the Creator as he is for creatures, then there will be a fundamental discrepancy between the God revealed in Jesus Christ and God as he is for himself.

Bulgakov believes that Aquinas's fundamental mistake comes with his distinction between *de Deo uno* and *de Deo trino* in the Summa. Bulgakov believes that this choice is more than a methodological tool, but rather a statement of Thomas's own partitioning out of the interplay between the economic and immanent Trinity. Bulgakov writes,

> At his point of departure Thomas Aquinas takes not the Christian dogma of the personal, trihypostatic God, but Aristotle's impersonal divinity. The trihypostatic dogma is added later, and this is done without influencing the fundamental cosmological conception, which is rather based on the purely Aristotelian relation of God and the world.[15]

This structure, according to Bulgakov, is entirely incompatible with Thomas's own notion of divine simplicity.[16] If the divine nature is the same as the divine life for Thomas, then Bulgakov cannot understand how he can simultaneously posit both the trihypostatic life of God in God's self, and a hypostatically indistinguishable life directed toward creation.

When Thomas treats God considered *de Deo uno* he says that one can distinguish between the operations of intellect and will in the divine life. He uses this distinction to trace the relationship among the following elements in our understanding of God: God considered simply according to the divine essence, God when considered as the content of God's own with respect to the truth that God knows, and the good that God desires. God is both the content of God's own intellect and the act of knowing that content. God is both the act of willing and the content of what God wills. Bulgakov's objection comes in when life and nature in God are construed in terms of power or operation rather than relation. This is especially problematic with Thomas's further distinction vis-à-vis the content of divine knowing

15. Bulgakov, *Bride*, 19.

16 Bulgakov endorses Thomas's understanding of divine simplicity: "In things not composed of matter and form, in which individualization is not due to individual matter—that is to say, to 'this matter'—the very forms being individualized of themselves—it is necessary the forms themselves should be subsisting *supposita*. Therefore *suppositum* and *natura* in them are identified. Since God then is not composed of matter and form, He must be His own Godhead, His own Life, and whatever else is thus predicated of Him." Aquinas, *Summa Theologica* (hereafter, *ST*), Ia.3.3.

and willing with respect to creatures. God understands creaturely reality as various ways of participating in his own being. With respect to God's intellect, the whole scope of creaturely reality, both actual and possible, is necessarily known by God as the ways of possible participation in his own essence.[17] With respect to the will of God, which brings creaturely reality into existence, God freely wills to bring a distinct set of ways of participating in his essence into actual existence.

Bulgakov argues that this way of distinguishing the operations of intellect and will within the divine life does violence to the personal nature of God. Moreover, he believes that Thomas's claim that the divine intellect knows the ideas of creatures necessarily while the divine will desires them freely is incoherent within an understanding of divine simplicity.

His first objection relates to the idea that, in a Christian doctrine of God, intellect and will are not primarily functions of an Aristotelian unmoved mover, but rather shared expressions of the triune life. One cannot abstract the notion of the divine intellect, either with respect to its function or content, from the relationship of Father, Son, and Holy Spirit. As such, both the act of knowing and the content of divine knowledge are equally constitutive of each of the divine persons, and can only be differentiated in the way that each of the persons "hypostatizes" them. Similarly, the act of willing and that which is willed must be considered simply with respect to content and as pertaining equally to each of the divine persons, again hypostatized uniquely. Both that which God knows and God's act of knowing, and that which God wills and God's act of willing must be considered simply and only differentiated with respect to the ways in which the divine persons live them uniquely in their eternal relation to one another. For Bulgakov, this rendering of the relationship between the divine will and intellect, and between persons and essence precludes any kind of distinction between the way in which God acts *ad intra* and *ad extra*. God's life is utterly simple as it is directed both toward himself and toward the creaturely "other."

---

17. "Hence many ideas exist in the divine mind, as things understood by it; as can be proved thus. Inasmuch as He knows His own essence perfectly, He knows it according to every mode in which it can be known. Now it can be known not only as it is in itself, but as it can be participated in by creatures according to some degree of likeness. But every creature has its own proper species, according to which it participates in some degree in likeness to the divine essence. So far, therefore, as God knows His essence as capable of such imitation by any creature, He knows it as the particular type and idea of that creature; and in like manner as regards other creatures. So it is clear that God understands many particular types of things and these are many ideas" (Aquinas, *ST*, Ia. 15.2).

Thomas's terminology permits a logical distinction between divine essence and nature, intellect and will, proper and participated being, possible and actual realities, freedom and necessity, logical and real relation, *de Deo uno* and *de Deo trino*, and divine activity *ad extra* and *ad intra*. Bulgakov believes these distinctions are really distortions. Within Bulgakov's sophiological paradigm, only two major distinctions are needed: the distinction between the content or world of the divine persons and creatures, divine Sophia and creaturely Sophia, and the distinction between the divine hypostases (or the particular acts which constitute the divine persons) and creaturely hypostases.

Thomas's assertion that the divine idea includes various modes of participation, both actually existing in creaturely reality as well as possible creaturely participations in the divine essence which are not actualized, is a way of retaining an infinite distance between the divine essence and creaturely being.[18] There is no way that creaturely being could fully reflect the infinity of the divine essence. Natural knowledge of God is therefore always analogous and in fact partial. Only the beatific vision gives a full, although not comprehensive, knowledge of God in himself. Bulgakov argues that Thomas's construal is "pure anthropomorphism." There can be no part of the divine idea that remains only possible while another part is actual. If God creates, then creation is the entire self-positing of divinity into an "other." There is no possible remainder. For Bulgakov then, what constitutes the infinite distance between God and creatures is not the limitedness of creation with respect to its participation in the divine essence, but rather the unlimitedness of the divine nature as it *is* an act of absolute self-donation. Creaturely existence is a participation, not in a distinct set of content so much as in the activity of infinite self-donation that constitutes the triune life. Thus, the basis for distinguishing between God and creation is provided by the full participation in and reflection of the divine essence by the whole of creation in the personal activity of infinite self-donation. God and creation can no more be conflated than the persons of Father,

---

18. "As ideas, according to Plato, are principles of the knowledge of things and of their generation, an idea has this twofold office, as it exists in the mind of God. So far as the idea is the principle of the making of things, it may be called an 'exemplar,' and belongs to practical knowledge. But so far as it is a principle of knowledge, it is properly called a 'type,' and may belong to speculative knowledge also. As an exemplar, therefore, it has respect to everything made by God in any period of time; whereas as a principle of knowledge it has respect to all things known by God, even though they never come to be in time; and to all things that He knows according to their proper type, in so far as they are known by Him in a speculative manner" (Aquinas, *ST*, Ia.15.3).

Son, and Holy Spirit.[19] However, creaturely hypostatization of the sophianic content, the act of absolute self-donation, is always a participated, finite, and contingent act. Only in Christ, the God-man, does creaturely Sophia acquire an integrity that would allow her to fully manifest her inner reality as the perfect reflection of the divine life in becoming.

A further difficulty arises for Bulgakov with Thomas's notion of the divine ideas. If God relates to creation through his nature, rather than tri-hypostatically, then what is to distinguish between the divine ideas as they exist in the mind of God and the divine ideas as they exist in the world? On this point Bulgakov goes so far as to accuse Thomas of pantheism:

> There is a kind of pantheism inherent in such a scheme. This kind of identification between God and the world is apparent in the definition of the relation between *Deus* (in the impersonal Aristotelian sense) and the world (*omnes res*).[20]

If God is in *omnes res* by his power, presence, and essence, and "innermostly," then what actually differentiates between God and creatures? Bulgakov believes that Thomas offers only two possibilities in response to this question. The first is that: "God in the world, or the world in God, is a gradation of being in the descending or ascending perfection of different steps of being, depending on the degree of nonbeing or imperfection that is added in . . . The multiplicity of creaturely being results from its imperfection,

---

19. "Relations multiplying ideas do not exist in created things, but in God. Yet they are not real relations, such as those whereby the Persons are distinguished, but relations understood by God" (Aquinas, *ST*, Ia.15.2). As I demonstrate in the second chapter, the concept of relation is central in Thomas's Trinitarian thought, and yet remains unexplored in Bulgakov's analysis of Thomas. The distinction between real and logical relations is particularly important, and Balthasar's incorporation of this distinction, I argue, allows him to situate Bulgakov's Trinitarian thesis within Thomas's Trinitarian Creator/creature distinction in a way that renders sophiology superfluous.

20. Bulgakov, *Bride*, 21 quoting Aquinas *ST*, I. 8. A.1: *Deus est in omnibus rebus, non quidem sicut pars essetiae, vel sicut accidens, sed sicut agens adest ei in quod agit. Cum autem Deus sit ipsum esse per suam essentiam, oportet quod esse creatum sit proprius effectus eius, sicut ignire est proprius effectus ipsius ignius. Unde oportet quod Deus sit in omnibus rebus et intime.* And,(*ST*, I. 8. A. 3): "God is in all things by his power, inasmuch as all things are subject to his power; he is by his presence in all things, as all things are bare and open to his eyes; he is in all things by his essence, inasmuch as he is present for all things as the cause of their being." *Deus est in omnibus, per potentiam in quantum omnia eius potestatis subdunter: et per paesetiam in omnibus in quantum omnia nuda sunt et aperta oculis eius: est in omnibus per essentiam, in quantum adest omnibus ut causa essendi.*

defectus."[21] In other words, the difference between God and creatures exists only in the finite mode, or lack of fullness of each individual's participation in the divine essence. A second possibility for distinguishing between God and creation stems from Thomas's distinction between the way in which divine ideas in creation are caused by the divine intellect versus the divine will, a distinction that Bulgakov finds intrinsically problematic as I have already mentioned.

> According to the general impersonalism of Aquinas's theology, which deduces the being of the hypostases solely from the distinctions and relations in divinity, the participation of individual persons in this causality takes place only *"secundem rationem suae processionis."* (45.6.) God is the cause of things through his mind and will; he is like an artist in relation to the things he produces. An artist creates through the word born in his mind and through the love of his will, which relates to something. Thus, God the Father established creation by his Word, which is the Son, and by his love, which is the Spirit. Therefore, the processions of the Persons are the types of the production of creatures inasmuch as they include the essential attributes of knowledge and will.[22]

For Thomas, because the creation of the world is not necessary with respect to the divine will, it is essentially different from the divine life itself, thus avoiding pantheism. However, Bulgakov believes that this solution is based in Thomas's original mistake, namely, taking the life or nature of God as power or operation rather than relation. If the processions of the persons are a result of the operations of divine intellect and divine will, and creaturely nature is "caused" by these operations in distinct ways, then 1) it would seem that it is the distinction between intellect and will rather than the divine persons that is most fundamental in Thomas's theology of God, and 2) the image of God in creation is primarily a matter of causality and power rather than an expression of the inner life of a tri-personal God.

Bulgakov notes that for Aquinas,

> Just as *"scientia Dei est causa rerum"* (Ia. 14.8), so *"voluntas Dei est causa rerum"* (Ia. 19.4). "God causes things by his intellect, since his being is his act of understanding; and hence his knowledge must be the cause of things, insofar as his will is joined to it" (Ia.

21. Ibid., quoting Aquinas, *ST*, Ia.14.5.

22. Ibid., 27 quoting Aquinas, *ST*, Ia.45.6. *Deus per intellectum suum causat res, cum suum esse sit suum intelligere; unde necesse est quod sua sceintia sit causa rerum, secudum quod habet voluntatem conjunctam.*

14.8). One should note that Aquinas uses both *intellectus* and *voluntas* without any reference to the personal God. Strictly speaking, he uses these terms not with reference to *Deus*, but with reference to *Deitas*.[23]

Thus the very basis for personal or hypostatic distinction within the triune life, namely the logical distinction between intellect and will, is treated in an entirely impersonal manner with respect to creation.[24]

A final difficulty that Bulgakov has with Thomas's construal of the relation between the divine ideas and creation is the concept of unrealized possibilities within the divine ideas. For Bulgakov, the concept of unactualized possibility in the content of divine ideas is "pure anthropomorphism." It renders the exemplary character of ideas as nonsense and introduces further difficulties with respect to the relationship of intellect and will in the divine life. He sums up his difficulties with this construal in the following quote:

> All of these additional clarifications, according to which not only the actual world but also its never-realized possibilities, as well as God's "speculations," are included in the idea of God, unnecessarily complicate and tangle the "exemplary" character of ideas. . . .

23. Ibid., 22.

24. Referring to Aquinas, *ST*, Ia. Q. 45, where Thomas says that God is the proximate and universal cause of creation, Bulgakov says: "Thus, the creative act is, on the one hand, defined in the spirit of emanative pantheism, while, on the other hand, it is wholly subsumed under the category of causality: God is the universal proto-cause. How can this idea be applied in relation to the trihypostatic God? Since creation belongs to God according to his being, it follows that, '*creare non ist proprium alicui personae, sed commune toti Trinitati,*' that is apart from hypostatic distinction." Bulgakov, *Bride*, 27. Not only this, but this distinction introduces a strange inconsistency within divinity where the will of God is only necessary with respect to God's self, and yet God's knowledge of created things is necessary both *ad intra* and *ad extra*. "From the distinction in God of *vella se* and *alia a se* it follows that, in the former, God *vult se ut finem*, whereas in the latter he wills *alia vero ad finem*. (*ST*, Ia. 19, 2). Here, God wants himself, his grace, with necessity, whereas on the contrary, *alia* is not *necessarium absolute* but *necessarium ex supposito* (Ia, 19, 3). as a means to a necessary goal. 'God's will is the cause of things and God acts by will, not by necessity.' (19, 4). 'Since God's being is the understanding of himself, his action preexists in him, *effectus secundum modum intelligibilem* and *per modum voluntatis*. For his inclination to action consists in the fact that what is perceived by the mind refers to will, and will is therefore the cause of things' (19, 4), whereas God's will itself 'does not by any means have causes.'" (a. 5) "This entire conception of Aquinas's, inspired by Christianity, is a torso without a head. The doctrine of the trihypostatic God appears here only after this doctrine of the Divine knowledge and will and of their relation to created things" (ibid., 23).

> Dubious is the inclusion in ideas of thoughts of God that never
> become a reality (contrary to Aquinas's own principle that the
> "*scientia rerum est causa rerum*").[25]

Ultimately, Bulgakov sees the problem with Thomas's construal as sophiological. When the divine life is taken as a simple act, the trihypostatic activity of kenotic love, then the "non-correspondence of ideas and things"[26] that Bulgakov argues is inherent within Thomas's understanding drops away.[27] The divine idea, the divine life, the three persons, for Bulgakov, all maintain their unity and simplicity as well as a real correspondence between their reality in God and their reality in creation.[28] This is the fundamental strength that Bulgakov sees in sophiology. "Sophiology is not only a doctrine of ideas as the prototypes of things but primarily a doctrine of the self-revelation of the Holy Trinity, and only subsequently of the revelation of the Holy Trinity in creation."[29] For Bulgakov, sophiology maintains the primacy of the Holy Trinity as the basis for understanding God, creation, and revelation.

BULGAKOV'S TRINITARIAN INSIGHT

In this section I look at three components of Bulgakov's Trinitarian insight: 1) the identification of divine activity and the divine essence through the

25. Ibid., 25–26.

26. Ibid., 26.

27. "The definition of these forms has, as its first principle, Divine wisdom, which conceived the order of the universe, which consists in the multiplicity of things. One must therefore say that the Divine wisdom, contains the images of all the things about which we spoke above in qu. 15.1, i.e., ideas, the exemplary forms of existence in Divine although. Although they become multiple in relation to things, these exemplary forms do not really differ from the Divine essence [*non sunt alia a divina essentia*] as it is perceived differently in different cases. Thus, God himself is *primum exemplar omnium*" (Bulgakov, *Bride*, 27 quoting Aquinas *ST*, Ia. 44.3).

28. Whereas Bulgakov writes that: "As we can see from the foregoing, Aquinas identifies ideas, the Divine essence, and God without any intermediary links, so that the *raison d'être* for a special doctrine of ideas even becomes incomprehensible." Ibid., 28. On the one hand, Bulgakov argues that Thomas' doctrine of the Divine ideas/Divine activity overly identifies the Divine essence and the creaturely world resulting in a kind of "emanantive pantheism." On the other hand, as we have seen, the disparity between the Divine Ideas in God and in the world of creaturely things creates an artificial break between the life of God *ad intra* and God's activity with respect to creation.

29. Ibid., 26.

concept of kenotic love, 2) the consistently tri-personal expression of the divine life both *ad intra* and *ad extra*, and 3) the continuity of the triune image, which allows for both identity and distinction across both the divine life and creation. Both divine and creaturely relations, or unique acts of hypostatization, consist in a kind of pathos or suffering, which is itself the glory or blessedness of the divine essence.

THE DIVINE ESSENCE IS KENOTIC LOVE

Balthasar summarizes Bulgakov's Trinitarian insight as follows: "The ultimate presupposition of the kenosis is the 'selflessness' of the Persons (when considered as pure relations) in the inner-Trinitarian life of love."[30] While Thomas describes the triune unity or essence in terms of being, Bulgakov contends that in the life of God, essence and nature cannot be distinguished even logically. In God "'*is*' [i.e., being] signifies not a relation of formal logic but the ontological link of love."[31] Rather than describing the divine persons according to the origin of the processions, Bulgakov describes a "trihypostatic personality, which in one personal consciousness of self unites all the modes of the personal principle: I, thou, he, we, and you."[32] The key for Bulgakov here is that the ousia, the hypostases, and the relations in the divine life can only be understood in terms of a dynamic activity. He explains:

> Fully manifested and actualized, the personal principle, the hypostasis, is a trihypostatic personality, in which the personal unity is revealed in the reality of three hypostatic centers, or hypostases, in triunity. Triunity is the divine number, not three and not one, but precisely triunity, Trinity. Such hypostatic being is realized not statically, as the unipersonal self-consciousness of the separate, isolated I in itself, reposing in its self-givenness (although this static and self-finished character is only apparent, for every I goes

30. Balthasar, *Mysterium Paschale*, 35.

31. Bulgakov, *Lamb of God*, 104. Aquinas also posits love as a uniting force in God. "So love is called the unitive force, even in God, yet without implying composition; for the good that He wills for Himself, is no other than Himself, Who is good by His essence, as above shown (Q[6], AA[1], 3)" (Aquinas, *ST*, Ia.20.1). As I argue in the second chapter, Balthasar takes love in this sense as the central transcendental in Thomas's understanding of the divine life, where both divine simplicity and the three divine persons are maintained with the notion of relation and the opposition of relations. Again, the Creator/creature distinction is preserved within this system by the distinction between real and logical relations.

32. Ibid., 94.

out into thou, we, you); rather it is realized dynamically, as the eternal act of Trinitarian self-positing in another. This dynamic self-positing is *love*: the flames of the divine trihypostasis flare up in each of the hypostatic centers and are then united and identified with one another, each going out of itself into the others, in the ardor of self-renouncing personal love.[33]

The three persons of the Trinity "are" love according to their own hypostases. Thus, the Father loves in begetting the Son, who loves in revealing the Father, and the Holy Spirit is the "accomplished act" of love between the Father and Son proceeding from the Father to and through the Son:[34]

> The Father acquires himself as His nature, not in Himself and for Himself, but in proceeding out of Himself and in begetting, as the Father, the Son. Fatherhood is precisely the form of love in which the loving one desires to have himself not in himself but outside himself, in order to give his own to this other I . . . The Father lives not in himself but in His Son's life; the Father lives in begetting, that is, in proceeding out of himself, in revealing himself.[35]

Bulgakov's Trinitarian theology depends upon a paradox. Each of the divine persons live through a kind of death, possesses through dispossession, enjoys the eternal blessedness of the divine life precisely in a "pre-eternal suffering." Bulgakov describes the Father's hypostatic activity as a "begetting power" that "is the ecstasy of a going out of oneself, of a kind of self-emptying, which at the same time is self-actualization through this begetting."[36] The Son's self-actualization is passive rather than active. It is:

> The sacrificial, self-renouncing humility of the Lamb of God . . . And if the Father desires to have himself outside himself, in the Son, the Son too does not desire to have himself for himself: He offers his personal selfhood in sacrifice to the Father, and being the Word, he becomes mute for himself, as it were, making himself the Father's word.[37]

33. Ibid., 94–95.

34. Ibid., 99–100.

35. Ibid., 98.

36. Ibid.

37. Ibid., 99. A consistent facet of Bulgakov's theology is the way in which activity and passivity are implied within the same act. The "begottenness" of the Son is the paradigmatic example of this paradox. The Son's "offering" of himself, his self-presentation as utterly transparent to the Father, is at once a kind of "self-negation" as well as an absolute positing of his identity as the Word of the Father. Balthasar embraces this paradoxical

Each of these acts of hypostatic love entails sacrifice or suffering. "The sacrifice of love, in its reality, is pre-eternal suffering[38]—not the suffering of limitation (which is incompatible with the absoluteness of divine life) but the suffering of the authenticity of sacrifice and of its immensity."[39] Unlike human suffering, which always entails a kind of resistance and limitation, divine suffering, which is divine blessedness, consists in the absolute openness of the divine persons toward each other.[40] Bulgakov admits that "this self-emptying and self-depletion would be a tragedy in God if it remained self-sufficient. But it is pre-eternally resolved in the bliss of suffering overcome."[41] The Holy Spirit is the joy of suffering overcome through sacrificial love, who ensures the all-blessedness of the divine life because he is the bond of love between the Father and the Son:

> In God there is no self-definition that is not hypostatic. Therefore, the recognition of his own nature as reality is the hypostatic act of the procession of the Holy Spirit . . . the Holy Spirit himself does not reveal the Son to the Father or the Father to the Son, but he unites them in the reality of the Divine nature . . . the Holy Spirit does not have his own particular content; rather, he proclaims that which the Son says in the name of the Father.[42]

So, each of the divine persons then possesses themselves only in their absolute self-gift to the others. The suffering that characterizes this self-offering entails a genuine sacrifice, but not a tragic one. The emptiness all of the

---

character of the triune kenosis so that it is an interpretation of the Thomistic notion of relational opposition.

38. Bulgakov's use of the term "pre-eternal" is odd. However, it is helpful to understand the term, not as a temporal designation, but rather as a sophiological statement. Pre-eternal suffering and pre-eternal humanity refer to the fact of these phenomena "in" the life of God absolutely. Their primary reference is not a creaturely reality, but the simple act of the divine life. Pre-eternal describes a facet of God's life that is impersonally identifiable with the divine nature (divine Sophia), and yet intrinsically related to an "other" (creaturely Sophia).

39. Bulgakov, *Lamb of God*, 99.

40. Bulgakov does not back away from the implications of his statement that the divine essence is suffering. He goes so far as to say that "one can define this state of sacrifice as voluntary hypostatic dying, under the condition that the concept of death is liberated from the meaning it has in temporal creaturely life, a meaning that has nothing in common with spiritual dying as a manifestation of eternal Divine life" (Ibid.).

41. Ibid.

42. Ibid., 100–101.

divine persons "suffer" as a result of their total self-donation is always already "filled" by their openness to and reception of the others:

> We know that the Trinity's love is mutually sacrificial as a mutual renunciation of the hypostases. Each hypostasis finds itself and realizes itself in the others in this renunciation. Therefore, the Trinity's love can be understood in this sense as a supra-eternal kenosis, but a kenosis that is overcome for each of the hypostases in joint Trinitarian love, in the all-blissfulness of this love.[43]

This kenotic love that is the personal activity of God has another aspect. "The trihypostatic God has his nature as the triune and uniTrinitarian act of the love of the Father and of the Son and of the Holy Spirit, the one nature of the three hypostases."[44] If the divine essence *is* the dynamic act of kenotic love, then Bulgakov argues that divine activity or nature *is* simply the expression of the triune life, both *ad intra* and *ad extra*.

Divine Nature as an Expression of the Triune Life

Bulgakov is concerned that Thomas isolates the divine nature, and by extension God's activity *ad extra*, from the triunity of the divine persons. Such a view of the divine nature, he argues, implies an abstraction of "nature" from the relation that is the triune life. "Nature" becomes a set of qualities, understood primarily in terms of "being" and "cause." Instead, Bulgakov proposes a concept of the divine nature as a trihypostatic self-revelation. God's nature is what God does, who God is, rather than something God "has."

> The formula that the Holy Trinity *has* one *nature* is, in this form, unsatisfactory in general. For what do this "nature" and this "has" signify? "Nature" in this case is invariably understood to mean the external factuality of things, specifically, a kind of single given of nature belonging to the three personal order of divinity. . . . However, "nature," to be sure, is divinity itself, God's own life in its self-revelation.[45]

43. Bulgakov, *Bride*, 49.

44. Ibid., 101.

45. Ibid., 42. Aiden Nichols provides a helpful summary of Bulgakov's construal of Sophia as the divine world. "The Wisdom of God is the divinity of God—not the personal existence of Father, Son and Spirit, but the living reality of the divine nature they share—the divine nature as a 'world' that is wonderfully coherent in itself (all the divine

Sophia, then, is a dynamic rendering of "nature" as a shared life that constitutes the divine persons in their uniqueness. It is the relation of the divine persons as they enact it for themselves. If it is the case that the divine nature, or Sophia, is the self-expression of the triune God in his simplicity, then how can one differentiate between the way in which this act manifests itself to God's self, and the way in which it manifests itself as creation?

The Image of the Trinity in Creation

For Bulgakov, the triune God is personal in both his existence for himself and his life for an "other." Divinity cannot be abstracted from the inter-hypostatic act of self-donation even when it turns *ad extra* as Creator. Bulgakov shies away from causal language in reference to the Creator/creature distinction precisely because it obscures the essentially Trinitarian nature of the relation:

> It is first necessary to point out that the idea of creation, in contradistinction to causality, is *personal* and presupposes a personal God. The idea of causality of the prime mover does not include creation and in a certain sense even excludes it, insofar as the latter is personal whereas causality, or motion, is mechanical and impersonal.[46]

If Bulgakov gains a positively personal relation between God and creation by situating the Creator/creature distinction in a triune context, the result of this construal is one of two things: either 1) by removing the "natural" distinction between God and the world he has set up a kind of pantheism (although he describes it as "panentheism"),[47] or 2) the concept of "person" will have to do the work not only of expressing a "bridge" or "relation,"

---

attributes and divine ideas fitting perfectly with each other), a world that is at the loving disposal of the divine hypostases, on which they can draw, with which, in which and from which they can act" (Nichols, *Wisdom from Above*, 25).

46. Bulgakov, *Bride*, 37.

47. If we believe that the world was created out of nothing, then, in the positive sense, this can mean only that God created the world out of himself. The whole power of the world's being belongs to divinity. This power is divine: "In him we live, and move, and have our being" (Acts 17:28); "For of him, through him, and to him, are all things" (Rom 11:36) (ibid., 44).

but also an infinite difference or distance that can apply, at least analogously, to both the inner triune relations as well as to the Creator/creature relationship.

The concept of "personhood" is pervasive in Bulgakov's thought. As we have already shown, for Bulgakov personhood is primarily "the kenotic self-positing of the three hypostases." Bulgakov extends this primary notion of personhood to the act of creation.[48] The creaturely world has its foundation in the divine world, or the triune act of kenotic, non-hypostatic self-positing.[49] But, as a true image of the triune life, creation possesses not only a "nature," but hypostases:

> In the creation of the world, God repeats his own being in Sophia, as it were. He repeats his nature, the Divine Sophia, in the creaturely Sophia, or in the world. In the creation of persons, of hypostatic spirits, human and angelic, God repeats Himself, as it were, creates *co-I's* for Himself in his hypostatic image, breathing into them the breath of his own divine life. He creates co-gods for himself, "gods by grace."[50]

As "gods by grace," creaturely hypostases are in the image of the triune God both by virtue of what constitutes their personhood as well as their relation to creaturely nature. Recall that in the divine life:

> "Nature," to be sure, is divinity itself, God's own life in its self-revelation. In no wise it is a property of this life to be a fact or a

48. "The relation of the hypostases of the Trinity to God's nature, Sophia, is just as kenotic as their interhypostatic self-determination, since the Divine Sophia herself, in her content as the divine world, is the kenotic self-positing of the three hypostases . . . This tri-hypostatic kenosis of love is manifested in yet *another* way in the relation of God to the divine world in the act of creation. Here, the Holy Trinity in Unity, or the Unity in Trinity, renounces, as it were, in its sacrificially kenotic love the possession of the divine world for itself and allows this world to have its own being. The Trinity in Unity has, or posits, this world outside itself, in separateness from itself, precisely as the world, as nonhypostatic self-being" (ibid., 49–50).

49. As Aiden Nichols clarifies, "The Wisdom of God is not itself hypostatic. But it is, if the neologism be allowed, 'hypostatizable'" (*Wisdom from Above*, 25). The important thing to note here is that Bulgakov's Trinitarian theology, the understanding that God's life is a tri-personally enacted self-donation, drives his understanding of divinity or Divine Nature. If Sophia seems like a "fourth hypostasis" it is because the relation that characterizes the Divine essence or the perichoretic activity of the persons is living and dynamic. "Though it differs from God's personal being yet it is inseparably bound up with it: it is not God, but divinity" (Bulgakov, *Sophia*, 30–31). "Sophia = Ousia = Glory" (ibid., 35).

50. Ibid., 87.

givenness of things. On the contrary, this life is divinity's eternal
act . . . God's nature is, in this sense, the creative self-positing of
divinity, God's personal—trihypostatic—act.[51]

Analogously, creaturely persons "have" their creaturely nature, not by that
nature consisting in a certain set of properties or a defective state of being.
Rather, creaturely nature is a participated and temporal hypostatization of
Sophia. Bulgakov distinguishes between divine and creaturely hypostatization of Sophia by saying that Christ is Son by nature, whereas humanity
has its sonship through participation in Christ. Humanity is the unique
mode of enacting kenotic love by receiving its life, not as its own nature or
possession, but as a wholly gratuitous gift.

WHAT IS SOPHIA?

Bulgakov adopts and adapts the concept of Sophia in the way he does precisely because he believes it provides an adequate and accurate language to
describe the reality of human experience.

Sophia is the divine nature and "love is the *natural* order of the divine world."[52] Sophia is not hypostatic or personal love; rather, as the life
of God, it is living love. For Bulgakov, Sophia posits the triune relation in
its concrete activity of mutual self-donation as fundamental rather than
an "abstract" notion of being or essence. For Thomas, the analogy of being
isn't a concretely existing thing, but rather a way of explaining how "being"
can be predicated of a number of things. It is a way of understanding both a
similarity and dissimilarity between various beings. God *is* in an unpartici-
pated way, whereas creatures receive their existence as participated beings.
Since every effect is similar to its cause we can somehow speak about God
by looking at creation, his effect. Because being is analogous rather than
univocal or equivocal, we can speak about God and know him through
his effects. Bulgakov takes this Thomistic concept and transposes it into a
relational or personal key. Creaturely reality participates in the act of relation that is constitutive of the triune life. Divine Sophia is the triune self-
revelation of the mutually kenotic perichoresis of the divine persons both
toward God's own self and towards all creatures. Creaturely Sophia is the
reception and participation of that relation by creatures.

51. Bulgakov, *Bride*, 42.

52. Bulgakov, *Lamb of God*, 107 (emphasis mine).

The creaturely world Bulgakov describes erupts with God's personal self-revelation. For Bulgakov, our reception of God's self-communication in Jesus' life and death, in the facts of history and creation, and in our own apprehension of our spiritual nature is itself already an assimilation into the divine life, the beginning of a reciprocal self-communication and offering that constitutes our deification. The kenotic act that *is* the divine ousia is also the foundation of the world grounded in the trihypostatic exchange of love. Thus the world is glorious; it is the personal revelation of God, not as a set of ideas or information, but the relation that is God's life extended to an "other." The point is that the world, as we apprehend it as creation, and God as Creator are engaged in a relationship that in various ways *is* the divine life. Bulgakov believes that his sophiological description of this life preserves the inherent relationality of a world to the triune God, the distinction between God and the world, and God's simplicity.

THE TRINITY AND SOPHIA

Bulgakov posits a system wherein the relational life of the three divine persons constitutes the whole of reality both within the divine life itself and with respect to a creation that participates in this life. Through the concept of Sophia, Bulgakov connects the aspect of the divine life that is not the trihypostatic act of self-donation with the contingent, creaturely world. Sophia is the "all-unity" of the content of the divine life. In God, Sophia is completely "hypostasized," or enacted by the divine persons in their eternal acts of reciprocal self-surrender. In creation, Sophia is the same divine life, yet given over into becoming and time to a contingent "other." Just as the handing over in love within the divine life is generative of personhood (although eternally and necessarily) in creaturely Sophia, this handing over is the ground for a participated hypostatization of the divine life, not a fourth hypostasis, but a dependant hypostatizedness.

Divine Sophia is nothing other than the divine nature, or *ousia*, shared by the three persons of the Trinity. When we speak of divine nature or substance, we are speaking of divine Sophia. Divine Sophia is the "ordered content" of God, the Father's revelation in the Son reposed upon and reflected by the Holy Spirit in its impersonal aspect. Two theological assumptions underlie Bulgakov's claim that the divine nature has an impersonal content or principle called Sophia.

First, Sophia can be understood as the divine nature in its impersonal aspect when "nature" is taken to be, not an essence or quiddity, but rather the "world" of a hypostasis. A hypostasis is a being that exists directly as a subject or agent, and hypostaseity is a capacity for being hypostasized in/by a hypostasis. Thus, Bulgakov distinguishes, but does not separate God's nature, or Sophia, from the three hypostases of the Trinity because the nature or world is that which is hypostatized by the three persons or hypostases.[53] The nature/world is the "place" where the hypostases live. The nature is itself alive, although impersonally, as the life of the Trinity.

> Sophia is the objective principle of the life of God, of the being of the One who is. This world is this life itself, and through it no extra-divine principle is introduced into Divinity. This life of God in his Divinity, or the divine world as an objective and living principle, is precisely what scripture calls Sophia, or the Wisdom of God.[54]

The divine nature is expressed trihypostatically, and there is no "part" of it that is not hypostasized in the three persons.[55] Hypostatically, the three persons of the Trinity are distinct. Father, Son, and Holy Spirit are equally God, but not identical to one another in their persons:

> It is the same way in the Divine life and self-revelation, in the Divine Sophia, as it is in hypostatic being. The Divine Sophia can be defined both in relation to the entire Holy Trinity in its unity (which is without separation) and in relation to each of the hypostases (which are unconfusable and inseparable).[56]

Divine Sophia is the unified self-revelation of "the Father in the Son and Holy Spirit"; divine Sophia is hypostatized rather than hypostatic.[57] "God's nature is, in this sense, the creative self-positing of divinity, God's personal—and tri-hypostatic—act. This act is divine Sophia, the self-positing and self-revelation of the Holy Trinity."[58]

---

53. Williams, *Sergii Bulgakov*, 165–66. See also Nichols, *Wisdom From Above*, 14–15 and Valliere, *Modern Russian Theology*, 304–5. Cf. Bulgakov's "Hypostasis and Hypostaticity."

54. Bulgakov, *Lamb of God*, 107.

55. For the triune dynamic in the divine nature see Bulgakov, *Lamb of God*, 108–12.

56. Ibid., 110.

57. Ibid., 110–11.

58. Bulgakov, *Bride*, 42.

The difference between hypostases and hypostaseity is rather obtuse, but Bulgakov's second assumption that "God is love" provides a bit more clarity. If divine Sophia is the "content" of the divine life, or the world of the persons, then it must be understood as kenotic love.[59] Each of the three persons "hypostatizes" this love in a unique way. The Father personifies that love by emptying himself entirely in the begetting of the Son. The Son is emptied by claiming no independent ground for himself except that which he receives from the Father. The Spirit is the "accomplished act" of love between the Father and Son proceeding from the Father to the Son.[60] The Second Person of the Trinity is particularly revealed in the divine Sophia because of his particular activity of love:

> In itself, the sonhood already represents a certain pre-eternal kenosis of the Son, his self-depletion in his love for the Father, the hypostatic sacrifice of the Lamb. This sacrifice of the Lamb is revealed also in the Divine Sophia—no longer as the personal self-definition of the Son in relation to the Father, but as his natural self-positing in the self-revelation of Divinity, in Sophia. The Son surrenders himself as the *Word of All and About All* to the Divine world; he serves the self-revealing Divinity, and he posits himself as the content of this self-revelation.[61]

The Son's surrender contains within it the "necessity of love" to "empty" itself not only within the triune life, but also into an "other." This "other" is creaturely Sophia.

The concept of divine Sophia as God's world, and the idea of the loving relationships of the Trinity expressed in that world, forms the basis for Bulgakov's understanding of creation. In what precedes, we have discussed Bulgakov's thought re God's life in its absolute sense. However, a God such as this cannot be solely absolute (that is, without relation to an "other"), but in the freedom of love *must* create, and is thus absolute-relative.[62] God is not compelled to create by anything outside his nature, nor does creation follow from "the proper life of Divinity and Divinity's own self-positing; there is no place for creation in Divinity itself . . . the creation of the world

59. Bulgakov, *Lamb of God*, 105–7.

60. Ibid., 100.

61. Ibid., 111.

62. In his discussion of this point, Rowan Williams includes an interesting footnote on the similarities and differences between Bulgakov and Hegel, and Bulgakov and Barth in the way that they conceive of the relationship between God and the world (Williams, *Sergii Bulgakov*, 169).

can only be the proper *work* of Divinity."[63] However, this work is not arbitrarily related to God's nature. It is an expression of that nature because "if God created the world, this means that he could not have refrained from creating it, although the Creator's act belongs to the fullness of God's life and this act contains no external compulsion that would contradict divine freedom."[64]

CREATURELY SOPHIA, ETERNAL HUMANITY, AND THE INCARNATION

In the eternal trihypostatic life of God there is all of the content of the creaturely world and history, not as a possibility, but as an already given-over reality. In a sense, then, the hypostaseity of created reality even in its temporal and contingent nature has an eternal aspect, as it is found in the content of the divine life. This eternal aspect is what Bulgakov calls "eternal humanity," as humanity is the proper hypostasis or spirit of creation. There is a way in which God himself, and in particular the hypostasis of the Son in his unique relation to Sophia, has within himself an "eternal humanity." This "natural" relationship between the hypostasis of the Son and creaturely and divine Sophia is the basis for the incarnation. Because of the personal continuity from the way in which the Son hypostatizes both divine and creaturely Sophia, one may say that the Son's self-revelation of the Father in the Spirit is utterly simple and consistent both in the divine life and in his incarnate life. The whole of creaturely reality is an eternal gift of the life of the Son who is eternally given for us. Creation becomes itself *within* the very life of God. In other words, the content of God's mind, or divine Sophia, receives its own being in becoming and multiplicity. God's eternal self-revelation becomes in time, and yet for God, creation "is present in exhaustive fullness as a single act in God's eternity."[65] However, creatures experience this fullness only as becoming in time.

63. Bulgakov, *Lamb of God*, 119. "God is not the Absolute—that is only his self-definition. He is *God*; that is, he is the Absolute existing for another—precisely for the world. To this degree this *other* of Divinity is included in the depths of the Divine life. This is panentheism, where all is in God or for God" (ibid., 121). See also Bulgakov, *Bride*, 30–31.

64. Bulgakov, *Bride*, 31.

65. Ibid., 59. It is important to note that Bulgakov makes a distinction between the inner triune life of God and his "work" in creation. He says "God is not diminished by this in his Divine immanence, but he goes beyond its limits into the world. In God's

CREATED SOPHIA AND HUMAN NATURE

Bulgakov explains creation in terms of Sophia in order to maintain a delicate balance between dualism and pantheism. Divine Sophia is the principle of kenotic love in the divine life that by its very *nature* must empty itself into another. There cannot be anything genuinely other than God; moreover, God already fully expresses kenotic love within the divine life. Therefore, the object of creative kenotic love must be distinct from God's eternal tri-personal life. Divine Sophia, as the content of the divine life, enters here as that which is both God and distinct from God, an "ontological bridge" between creature and Creator.[66] Creation is Sophia, not as she exists eternally hypostatized by the three persons, but in another mode. Creaturely Sophia is the positing of divine Sophia into "becoming" or time. In eternity she is one and complete. In time she exists in multiplicity, although taken as a whole she is the precise image of divine Sophia. As Bulgakov explains, "The [created] world is the altero-being of the Principle, the creaturely mode of the divine being. Eternity becomes the foundation for temporal-spatial multiple being. In the creaturely world, the divine world is clothed in becoming."[67] However, if the creaturely Sophia or world is an

---

self-definition this fact is not primary but secondary, in the sense that his love in the Holy Trinity, his being in himself, is the foundation for his love outside himself, for his creative kenosis. The creation of the world is therefore not an inner self-positing of Divinity, which is God in the Holy Trinity, but a certain work of God" (Bulgakov, *Lamb of God*, 128). This distinction between "work" and divine immanence becomes especially important in his discussion of the Son's kenosis in the incarnation (see *Lamb of God*, 223). Paul Valliere does not take this distinction into account, and ends up comparing Bulgakov's idea of sophianization to "Anglo-American process theology" (*Modern Russian Theology*, 332). Nichols, on the other hand, is careful to highlight Bulgakov's distinction between the way creation is included in God's self-definition and the fact that "insofar as creation constitutes outside of God a reality other than God, it is the work of God, and to say this is to speak of creation as found essentially in time, in becoming" (Nichols, *Wisdom From Above*, 38).

66. Bulgakov, *Lamb of God*, 220.

67. Bulgakov, *Bride*, 53. "Creation and relatedness to creation are an integral part of the very idea of God. They cannot be rejected as contingent, non-essential, as if they might or might not have existed. It is impossible for them not to exist. The Absolute, God in himself, unrelated to creation, as conceived by theology, is a conventional abstraction by which we examine the question of God's nature. Concretely, there is no such thing, because relation to the world, being for the world, belong to that nature and are inseparable from it. 'The Absolute' is God, and does not exist and cannot be understood except in relation to the world. God exists as creator, not as a frozen 'Absolute' closed upon itself. 'God' is a relative concept, containing in itself his relatedness to the world" (Williams, *Sergii Bulgakov*, 185).

image of the divine world, then it must also have a hypostasis or hypostases to hypostatize it. The proper hypostases for creaturely Sophia are human persons who are distinct and yet, by *nature*, united.

The logic of Bulgakov's relationship between God and the world depends upon extracting the relationship from the categories of causality and motion.[68] God is related to the world as a "doer" rather than as a cause. "To determine the actual relation between God and the world, another category must be used, a category for which there is no place in the immanence of the world . . . This category must preserve both the positive connection between God and the world and the ontological distance between them. This category is . . . *creation* and *createdness*."[69] Creation presupposes a Creator, a personal God, and has its foundation in the triune relation that God *is*. Bulgakov argues that *creatio ex nihilo*, when conceived as "a sack into which, later, upon creation, all the forms of being were poured," entails not only change in the divine nature, but a kind of depersonalization of the relationship between God and creatures. When conceived in a Trinitarian, sophiological manner:

> One must include the world's creation in God's own life, coposit the creation with God's life, correlate God's world-creating act with the act of His self-determination. One must know how to simultaneously unite, identify, and distinguish creation and God's life, which in fact is possible in the doctrine of Sophia, Divine and creaturely, identical and distinct.[70]

The creaturely world or creaturely Sophia is the self-emptying of the divine world into another mode of being, "the self-revelation of the Divine Sophia in the creaturely Sophia."[71] Thus, creation has its foundation in God's own life as an activity rather than a content. For Bulgakov, creation is each hypostasis loving divinity into nothingness: the Father loving his self-revelation in the Son; the Son loving the Father revealed in himself; the Holy Spirit ratifying and reposing upon divine Love, and pouring this

---

68. Bulgakov, *Bride*, 36. Here Bulgakov addresses Aquinas in particular: "The doctrine of God as the prime mover or first cause of the world is completely unconnected with the Divine Person. (The personal properties are introduced in Aquinas later and do not have a determining significance for this question)."

69. Ibid.

70. Ibid., 44.

71. Ibid., 60.

love out into an "other."[72] Such a sophianic description of the relationship between God and the world establishes a correlation between the triune, relational nature of God and God's self-disclosure in creation.

Only such a "personal" triune foundation for creation forms a sufficient basis for the image of God in human persons. It is the inner-triune act of kenosis that constitutes the divine persons, and participation in this act is the basis for the hypostaseity of creation. "This self-revelation is accomplished by God as the foundation of man's being and, in man, of the being of all creation."[73] Humanity bears the image of God both in being hypostatic, as well as in being the hypostasis for the creaturely world/human nature. The image of God in humans is "an ontological bridge between the Creator and his creation and from the beginning it establishes a positive relation between the Image and the Proto-Image."[74] Hypostaseity, or personhood, *is* in relation to the "other" by being an act of self-donation, the content of which is the "nature" of the hypostasis. Just as God is trihypostatic and has his own nature/divine Sophia in an eternal and fully hypostatized way, so human hypostases are personal and hypostatize creaturely Sophia in time. While the divine Sophia may be open to creaturely participation, this participation neither changes nor diminishes the way in which God possesses God's self. Thus, humanity in time and becoming can have its foundation and end in the divine nature itself as "Image" or fullness of humanity, without implying that God needs human perfection to complete God's own life.

HUMAN NATURE

If the divine nature is pre-eternal humanity, then human nature, like divine, must be one. Unlike Aquinas, who argues for individual human natures, Bulgakov thinks humanity is one nature with multiple hypostases.[75] Nature in this sense extends beyond a particular body or species. For Bulgakov, human nature is, like divine nature, a world. As such, humanity extends across

---

72. Bulgakov calls this "panentheism"—the idea that the world is in and for God. He argues that "reducing the world solely to an accident inwardly unconnected with God . . . impoverishes Divine Love, transforms it into an abstraction, and even blasphemes against it" (*Lamb of God*, 122).

73. Ibid., 112.

74. Ibid.

75. Ibid., 204–5. Aquinas, on the other hand, follows an Aristotelian idea of human nature existing only in particular substances. For him there is no such thing as a universal human nature that Christ could assume (*ST*, IIIa.4.4–5).

the boundaries of species, space, and time. Human nature is the entirety of divine nature as it exists in becoming and multiplicity—it is all of creation throughout all of time. Human persons are the hypostases of that one nature. In fact, Bulgakov believes that the Chalcedonian definition supports this idea when it says that Christ is "perfect in humanity . . . consubstantial with us according to humanity." Bulgakov understands "homoousios according to humanity" to mean that, just as with divinity, an integral humanity must exist which is hypostatized by individual humans. He says:

> Every person not only has certain universally human traits, or participates in humanity. Every person is also an all-man: I am a man and nothing human is foreign to me. That is the fundamental anthropological axiom which lies at the basis of the idea of original sin and God's incarnation and, finally, redemption . . . The new Adam redeemed the whole old Adam and in this sense replaced him with himself. And no *pars pro toto*, or series of successive and partial redemptions could correspond to this task, which is a universal one.[76]

The impersonal aspect of the divine Sophia, hypostatized by the three divine persons, is analogous to the impersonal aspect of human nature, hypostasized by all humanity. Therefore, the Second Person of the Trinity assumed not "a" human nature, which he united to himself in his person, but rather, the one human nature that constitutes all of creation.

THE GOD-MAN

Bulgakov's definitions of hypostasis and nature have thus far allowed him to posit divine Sophia or divine nature and creaturely Sophia or nature as building an ontological bridge between God and humanity.

> Again, the Logos became the hypostasis for this nature not in virtue of abstract omnipotence but because precisely the human nature was called to be hypostatized by the hypostasis of the Logos. . . . From the beginning, the Logos finds himself in a positive relation with the human nature, just as, in its depths, the human nature bears His image and awaits His coming into the world.[77]

76. Bulgakov, *Bride*, 111.
77. Bulgakov, *Lamb of God*, 196.

In God, the divine nature is fully hypostatized and the divine life is fully accomplished. However, the creaturely world, or humanity, remains fragmented in itself and separated from its proper life in God, its image and foundation. Humanity could only be brought into the divine life by the one who is Divine Life, the Person of the Word. In his divine nature the Word is already humanity in its fullness and unity and this is exactly what allows human nature to be assumed by the Logos in the incarnation:

> The assumption of the integral humanity signifies not the abstract assimilation of certain human properties, corporeal and psychic, but the concrete assumption of me, you, them . . . The Lord took his humanity not from impersonal nature, but from each of us personally. He thus became one with his humanity, introducing it into his own hypostatic being.[78]

In the incarnation Christ's humanity is a "multi-hypostatic all-unity." He is human with us as we are human, not homoiousianly, but homoousianly as simultaneously "personal and all-human."[79] The Son is in fact the fulfillment, or full actualization of human nature, for only the Son can fully hypostatize creaturely Sophia. Hypostatization, the kenotic self-donation to the "other," in its absolute sense requires the absolute handing over of the one's self to the other, an act that requires the full "possession" of a nature. Only the Son, who *is* in himself the Word or ordered content of creaturely nature, is able to fully offer that nature over to God in kenotic obedience, and thus to fully hypostatize creaturely nature or Sophia. Only the Son can fully "hypostatize" both divine and creaturely Sophia in a personal act of self-donation that orders the content of both natures as a transparent "gift" to the Father in the Spirit.

In the incarnation, the union between humanity and divinity in Christ is accomplished through divine self-emptying, or kenosis, which is itself Christ's hypostatization of human and divine natures. In the union of natures, both divinity and humanity must remain intact. "God does not stop being God; even after descending from heaven, he remains in heaven. Likewise, man does not stop being man after he receives God into himself."[80] Although the ontological and substantial fullness of the divine

78. Bulgakov, *Bride*, 109.

79. Ibid., 110.

80. Bulgakov, *Lamb of God*, 220. This issue is central in Weinandy's critique of the modern kenotic theology Bulgakov draws upon. Weinandy argues that the kenotic theology of Gess, Godet, Gore, and even Thomasius is inherently compositional (Weinandy, *Does God Change*, 101–14).

life is unchanging and undiminished, Bulgakov thinks that the *fullness* of the divine life, or the living out of its bliss, can be limited "not by something from outside, but by Divinity's own proper will."[81] The kenotic act does not begin in the incarnation, but "expresses the general relation of God to the world . . . but this kenosis is revealed in a wholly new way in the humiliation of the Word, who is united with creation, becomes man."[82]

In the incarnation, the Son empties himself of the divine life and his hypostasis is made manifest in humanity. "His life becomes not his own any longer but comes to belong to the Paternal hypostasis: the Father sends. The Father is revealed in the Son, who thus becomes perfectly transparent for the Paternal Hypostasis . . . The Son is the hypostatic obedience to the commands of the Father, accomplished by the power of the Holy Spirit reposing upon him. Outside of and apart from this the Son does not have himself."[83] The Son who, as God, lives in the divine nature, now lives as a human "I." The human "I," however, is by its own nature a "supratemporal I" with its foundation in the divine nature and eternity.[84] This simultaneous eternality and temporality in every human "I" means Jesus lived a human life such that:

> His life on earth was a constant kenosis both exteriorly in what he did and suffered and interiorly, in his own self-awareness. He was aware of his own divinity to the extent that his human essence could receive and contain that divinity. It is in that limitation that the incessant kenosis consisted.[85]

---

81. Ibid., 221. Bulgakov resembles Thomasius here in his emphasis on the difference between the economic and immanent Trinity with respect to kenosis. "The immanent Trinity is invariably present in the economic Trinity. The immanent Trinity is itself in its proper depths and foundation, but it is also other than and in this sense transcendent to the life of the economic Trinity" (ibid., 222). This idea coincides with the distinction of the triune life "in itself" and "for itself." Nichols explains this as "the distinction between what a reality is in its own inherent character and the manifestation of that reality to itself" (Nichols, *Wisdom From Above*, 102). It can also be compared to Thomas's essence and act distinction.

82. Bulgakov, *Lamb of God*, 223. Will is not distinct from the eternal triune activity of love and its expression in the divine life.

83. Ibid., 225.

84. Ibid., 260–61.

85. Nichols, *Wisdom from Above*, 105.

The two natures in Christ are distinct; his human nature is not merely an instrument but cooperates in its own divinization.[86] On the other hand, divinity "must allow itself to be in a condition of continuous self-adjustment to what the human nature can accept."[87] The human and divine natures are always inseparable, unconfusable, and unchangeable, but in the life of Christ, the God-Man, they are also united "in virtue of the hypostatic center of this life."[88]

The foundation for Christ's kenotic life, his divine experience of the human world/nature, lies in his eternal identity as the Word/Wisdom in the life of God. From eternity the Son is the divine-humanity such that "Jesus is not Son of God without relation to his humanity nor Son of Man without relation to his divinity. Nor is he God and man, as although these could be alternated or separated."[89] Jesus is co-man with humanity and he proclaims his divine sonship to his fellow humans. Thus, the Son opens the possibility for human nature to participate in the glory of the divine nature, or creaturely Sophia into the life of divine Sophia. Creaturely participation in the divine life is the co-enactment with the Son of his kenosis.

In Christ, God enters as man into the real relationship established between God and humanity at creation. Bulgakov is able to posit both a reciprocal and a perichoretic relationship between God and humanity on the ontological basis of divine and creaturely Sophia as divine and human nature hypostatized—on the one hand, eternally in the divine life and on the other, temporally in becoming. The divine Word assumes his own nature (divine Sophia) hypostatically (a human "I") as it is in becoming (created Sophia/human nature). The Word's personal act of self-emptying in the incarnation is parallel to his impersonal act of self-emptying in creation. For Bulgakov, the difference between God and humanity does not lie in human and divine natures as it does for Aquinas. Rather, the mystery of the difference in the Son's life in creation and the incarnation lies in the

---

86. This kind of two-sided real relationship entails a mutual *communicatio idiomatum*. "Being God by hypostasis and nature, but humbling himself to the point of union with man and emptying himself, he actualizes his divinity for himself only in inseparable union with the human nature, as a function of its receptivity. Therefore, the perichoresis, the communication of the properties of the two natures in the God-Man, goes in both directions: not only from the Divine to the human but also from the human to the Divine" (Bulgakov, *Lamb of God*, 256).

87. Nichols, *Wisdom from Above*, 110.

88. Bulgakov, *Lamb of God*, 196.

89. Nichols, *Wisdom from Above*, 114.

difference between time and eternity. God empties himself into time in an act of communicative love that is creation. God comes to his own Image, in becoming as the perfection and completion of that Image thereby opening humanity to its telos, the union of created and divine Sophia and a hypostatized life in God.

The universe is personified and relational in humanity, and human nature extends throughout history, across species, and especially as it is shared by all human persons. Human nature, as a historical reality, is always a fragmented image of the divine nature, but there is a real correspondence between Image and image.[90] God will be all in all when creaturely Sophia becomes a true image of divine Sophia. The goal of creation is the union of creaturely and divine Sophia, when creation will be a true image of the divine life. The process of unification between creaturely and divine Sophia is called sophianization. This union between creaturely and divine Sophia is what is meant when we speak of the marriage between the Lamb of God and his Bride, the church. Bulgakov's ecclesiology posits the church as "the fulfillment of God's eternal plan concerning creation and the salvation, sanctification, glorification, deification, and sophianization of creation. In this sense it is the very foundation of creation, its inner entelechy."[91] The church is the proper activity of creation, her self-surrender to the Father in the Son, by the power of the Holy Spirit.

SALVATION HISTORY: HUMANITY AND THE CHURCH

If the "inner entelechy" of creaturely nature is the church, or the participation in the kenotic love that constitutes the triune life, then we must ask who

90. "The initial axiom of this revelation consists precisely in there being a conformity or co-imagedness between Divinity and humanity. In other words, the Divine Sophia, as the pan-organism of ideas, is the pre-eternal humanity in God, as the divine proto-image and foundation for men's being" (ibid., 113). Here, Bulgakov accomplishes two things: First, divine nature is available for participation by creatures as the foundation of creaturely nature, and creaturely nature is not alien to divinity, such that a real, two-way relationship is possible. Second, the openness of the triune life to creaturely participation does not impinge upon the immanent Trinitarian life. God possesses the divine Sophia eternally and completely in the three persons. While the divine Sophia may be open to creaturely participation, this participation neither changes nor diminishes the way in which God possesses it. Thus, humanity in time and becoming can have its foundation and end in the divine nature itself as "Image" or fullness of humanity without implying that God needs human perfection to complete God's own life.

91. Bulgakov, *Bride*, 253.

is the agent of this kenosis? If humanity is the agent of "sophianization" for creaturely Sophia, then does the triune life become in some way contingent upon human freedom? If God is the agent of creaturely participation in the triune life, what role, if any, does human agency play in the history of the world? At the heart of these questions is the question about the nature of personhood in general. What sort of freedom in self-surrender does a person possess, both within the divine life, and in the creaturely world created in the triune image?

Bulgakov sees the antinomy between freedom and necessity with respect to God and humanity as a misconception of hypostatic life. The nature of a hypostasis is love. "All life in God, in itself, is love."[92] Bulgakov's notion of personhood is consistent throughout his theology. In God there is a "necessity of love" that characterizes the relations between the divine persons. This necessity of love is identified with absolute freedom. For Bulgakov, freedom does not consist in alternate possibilities, or even the absence of necessity. It is the full exchange of self-giving love, the absolute outpouring of personal content given and received.[93] Therefore, there is no need to maintain a kind of openness in content or freedom from necessity in order to preserve either divine or creaturely freedom. Just as the content of the divine life, or Sophia, is given and necessary, so the relationship between God and creation contained within that content is given and necessary. "God is a relational concept" both *ad intra* and *ad extra*. Just as the

92. Bulgakov, *Sophia*, 35. "In this sense we can speak of love in God not only in the mutual relationship of the three hypostases and in the relationship of God to his Godhead, but in like manner in the love of the Godhead for God. Thus if God loves Sophia, Sophia also loves God. Apart from this the tri-hypostatic relation between God and his ousia is inconceivable. To sum up, the nature of God (which is in fact Sophia) is a living and, therefore, loving substance, ground, and 'principle.' But it might be said, does this not lead to the conception of a 'fourth hypostasis?' the reply is 'certainly not,' for this principle in itself is non-hypostatic, though capable of being hypostatized in a given Hypostasis, and thereby constituting its life" (ibid).

93. "The notion, freely accepted by Aquinas and others, that God, by virtue of this 'freedom' of his, could have refrained from creating the world must be rejected as not appropriate to his essence. If God created the world, this means that he *could not have refrained from creating it*, although the Creator's act belongs to the fullness of God's life and this act contains no external compulsion that would contradict divine freedom. And if one can speak of the *will* to create in God, this will, as synonymous with freedom, is not an anthropomorphic will, which can desire or not desire, but the divine will, which invariably and absolutely desires. In general the distinction between God's being and his creation, defined according to the feature of freedom and understood in the sense of different *possibilities*, must be completely eliminated, for such a distinction does not exist" (Bulgakov, *Bride*, 31).

Son in a certain sense possesses an eternal humanity that is worked out and revealed to creatures in the incarnation, so the hypostatization of creaturely Sophia by human nature, a synergistic activity Bulgakov calls "grace," has a kind of givenness to it, or a foregone conclusion. The cosmos does possess an openness and freedom toward its end, but this is not the openness of various possibilities or the freedom of surprise between one person and another. The freedom of creatures consists in the process of working out the irresistible call of creaturely nature to be unified and hypostatized into the divine life as the creaturely image of divine Sophia.

CREATURELY SOPHIA, ETERNAL HUMANITY]CHURCH: SOPHIA AND SOBERNOST

For Bulgakov, the church is in one aspect "eternal with the eternity of God, for it is the Divine Sophia herself."[94] In this sense the church is the "very foundation of creation, its inner entelechy"[95] moving toward an eschatological union of divine and creaturely Sophia, a "conjugal syzygy" of the Lamb and his Bride.[96] Both divine and creaturely aspects are described as *sobernost*, or gatheredness. The divine Sophia is "universal cosmic *sobernost* or concrete all-unity in divine love."[97] That is, the shared life of the divine nature. In a second aspect, the church is equivalent to the creaturely Sophia in that:

> God created the world for the sake of the Church. That is as much as to say that it is at once the ground and goal of the world, its final cause and entelechy. The world of humans by its creation is already designated for deification, in the incarnation and Pentecost. And this deification, which whether virtual or actual is the supreme actualization of the world, is effected through the Church, which thus appears as a ladder joining heaven and earth and conveying divine life to the creation.[98]

Indeed, if creaturely Sophia is the divine life emptied into becoming and multiplicity, then all creaturely existence must be included within her as an

94. Ibid., 253.
95. Ibid.
96. Ibid., 254.
97. Bulgakov, *Lamb of God*, 104.
98. Bulgakov, *Sophia*, 134.

organic, living, multi-unity headed by Christ and quickened by the Holy Spirit.[99] The church as the foundation and telos of creation is the principle of *sobernost* or gatheredness at work uniting the creaturely nature in and through Christ. She is the fullness of Christ, who by virtue of his incarnation brings all things together in himself and "accomplishes the unification of divine and creaturely life, man's deification, which is precisely the power of the heavenly Church manifested in the earthly Church."[100]

Within this paradigm the reality of sophianization, or the hypostatization of creaturely Sophia in the divine life, is accomplished by a dual movement of Sophia, both within and other than God moving with and toward one another.[101] This movement is a synergistic grace that draws creation into the eternal *sobernost* of the Trinity.[102] The eternal Sophia and creaturely Sophia are united through the incarnation of Christ. Now the presence of the incarnate Lord and the Holy Spirit fill the earthly church with the power of the heavenly church, its own proper end. Thus, the church as divine-humanity, as the body of Christ and the temple of the Holy Spirit, is a union of divine and creaturely principles, their interpenetration without separation or confusion.[103]

Human nature, and through it all of creation, is caught up in this inexorable telos through the incarnation. "The Incarnation of the Lord as the divine-human person of Christ consisted in the assumption of the whole Adam, 'perfect' humanity. There are no limits to this assumption, either external or internal. Christ's humanity is the inner human condition of every human being."[104] For Bulgakov, this means that grace is received simply in creatures being what they are, the creaturely Sophia whose being

---

99. Bulgakov, *Bride*, 257.

100. Ibid., 257–58.

101. Ibid., 264. "Heavenly and earthly, the Church is one in ground and limit, in entelechy, but she remains dual in the world process until the end of the world."

102. Ibid., 255. "The sophianization of the world is accomplished through the redemption given by the Lord Jesus Christ in his Incarnation by the Holy Spirit. This general relation between the Divine and creaturely principles, sophianization *in actu*, is defined as grace in all the different senses of the term."

103. Bulgakov distinguishes between Christ and the church, or between divine and creaturely Sophia, by saying that Christ is Son by nature, whereas the church has its sonship through participation in Christ. Recall again that according to Bulgakov, creaturely Sophia is not a fellow hypostasis in the divine life; rather she is hypostatized.

104. Ibid., 266.

is anchored in the divine life.[105] There is no possibility for a "pure human nature," or human perfection or fulfillment apart from God. Creaturely Sophia, human nature *in toto*, has its foundation and finality in the union of creaturely and divine Sophia.

For Bulgakov, the incarnation makes the church coextensive with human nature. Human nature is the entirety of divine nature/Sophia as it exists in becoming and multiplicity—it is all of creation throughout all time, and human persons are the hypostases of that one nature.[106] This does not imply that the whole maintains a priority over the members or vice versa. Bulgakov resolves this tension with his distinction between individual human hypostases and the unity of humanity, "first in the old Adam, and then in the New Adam."[107] "Every hypostasis is a personal *how* of the universal *what* and, as such, belongs to the fullness, the pleroma."[108] Each hypostasis belongs to Christ as head of the church. But Christ as head is not the equivalent of any other member, or even of all the members combined. "The head abides *above* the members. It is the foundation, in which all the different members find themselves as multiple in unity: Christ, the head, is not only a man; He is the All-man."[109] Christ expresses both the triune life and all of creaturely existence in himself. "He testifies that he is present in every person (and therefore not a single person is excluded from this presence)."[110] Every human hypostasis participates in the universal human nature or Sophia such that each person is an "all-man." Rather it can be said of each of us, "I am a man and nothing human is foreign to me."[111] Thus, in the one human nature assumed in the incarnation, the Logos takes up the whole of humanity, and through it, the cosmos. The church, then, as a creaturely reality is already accomplished with the incarnation, as Christ joins human nature, which is creaturely Sophia, to his divine nature, which is the divine Sophia. The result of the incarnation is that the church does

---

105. Ibid., 295.

106. In fact, as noted earlier, Bulgakov believes that the Chalcedonian definition supports this idea when it says that Christ is "perfect in humanity . . . consubstantial with us according to humanity." Bulgakov understands "homoousios according to humanity" to mean that, just as in divinity, an integral humanity must exist.

107. Bulgakov, *Bride*, 260.

108. Ibid.

109. Ibid.

110. Ibid., 261.

111. Ibid., 111.

not mediate Christ to human nature, but rather the church is, in Christ, equivalent to human nature.

> Thus the doctrine of the Church as the body of Christ, as the temple of the Holy Spirit, has, first of all, an anthropological significance. This doctrine affirms a certain panchristism and panpneumatism, to which no limits are set. In this aspect this doctrine contains the idea that, after the Incarnation and the Pentecost, Christ is the head of humankind and therefore lives in all humankind. The same thing is affirmed concerning the Holy Spirit.[112]

The unmediated and universal presence of Christ and the Holy Spirit in all of humanity, calling it into a shared participation in creaturely Sophia, is also a participation in the divine Sophia, or a "cosmic universal sobernost." Bulgakov thus defines his ecclesiology as "the doctrine of the sobornost of the Church, understood, both ontologically and pragmatically, as the principle of gathering and gatheredness in love."[113] Christ and the Holy Spirit gather together the multiplicity of creatures together into this sobernost wherein, as church, we respond with creaturely love. The question remains, however, whether creaturely love so permeated with the seeds of divinity is in any way a genuine response. Is the wedding feast of the Lamb a celebration of true love, or the product of an arranged marriage? Bulgakov claims that the church's response is a synergism that is grace, yet that grace overwhelms human and natural/historical reality. The *pleroma* or fullness overtakes history. Bulgakov's panentheism, panchristism, and panpneumatism leave no space for genuine creaturely activity and no need for transformation. The church is only unfinished in the sense that, from the church's perspective, she still awaits the eschatological union with, or hypostatization in, the divine Sophia that will occur at the end of history.[114]

---

112. Ibid., 261.

113. Ibid., 262.

114. The full extent of human determination which results from Bulgakov's characterization of human nature as creaturely Sophia is only fully developed in his detailed treatment of the soul's experience of life after death. He believes that each soul will be confronted with the Truth of Christ in such a way that they will eventually (although the experience is actually outside of time) come to love him and take their place in/as creaturely Sophia.

CONCLUSION

Bulgakov's theology hinges upon a set of variations on the theme of the triune life as kenotic love expressed uniquely in the relations of the divine persons. As we have seen, he is careful not to obscure the personal activity of God with other distinctions, such as the distinction between nature and essence or between divine acts *ad intra* and *ad extra* that he sees as poisoning Thomas's theology of God. All of reality has its foundation in the tri-personhood of God. Bulgakov's doctrines of the Trinity, the incarnation, and the church as human history all reflect this Trinitarian dynamic. His concept of Sophia is not so much the focus of his work, as what enables him to maintain continuity with the Orthodox tradition while making a kenotic Trinitarian theology central to all of reality. As a shared life given over to the "other," primarily in God, but also participated in by creaturely life, Sophia is dependent upon the notion that divine blessedness, or glory, is equivalent to suffering, or kenosis, and this suffering/glory *is* the love that is the divine essence.

Bulgakov's construal of the divine act *ad extra* as a self-donation of the triune God allows him to articulate two crucial theological points. First, Christ's suffering and death can be a genuine expression of the immanent Trinitarian life. Second, there is an infinite distance between Creator and creature that constitutes both the possibility of relation and the possibility of genuine freedom, Bulgakov's Trinitarian insight provides a foundation for recognizing all of reality as an image of the triune life, a thesis Balthasar places at the heart of his own corpus.

2

Thomas Aquinas on Triune Relation

INTRODUCTION

In the previous chapter I explained the interaction between Bulgakov's Trinitarian theology and his sophiology, particularly as it is a reaction to Thomas Aquinas. In this chapter I demonstrate that Balthasar reads Thomas with relation rather than the essence/nature *ad intra/ad extra* distinction as the primary concept. If Thomas is taken to mean that relation *is* the divine essence, which determines the divine persons and divine activity, then Balthasar believes that Bulgakov's bridging concept of Sophia is superfluous. However, Balthasar understands the Thomistic Trinitarian theology, particularly the concept of relation, in a distinctly Bulgakovian light: The act of relation is the absolute self-donation of self to the "other," which constitutes both divine simplicity, the infinite distance/difference between the three divine persons as well as the analogously infinite distance/difference between God and creation.

Bulgakov's Trinitarian theology requires a "space between" the divine persons. The very act of personhood is a ceaseless offering of self to another, "across" or "into." The metaphorical language of distance or space is Bulgakov's way of dealing with the unity and difference inherent within the triune life as well as the difference and identity between God and a contingent other. Bulgakov, however, goes on to name this distance or space between as Sophia. Sophia is the impersonal "setting" for the drama of the triune life. In adopting Bulgakov's Trinitarian theology, Balthasar must account for the "distance" between divine persons required by the very activity of self-donation that constitutes personhood. Whereas Bulgakov looks to ground a "personal space" for the triune dynamic in the impersonal self-revelation of God, Balthasar believes that Sophia is unnecessary. Balthasar believes that the notion of relation, as it is presented in Thomas's Trinitarian theology, is sufficient to describe not only unity and difference within the triune life, but the analogous "space" between Creator and creature.[1] "Space" in terms of relation is not emptiness devoid of content, nor should it be sophiologically considered as a kind of extra-personal positing of content. "Space," or distance for Balthasar, is relation primarily characterized as an "encounter" or the "interaction of (positive) centers of freedom."[2] It is the activity or encounter, the *relation*, between subject and object that entails a "genuine mutuality."[3] Again, this "space between" is neither separable from the agents, nor can it be reduced to a kind of "thing" between them. It is in the unique category of relation.

1. "Relation" functions analogously for Balthasar in his epistemology. D. C. Schindler discusses Balthasar's "Dramatic Structure of Truth" by posing the question "Whether the transcendence of the act of knowing is accounted for wholly by the subject, or whether it is something the object coenables . . . if the ground of the object's objectivity is nothing other than the 'transcendental' striving of the subject, then the subject's openness ends where the object begins; the object's otherness is lost precisely to the extent that the subject's union with it is consummated" (D. C. Schindler, *Hans Urs Von Balthasar*, 4). The act of knowing requires a mediation between subject and object that is not other than subject and object; it requires the relation between subject and object. Schindler examines the "structure of truth" as an activity that entails the "reciprocity of union and difference in knowing" (ibid., 5). Schindler points out the important difference between Balthasar and Heidegger on this point. Heidegger establishes the "subject-object-relation" on "the ultimate reciprocal relation of being and the human essence" (*das Sein und das Menschenwesen*) (Heidegger, *Zur Seinsfrage*, 28). Ultimately, Schindler contends that this basis "degenerates into merely the final horizon of human consciousness" (D. C. Schindler, *Hans Urs Von Balthasar*, 6). Both the unity and the difference entailed in the term "relation" collapse into negativity. Schindler notes that, for Balthasar, the relation between subject and object retains a "positive and abiding otherness" that preserves its character as "mystery" (ibid.).

2. D. C. Schindler, *Hans Urs Von Balthasar*, 6.

3. "The mystery of being is revealed, that is, made *immediately apparent,* in and through the mediation of the encounter of particular beings in their simultaneous unity and difference. The mystery of being is, for Balthasar, not the murky night of ambiguity in which being and man dissolve into one another, but it is instead the translucent joy of genuine mutuality" (ibid.).

Aiden Nichols, in *No Bloodless Myth*, outlines this relational structure in Balthasar's conception of the analogous relation between the triune God and humankind. The defining fact of humanity is the capacity for relational space.

> In that finite image of the Trinity which is human being, unique-
> ness was given me so that, through the medium of the nature I
> share with my species, I can communicate with those others who
> have also been divinely "called by name." . . . I make my most basic
> act of self-possession in and with my universal opening to all be-
> ing whatsoever.[4]

In this quote we see not only how the bridging concept of relation is grounded in the infinite triune relation. The way in which "relation" serves to both identify and differentiate between human hypostases is an "echo" or analogy of the triune life. The notion of relation is an analogous notion that operates for Balthasar across his understanding of the transcendental as they exist in both God and creation; Truth, beauty, goodness, being, one-ness, and, ultimately, love are constituted by the perichoretic relation that is the life of God.

In this chapter I present a very different reading of Aquinas from that of Bulgakov. I rely for this analysis chiefly on the work of Gilles Emery. Unlike Bulgakov, Emery takes Thomas's separation of the *de Deo uno* from *de Deo trino* as a methodological tool rather than a theological statement. By doing so, he is able to use the concept of relation to bridge the apparent gap between the divine life *ad extra* and *ad intra*. I then present a brief argument as to why this particular reading of Aquinas is compatible with Balthasar's Trinitarian theology.[5]

This chapter provides a background for understanding how Thomas's notion of triune relation operates within Balthasar's Trinitarian theology, and forms the basis for definition of human persons. Balthasar develops Thomas's concept of relation with Bulgakov's to construct a theology of the

---

4. Nichols, *No Bloodless Myth*, 67. Balthasar follows Thomas in asserting the utter simplicity of divine being and divine freedom. Balthasar, however, points to a "space between" where God's freedom is identical with God's nature, and both freedom and nature are an activity where "self-possession" is the activity of "openness."

5. Obviously, a lot could be said about the relationship between Balthasar and Aqui-nas with respect to Trinitarian theology. For the purpose of this discussion, I merely wish to demonstrate that it is vital to read Balthasar with Thomas's Trinitarian theology, particularly his use of the concept of relation, in the background.

divine life both *ad intra* and *ad extra*, as well as the analogy between creaturely being and God.

BALTHASAR'S READING OF THOMAS ON TRINITY AND DIVINE/CREATURELY RELATION

Bulgakov's assertion that Thomas Aquinas obscures the personal Trinitarian nature of God with the distinction between God's nature directed *ad intra* and *ad extra* would seem to be of vital interest for Balthasar as well. After all, Bulgakov's Trinitarian insight establishes the perichoretic, triune kenosis as *the* fundamental characteristic of God's own life and the foundation of the creaturely world. Any real difference between God vis-à-vis God's self and God vis-à-vis the world would then compromise not only divine simplicity, but also the revelatory character of the Son's incarnate life. If Balthasar takes Bulgakov's Trinitarian insight as pivotal for his own work, then it seems likely that he too would find Thomas's Trinitarian theology at best inadequate. Instead, in *Theo-Logic* II, we see Balthasar turns to Aquinas to establish the continuity between the triune life in God and the triune life as it is the foundation of the world. In fact, he frames Bulgakov's thesis about the kenotic character of the triune act in distinctly Thomistic language. How does Balthasar overcome the apparent incongruity between these two thinkers? As I will show, Balthasar reconciles Bulgakov's Trinitarian insight with Thomas's distinction between the divine nature (activity) and essence by recognizing the role of "relation" within Thomas's Trinitarian logic. Balthasar's use of Thomas does not deal with this issue directly, but rather presumes a certain reading of Thomas's Trinitarian theology where the concepts of relation and opposition are "ways of being" that ground both unity and difference in the triune life.[6]

In order for the concepts of relation and analogy to function as both a "bridge" as well as an infinite difference, Balthasar wants to situate the analogy of being as the analogy of specifically triune being. To this end, Thomas must be read with his Trinitarian theology, particularly the notion of relation, in harmony with his discussion of being. In other words, the *de Deo uno* needs to be read together with the *de Deo trino*. When God's works "*ad extra*" are understood as expressions of the "relation" that constitutes the divine life, then "we must take in all seriousness the question of the image of the Trinity in created being, even if this question has been seldom

6. López, "Eternal Happening," 87.

posed in the history of theology."[7] This is because the basis for difference within the triune life, when the divine essence is understood as relation, is the basis for the difference between God and creation, and between creaturely persons. Though Aquinas himself does not explicitly establish this connection,[8] I will now outline his Trinitarian theology in a way that does in fact support Balthasar's project.

Thomas Aquinas and the Trinity

Whereas Bulgakov believes that Thomas's Trinitarian theology is secondary to his Aristotelian adaptation of God as First Cause, when we place the concept of relation at the heart of his Trinitarian theology it is clear that Thomas's separation of the *de Deo uno* from *de Deo trino* is in fact a methodological tool rather than a theological statement. In this reading of Thomas, the concept of relation bridges the apparent gap between the divine life *ad extra* and *ad intra*.

Essence and Nature

I want to focus on Gilles Emery's discussion of six terms that Thomas employs to understand the triune life in God: essence, nature, relation, procession, operation, and person.[9] Thomas explains these terms with respect to divine simplicity, where God's existence and essence are the same. God is God's own being. In *ST* Ia.39.1, Aquinas explains how the three persons or relations are related to the divine essence: "In God relations are subsistent, and so by reason of the opposition between them they distinguish the 'supposita;' and yet the essence is not distinguished, because *the relations themselves are not distinguished from each other so far as they are identified with the essence*" (emphasis mine).[10] When the three persons are understood in God, they each pertain in the same way to the essence such that one can say that the Father is the essence or the Son is the essence, or any combina-

---

7. Balthasar, *Truth of God*, 173.

8. "Medieval theology admittedly entered into this area of discussion with a certain hesitancy; leaving in the background the question of the relationship between Trinitarian difference and the fundamental difference within worldly being" (ibid).

9. In this section I rely on the work of Gilles Emery OP, particularly his summary of Thomistic Trinitarian theology in *The Trinitarian Theology of St Thomas Aquinas*.

10. Thomas Aquinas, *Summa Theologica*, Ia.39.1.

tion of the three are the essence, and that the essence is the three persons. While the three persons remain always distinct in relation to one another, essentially (*ad essentiam comparata*), they are the same. However, this does not imply that triunity is collapsed into static or impersonal oneness. On the contrary, the identification of essence and person allows Aquinas to say that God's one being *is* being three persons.[11]

The divine *essentia* is not only really the same as one person, but it is really the same as the three persons. Whence, one person, and two, and three, can be predicated of the *essentia* as if we were to say "the *essentia* is the Father, and the Son, and the Holy Ghost." And because this word "God" can of itself stand for the *essentia*, as above explained (A[4], ad 3), hence, as it is true to say "the *essentia* is the three *persona*"; so likewise it is true to say "God is the three persons."[12]

---

11. "One person in God is related to two persons—namely, the person of the Father to the person of the Son and the person of the Holy Ghost. This is not, however, by one relation; otherwise it would follow that the Son also and the Holy Ghost would be related to the Father by one and the same relation. Thus, since relation alone multiplies the Trinity, it would follow that the Son and the Holy Ghost would not be two persons. Nor can it be said with Prepositivus that as God is related in one way to creatures, while creatures are related to Him in divers ways, so the Father is related by one relation to the Son and to the Holy Ghost; whereas these two persons are related to the Father by two relations. For, since the very specific idea of a relation is that it refers to another, it must be said that two relations are not specifically different if but one opposite relation corresponds to them. For the relation of Lord and Father must differ according to the difference of filiation and servitude. Now, all creatures are related to God as His creatures by one specific relation. But the Son and the Holy Ghost are not related to the Father by one and the same kind of relation. Hence there is no parity. Further, in God there is no need to admit any real relation to the creature (28, 1,3); while there is no reason against our admitting in God, many logical relations. But in the Father there must be a real relation to the Son and to the Holy Ghost. Hence, corresponding to the two relations of the Son and of the Holy Ghost, whereby they are related to the Father, we must understand two relations in the Father, whereby He is related to the Son and to the Holy Ghost. Hence, since there is only one Person of the Father, it is necessary that the relations should be separately signified in the abstract; and these are what we mean by properties and notions" (Aquinas, *ST*, Ia.39.2).

12. Ibid., Ia.39.7. Also, "Some have thought that in God essence and person differ, forasmuch as they held the relations to be "adjacent"; considering only in the relations the idea of "reference to another," and not the relations as realities. But as it was shown above (Q[28], A[2]) in creatures relations are accidental, whereas in God they are the divine essence itself. Thence it follows that in God essence is not really distinct from person; and yet that the persons are really distinguished from each other. For person, as above stated (Q[29], A[4]), signifies relation as subsisting in the divine nature. But relation as referred to the essence does not differ there from reality, but only in our way of thinking" (Aquinas, *ST*, Ia.39.1).

As we can see here, relation allows Thomas to ground both simplicity and difference in the same concept. However, further distinctions are necessary. When the divine essence is considered as relation, "there must also be some abstract terms whereby we may answer that the persons are distinguished; and these are the properties or notions signified by an abstract term, as paternity and filiation. Therefore the divine essence is signified as 'What'; and the person as 'Who'; and the property as 'Whereby.'"[13]

If the divine essence is relation and the diverse relations in God constitute the persons, how does Thomas talk about the activity of God? In the following quote, from the question on divine simplicity, both suppositum and nature refer to what is one in God. The suppositum is that which individualizes and actualizes a nature, and the nature is that by which the supposit has its life and proper activity.

"In things not composed of matter and form, in which individualization is not due to individual matter—that is to say, to "this" matter—the very forms being individualized of themselves—it is necessary the forms themselves should be subsisting *supposita*. Therefore *suppositum* and *natura* in them are identified. Since God, then, is not composed of matter and form, he must be his own Godhead, his own life, and whatever else is thus predicated of him."[14]

God's essence and nature, however, can be distinguished logically. The *essentia* is that by which God is, and the *natura* "designates the principle of action."[15] Again, these are the same in terms of simplicity, but both concepts are vital for understanding Trinity and unity in God's life. When speaking of divine unity, "the divine unity is better described by saying that the three Persons are 'of one essence,' than by saying they are 'of one nature.'"[16] The persons cannot be differentiated according to essence, but they each express the divine nature differently, or "appropriate" different characteristics according to their relation. In this sense, nature describes different "operations" within God's one act of existence. God's activity can logically be divided into two internal "operations," intellect and will, and one external

---

13. Ibid., Ia. 39.2.

14. Ibid., Ia.3.3.

15. "Because 'nature' designates the principle of action while 'essence' comes from being [essendo], things may be said to be of one nature which agree in some action, as all things which give heat; but only those things can be said to be of 'one essence' which have one being" (ibid., Ia.39.2).

16. Ibid., Ia.39.2.

operation, power.[17] While essence only allows us to speak of the one being shared by the three divine persons, nature in terms of operations giving rise to the processions allows us to speak of the supposita individually.

> So when we say, "Trinity in Unity," we do not place number in the unity of the *essentia*, as if we meant three times one; but we place the persons numbered in the unity of *natura*; as the *supposita* of a nature are said to exist in that *natura*. On the other hand, we say "Unity in Trinity"; meaning that the *natura* is in its *supposita*.[18]

The three persons share in the one nature as essence, but the nature, as principle of activity, *is* in each of the supposita uniquely.

Relation

Thomas defines relation as follows: "Relation itself must be founded in the origin of the Persons, that is, in an action giving rise to a procession."[19] Real relations are founded in the activity between agent and end; they have a concrete existence in the divine nature. Thomas says that "relation in God is something that inheres. It is what God is."[20]

> Some have thought that in God essence and person differ, forasmuch as they held the relations to be "adjacent;" considering only in the relations the idea of "reference to another," and not the relations as realities. But as it was shown above (Q[28], A[2]) in creatures relations are accidental, whereas in God they are the divine essence itself. Thence it follows that in God essence is not really distinct from person; and yet that the persons are really distinguished from each other. For person, as above stated (Q[29], A[4]), signifies relation as subsisting in the divine nature. But relation as referred to the essence does not differ there from reality, but only in our way of thinking.[21]

The concept of relation enables us to speak of both the divine essence in its simplicity as well as the persons in their uniqueness. The concept of relation, for Aquinas, serves to distinguish between the divine persons as

17. Ibid., Ia.14, preface.
18. Ibid., Ia.31.1.
19. Emery, *Saint Thomas Aquinas*, 51 quoting Summa Contra Gentiles IV, 24.
20. Aquinas, *ST*, Ia. 28.2.
21. Ibid., Ia.39.1.

well as describe the divine unity. The relations in God can be conceived in terms of relative opposition.

> Relative opposition consequent on origin does not just put the real distinction of the divine persons on show. It also exhibits the inseparability of the persons, because a relative, as such, cannot exist without its correlate . . . as to the distinction of the persons, which is by relations of origin, knowledge of the Father does indeed include knowledge of the Son, for He would not be Father, had he not a Son; and the Holy Spirit is their mutual bond. (STII-II 1.8.) In this way, relative opposition shows that the persons are distinct and inseparable.[22]

There are two relative oppositions: paternity-filiation and spiration-procession. The first is the opposition between Father and Son and the second is the opposition between Father and Son as spirating and the Spirit processing. One cannot conceive of the Father without the Son or the Holy Spirit without the Father and Son. These relations are based in the origin of the processions.

> Relations in God are the divine essence itself. It follows from this that relations in God the essence is not really distinct from the person even though the persons are really distinguished from one another . . . person signifies relation insofar as this relation subsists in the divine nature. But, considered in comparison to the essence, relation only differs from it conceptually; and, in comparison to the opposed relation, it is really distinguished by virtue of this relative opposition. Thus there is one essence and three persons.[23]

Relations "imply a relative opposition according to origin."[24] As such, there are four relations: Fatherhood, Sonship, "active spiration," and passive spiration. With respect to the proper nature of the relation, it refers to the relation of origin. Relation and essence can't be separated. "Everything converges in relation, because the divine relation contains both the element of personal distinction (ratio), and the element of the hypostatic divine substance (esse). These two aspects together constitute the theological notion of a divine person."[25] So, for Aquinas, both the divine essence and the

---

22. Emery, *Saint Thomas Aquinas*, 99.

23. Aquinas, *ST*, Ia.39.1.

24. Ibid., Ia.28.3.

25. Emery, *Saint Thomas Aquinas*, 54.

divine persons must be understood in terms of relation.[26] Now we turn to a closer examination of Thomas's notion of "person" especially as it concerns the origin of the person from the operations of the divine nature.

Operations

With the idea of operations we can look more closely at Bulgakov's critique. How do the operations of the divine nature, intellect, and will relate to the divine essence and the divine persons? Is there merely an arbitrary distinction between these powers that gives rise to an impersonal concept of divinity? Thomas argues that will, or an impulse to either obtain or maintain the good, is characteristic of every being, but that in intellectual beings it follows as a necessary feature of the intellectual act.[27] In God, then, knowing and loving the highest good are intrinsic features of God's existence as intellectual being.[28] In God, these immanent acts or operations are the basis of the processions. Thomas's doctrine of the processions demonstrates that God's self-knowledge is not a static self-contemplation, nor is God's self-love a static self-satisfaction, but rather these operations give rise to the processions that constitute the relations. God the Father knows himself eternally in a procession of the intellect, his Word. Father and Son as knower and known love, or "spirate," eternally in the procession of the Holy Spirit. Intellect and will are only logically distinct properties in the divine life, but the actions which proceed from them give rise to really distinct relations.[29]

26. "Since the real plurality in God is founded only on relative opposition, the several properties of one Person, as they are not relatively opposed to each other, do not really differ. Nor again are they predicated of each other, because they are different ideas of the persons; as we do not say that the attribute of power is the attribute of knowledge, although we do say that knowledge is power" (Aquinas, *ST*, Ia. 32.3).

27. "In no wise has the will of God a cause. . . . Now as God by one act understands all things in His essence, so by one act He wills all things in His goodness" (Aquinas, *ST*, Ia.19.5).

28. "In things willed for the sake of the end, the whole reason for our being moved is the end, and this it is that moves the will, as most clearly appears in things willed only for the sake of the end. . . . Hence, although God wills things apart from Himself only for the sake of the end, which is His own goodness, it does not follow that anything else moves His will, except His goodness. So, as He understands things apart from Himself by understanding His own essence, so He wills things apart from Himself by willing His own goodness" (ibid., 19.2).

29. "There are two processions in God; the procession of the Word, and another. In

60

The first operation of the divine nature is intellect. God is intellect thinking the highest good and loving it, which is the second operation.

> And since one kind of operation is immanent, and another kind of operation proceeds to the exterior effect, we treat first of knowledge and of will (for understanding abides in the intelligent agent, and will is in the one who wills); and afterwards of the power of God, the principle of the divine operation as proceeding to the exterior effect.[30]

Thomas does not follow Aristotle here in positing a static self-contemplation. Rather, the Father begets the Son *per modum intellectus*. The Son is the full revelation of the Father, the content of the divine mind, or God's own Word about himself.[31] Word is a very important concept for Thomas. It is both a person (Idea) and the "impersonal" content of the divine life (divine ideas) expressed by that person:

> With regard to any sort of word, two points may be considered: viz. the word itself, and that which is expressed by the word . . . So then in God the Word conceived by the intellect of the Father is the name of a Person: but all things that are in the Father's knowledge, whether they refer to the Essence or to the Persons, or to the works of God, are expressed (*exprimuntur*) by this Word, as Augustine declares (De Trin. xv, 14).[32]

Here Thomas says that the Word, or Second Person of the Trinity, is the divine self-expression. The Son expresses the Father both personally and impersonally in the inner triune life, as well as personally (agent) and impersonally (content) in creation. Recalling that Thomas said supposita and nature are identified in God, and "since God then is not composed of matter and form, He must be His own Godhead, His own Life, and whatever

---

evidence whereof we must observe that procession exists in God, only according to an action which does not tend to anything external, but remains in the agent itself. Such an action in an intellectual nature is that of the intellect, and of the will. The procession of the Word is by way of an intelligible operation. The operation of the will within ourselves involves also another procession, that of love, whereby the object loved is in the lover; as, by the conception of the word, the object spoken of or understood is in the intelligent agent. Hence, besides the procession of the Word in God, there exists in Him another procession called the procession of love" (ibid., Ia. 27.3).

30. Aquinas, *ST*, Ia.14, preface.

31. Emery, "Trinity and Creation," 64.

32. Aquinas, *ST*, Ia.IIae.93.1.

else is thus predicated of Him."[33] In one sense, the Son, as the operation of divine intellect, seems to "be" the divine nature.[34] If the Son is the divine intellect then what Thomas asserts of the divine intellect in Ia.18.4. can be said of him both personally/essentially and impersonally as the content or product of his activity.

> In God to live is to understand, as before stated (A[3]). In God intellect, the thing understood, and the act of understanding, are one and the same. Hence whatever is in God as understood is the very living or life of God. Now, wherefore, since all things that have been made by God are in Him as things understood, it follows that all things in Him are the divine life itself.[35]

Thus, the Son is most properly associated with the divine nature as its content and life. The second operation of divine nature, will, is directed toward and proceeds from the Son as the divine self-revelation. The goodness of the Father, revealed in the Son, compels the divine will to love that good. The Love which spirates from and reposes upon God's self is a person, God the Holy Spirit. So, the supposita or hypostases in God pertain to the nature as eternal dynamic instantiations of the operations of divine nature acting upon itself.[36]

33. The Son "is" the divine nature here both personally/essentially, in that in God "relation subsists by virtue of the divine essence with which it is identical, and it distinguishes each person by virtue of the connection ad aliud which constitutes its ratio" (Emery, *Saint Thomas Aquinas*, 55), and impersonally as "a 'fruit of God's intelligence and will, that is an immanent 'term'" (ibid., 52).

34. Aquinas, *ST*, Ia. 3.3.

35. Ibid., Ia.18.4.

36. "But, as shown above (3, 3, ad 1), the use of concrete and abstract names in God is not in any way repugnant to the divine simplicity; forasmuch as we always name a thing as we understand it. Now, our intellect cannot attain to the absolute simplicity of the divine essence, considered in itself, and therefore, our human intellect apprehends and names divine things, according to its own mode, that is in so far as they are found in sensible objects, whence its knowledge is derived. In these things we use abstract terms to signify simple forms; and to signify subsistent things we use concrete terms. Hence also we signify divine things, as above stated, by abstract names, to express their simplicity; whereas, to express their subsistence and completeness, we use concrete names . . . Although the persons are simple, still without prejudice to their simplicity, the proper ideas of the persons can be abstractedly signified" (ibid., 32.2).

Processions

Thomas says "It is only the order of the processions, which arises from their origin, which multiplies processions in God"[37] The processions also allow us to distinguish activity between the persons. The idea of "notional action" indicates one action with two relations, namely paternity-filiation, or spiration-procession. This kind of action results in the relative opposition between the relations. The relation is a shared activity that is distinct only because of who performs it. The persons possess the relation based on the procession.[38] These processions are not contingent. The activity is intrinsically defined by the one acting, and the identity of the agent is constituted by the action. The Father does not will the Son. The Father is Father in begetting the Son. The power of begetting the Son is simply the divine nature as it is in the Person of the Father. The spiration of the Spirit is the shared relative opposition of the Father and Son in the divine nature.[39]

37. Aquinas, *De Potentia*, 10.2.

38. "In God the notions have their significance not after the manner of realities, but by way of certain ideas whereby the persons are known; although in God these notions or relations are real, as stated above (Question 28, Article 1). Therefore whatever has order to any essential or personal act, cannot be applied to the notions; forasmuch as this is against their mode of signification. Hence we cannot say that paternity begets, or creates, or is wise, or is intelligent. The essentials, however, which are not ordered to any act, but simply remove created conditions from God, can be predicated of the notions; for we can say that paternity is eternal, or immense, or such like. So also on account of the real identity, substantive terms, whether personal or essential, can be predicated of the notions; for we can say that paternity is God, and that paternity is the Father" (Aquinas, *ST*, Ia.32.2).

39. "A notion is the proper idea whereby we know a divine Person. Now the divine persons are multiplied by reason of their origin: and origin includes the idea of someone from whom another comes, and of someone that comes from another, and by these two modes a person can be known. Therefore the Person of the Father cannot be known by the fact that He is from another; but by the fact that He is from no one; and thus the notion that belongs to Him is called 'innascibility.' As the source of another, He can be known in two ways, because as the Son is from Him, the Father is known by the notion of 'paternity'; and as the Holy Ghost is from Him, He is known by the notion of 'common spiration.' The Son can be known as begotten by another, and thus He is known by 'filiation'; and also by another person proceeding from Him, the Holy Ghost, and thus He is known in the same way as the Father is known, by 'common spiration.' The Holy Ghost can be known by the fact that He is from another, or from others; thus He is known by 'procession'; but not by the fact that another is from Him, as no divine person proceeds from Him. Therefore, there are Five notions in God: 'innascibility,' 'paternity,' 'filiation,' 'common spiration' and 'procession.' Of these only four are relations, for 'innascibility' is not a relation, except by reduction, as will appear later (33, 4, ad 3). Four

Person

The persons are the subsistent relations outlined above. For Thomas, a divine person exists through itself (substance), in an irreducible way (individuality), with a freedom of action drawn from its essence (intellectual nature). Though St. Augustine said that "person" could be applied to the divine essence in the same manner as "God," Thomas's construal does not allow him to do this. To posit "person" of the divine essence could lead to Sabellianism. Instead, Thomas says that relation can apply to the divine essence as its mode of existing, and person can be applied to the three subsistent relations. So person can be applied to the essence as a mode of existence that subsists, but not directly as equitable with existence as such. By using the concept of relation to both distinguish and unite the divine persons, Thomas makes the concept of personhood dynamic. Personhood implies the activity of relation; it is constitutive of divine activity *ad intra* and by extension, *ad extra*. Relation entails both infinite distance and perfect unity. Because the persons are conceived only in their relational properties and the relations are, in a sense, the divine essence, Thomas can say that the persons are distinct from one another, yet not distinct from the essence. "The divine essence is not something other than the three persons; so there is no quaternity in God."[40] The "space" in which the divine persons enact the divine essence is not something other than the relation that constitutes them.

Divine Activity: Ad Intra

When it comes to divine activity as well, Thomas is able to both unite and distinguish through the concept of relation. As was pointed out above, the same action belongs to the persons according to their relations. So the act of spiration belongs to the Spirit as proceeding and the Father and Son

---

only are properties. For 'common spiration' is not a property; because it belongs to two persons. Three are personal notions—i.e. constituting persons, 'paternity,' 'filiation,' and 'procession.' 'Common spiration' and 'innascibility' are called notions of Persons, but not personal notions, as we shall explain further on (40, 1, ad 1) . . . The divine essence is signified as a reality; and likewise the persons are signified as realities; whereas the notions are signified as ideas notifying the persons. Therefore, although God is one by unity of essence, and trine by trinity of persons, nevertheless He is not quinary by the five notions" (ibid., 32.3).

40. Emery, *Saint Thomas Aquinas*, 146, quoting *Super II Decret*, Leon. ed., vol. 40, E43.

as spirating. Another way in which an action can "belong" to a person is through attribution: a certain likeness between the notion of the person and the attribute, e.g., Gift to the Spirit or Word to the Son. This attribution inheres in the relation itself not merely in our minds. Divine activity, like the divine essence, is simple, but that simplicity is constituted in relation. This activity *ad intra* is a perichoresis, or mutual indwelling by common nature and mutual relations. Each person is the divine essence as a subsisting relation and is in the other persons by virtue of the relation that constitutes them as a person. The Father is in the Son as the content of his Word and the Son is in the Father by existing in the one who utters the Word. Therefore, there is no divine act, whether *ad intra* or *ad extra*, in which the triune relations are not a relevant topic of discussion.

Divine Activity: Ad Extra

When Thomas discusses divine activity *ad extra* it proceeds from his insights into the divine activity directed *ad intra*. Divine activity always occurs simply and from the one divine nature, but the activity is no less personal for its unity as an expression of the divine nature. It would be just as impossible for Thomas to conceive of God acting somehow apart from the divine relations that are the divine essence as it would be for him to imagine the three persons engaged in activities distinct from one another. In the one activity of the divine nature *ad extra* each of the three persons acts within their distinct mode of relationship to the other persons. The Father acts through and in the Son. The Spirit acts as an impulse or procession from the unity of Father and Son. The Son acts as an expression of and in obedience to the Father. These appropriations are continuous with the triune activity *ad intra*.

With respect to creatures, divine activity can be spoken of in terms of the specific missions of the persons that correspond to their appropriations. The mission is the eternal procession of the person being made present in a new way to the creature.[41] The donation of the person is the created effect

---

41. Aquinas, *ST*, 43.2. "For a thing is sent that it may be in something else, and is given that it may be possessed; but that a divine person be possessed by any creature, or exist in it in a new mode, is temporal. Hence 'mission' and 'giving' have only a temporal significance in God; but 'generation' and 'spiration' are exclusively eternal; whereas 'procession' and 'giving,' in God, have both an eternal and a temporal signification: for the Son may proceed eternally as God; but temporally, by becoming man, according to His visible mission, or likewise by dwelling in man according to His invisible mission."

of the mission being really possessed in a new way by the creature.[42] This is a logical relation for God (a relation that is found elsewhere really in the world but is applied by the mind to the relation), and a real relation for the creature, (one that inheres in the subject). However, the relations between the persons of the Trinity are no less real for being only logical in their application to creatures. The question of whether Bulgakov's understanding of the Trinity (and Balthasar's) is compatible with Thomas's doctrine of appropriations is not whether there is a triune dynamic present in divine activity directed *ad extra*, but whether their construal of that activity can be understood as identical to the divine life, that is, to the act of relation that constitutes the divine essence.

When the divine nature acts externally, distinctions between intellect and will or between the divine persons are only logical, and this external act is the operation of divine power. However, this does not imply that the external act of creation is not triune. On the contrary, Aquinas says, "the eternal procession of the divine persons is the cause, the reason, the motive, the model of the procession of creatures."[43] In the creative act of the divine power, the Son is the content of creation, impersonally, as both the Word of God and as ordering principle of divine wisdom.[44] The Holy Spirit acts as the will of God confirming and enacting the procession of creation. The three persons are the cause of the diversity in creation, but only simply, as creation is the communication of the divine nature as act (divine intellect and will in the one external operation of divine power). Thus, when speaking of relation with respect to the triune life and creation, a further distinction must be made. God *is* relation in God's essence, and the opposition

---

42. Ibid., 38.1. "The word 'gift' imports an aptitude for being given. And what is given has an aptitude or relation both to the giver and to that to which it is given. For it would not be given by anyone, unless it was his to give; and it is given to someone to be his. Now a divine person is said to belong to another, either by origin, as the Son belongs to the Father; or as possessed by another. But we are said to possess what we can freely use or enjoy as we please: and in this way a divine person cannot be possessed, except by a rational creature united to God. Other creatures can be moved by a divine person, not, however, in such a way as to be able to enjoy the divine person, and to use the effect thereof. The rational creature does sometimes attain thereto; as when it is made partaker of the divine Word and of the Love proceeding, so as freely to know God truly and to love God rightly. Hence the rational creature alone can possess the divine person. Nevertheless in order that it may possess Him in this manner, its own power avails nothing: hence this must be given it from above; for that is said to be given to us which we have from another source. Thus a divine person can 'be given,' and can be a 'gift.'"

43. Aquinas, I *Sent.*, 10,1,1.

44. Aquinas, *ST*, Ia.IIae.93.1.

of relations within God is understood as the basis for triunity. However, God *is* in relation to creation in a different way. There is no opposition of relation between God and creation; creatures do not enact the divine essence as a divine hypostasis, but rather in a participated sense. For this reason, whereas the persons in the Trinity are constituted by the opposition of real relations, there is no real relation between God and the creature.

> As the creature proceeds from God in diversity of nature, God is outside the order of the whole creation, nor does any relation to the creature arise from His nature; for He *does not produce the creature by necessity of His nature, but by His intellect and will*, as is above explained (Q[14], AA[3],4; Q[19], A[8]). Therefore there is no real relation in God to the creature; whereas in creatures there is a real relation to God; because creatures are contained under the divine order, and their very nature entails dependence on God. On the other hand, the divine processions are in one and the same nature. Hence no parallel exists.[45]

Creatures have a real relation to God since creaturely reality is an effect of, or participation in the divine nature. However, creatures do not constitute a real relation in God, they do not "proceed from a principle of the same nature"; creation is not an internal operation of the divine nature like intellect or will, but a contingent effect of the divine nature.[46] In this way the concept of relation serves both to distinguish and to unite the divine persons with respect to the divine essence, as well as distinguish between God

---

45. Ibid., Ia.28.1.

46. "Relations exist in God really; in proof whereof we may consider that in relations alone is found something which is only in the apprehension and not in reality. This is not found in any other genus; forasmuch as other genera, as quantity and quality, in their strict and proper meaning, signify something inherent in a subject. But relation in its own proper meaning signifies only what refers to another. Such regard to another exists sometimes in the nature of things, as in those things which by their own very nature are ordered to each other, and have a mutual inclination; and such relations are necessarily real relations; as in a heavy body is found an inclination and order to the centre; and hence there exists in the heavy body a certain respect in regard to the centre and the same applies to other things. Sometimes, however, this regard to another, signified by relation, is to be found only in the apprehension of reason comparing one thing to another, and this is a logical relation only; as, for instance, when reason compares man to animal as the species to the genus. But when something proceeds from a principle of the same nature, then both the one proceeding and the source of procession, agree in the same order; and then they have real relations to each other. Therefore as the divine processions are in the identity of the same nature, as above explained (27, 2, 4), these relations, according to the divine processions, are necessarily real relations" (Aquinas, *ST*, Ia. 28.1).

in God's self, and God in relation to creation. The question remains, however, as to whether a relation that is real from the perspective of creatures, yet "only" logical in the other direction, can be an adequate bridge between the triune God and creation. Is God's activity *ad extra* genuinely personal? Is there a real *imago trinitatis* in creaturely nature? Can we speak of an impersonal *analogia entis*, or does being itself already entail an *analogia relationis* as a participation in the triune God? By ordering the transcendentals, both as they exist in God and as they exist analogously in creatures, with kenotic love as the transcendental "par excellence," Balthasar is able to propose an *imago trinitatis* in creation that both preserves the simplicity of the divine act *ad extra* and *ad intra* as well as preserves the infinite distance between God and creatures (or Thomas's distinction between real and logical relation). Balthasar does this by appropriating Thomas's Trinitarian concept of relation in light of Bulgakov's Trinitarian insight that the divine persons are the act of infinite self-donation.

3

Balthasar's Appropriation of Thomas

How does "relation" in a Thomistic sense provide the basis for a kenotic communion across an infinite distance in a Bulgakovian sense? Balthasar wants to hold these ideas together to preserve the infinite distance or difference between God and creation while establishing the foundation and goal for creation within the inner-relation of the triune life. Like Bulgakov, Balthasar wants to avoid a notion of God's activity *ad extra* that would in any way obscure the relational nature of the divine essence or posit the image of the Trinity as extrinsic to created nature. Like Thomas, Balthasar sees the opposition of relation as constituting personhood and thus requiring an infinite distance even within a shared essence, let alone between the absolute and the participated, or infinite and finite being. In *Theo-Logic* II, Balthasar brings together the Trinitarian theologies of Aquinas and Bulgakov to accomplish this precise combination.

Both Bulgakov and Balthasar seek to answer the question: How can God's works *ad extra* be a genuine reflection of the triune life if they are performed in common? The urgency of this question becomes especially acute with Christ's suffering, death, and descent into hell. As we saw in the first chapter, Bulgakov believes the only way of preserving the genuine revelatory nature of Christ in his incarnation, death, and descent while maintaining divine "impassibility" and simplicity is to posit Sophia as a kind of bridge between divine and creaturely nature. Balthasar, however, looks for this "bridge" in the analogy or participation of creaturely being in the divine triune life. Balthasar is able to read Bulgakov's notion of person together with Aquinas's notion of relation in such a way that the Person of the Son himself is a sufficient "bridge" between God and creation, yet in such a way that does not blur the infinite difference between them. If the descent into hell is, for Balthasar, the ultimate expression of the triune relation then:

> The descent must be planned out with a great deal of caution lest it start—and stop—with anything secondary . . . We must risk beginning with something more universal, namely, with the question of how God's absolute being, which—even though the *opera dei "ad extra"* [works of God outside] (if indeed God has any works *ad extra*) are performed in common—can occur only in Trinitarian form, is reflected in the world's being.[1]

Balthasar begins by analyzing Thomas's thesis that the divine nature acts *ad extra simpliciter.* If this is the case, then what might we expect to find with respect to the activity of the persons in the image of created being, and ultimately, in the Son's incarnate life? Balthasar looks to the *imago trinitatis* in creation with respect to the transcendentals. He finds that:

> The transcendentals cannot be ascribed exclusively to the divine essence as such, since *imago,* hence, exemplarity with respect to all that can be created, is a proper name of the Son, just as *liberalitas,* hence the ground of the very reality [*wirklich*] of the creation in the first place, is a proper name of the Holy Spirit. Therefore, even though the "emanation" of worldly being from God is effected by the Divine Persons in common, each Person operates therein in accord with his property.[2]

Balthasar thus prepares us to think about creation as a Trinitarian act by situating a discussion of the transcendentals within Thomas's doctrine of the divine appropriations of the persons. The doctrine of appropriation allows Balthasar to talk about the transcendentals within the divine essence as already expressive of the triune life "anchor[ed] in the process of the hypostases."[3] Any expression of the divine essence must reflect the relation

1. Balthasar, *Truth of God,* 173. In the following chapter we will explore in more detail the way in which the distance in the triune opposition of relation forms the basis for the difference between God and creation. Balthasar's rendering of the descent into hell is an inherently Trinitarian thesis. It is the ultimate "enactment" of the divine essence as relation where unity and distance are reciprocal or the opposite terms that constitute a relation.

2. Ibid., 176 quoting Aquinas, *ST,* Ia 45.1, 2 and 44.2.

3. "Whether we think philosophically in terms of worldly being or theologically in

that constitutes the divine essence. Rather than describing the essence in its relational character as a result of the operations which give rise to the processions, Balthasar turns to Bulgakov's Trinitarian thesis: "The identity of the divine essence is found in the positive self-expropriation of the Divine Persons, which in all three is one, true, good."[4]

It is important to emphasize that Balthasar sees Bulgakov's dynamic Trinitarian description of the divine essence as contiguous with Thomas's discussion of the simplicity of the divine act *ad extra*. The concept of relation links the positive self-expropriation of the divine persons in the simplicity of the operation of the divine nature. However, in order to conceive of the divine essence as the act of self-expropriation, Balthasar must find a way of describing that relation in terms of the transcendentals. Can there be a transcendental "personal act" that can be ascribed to the divine essence both simply and tri-personally? Again, Balthasar finds the solution in Bulgakov:

> We can understand this only if we dare to speak, with Bulgakov, of a first, intraTrinitarian *kenosis*, which his none other than God's positive "self-expropriation" in the act of handing over the entire divine being in the processions.[5]

When we look at the act that constitutes the divine relation or divine essence, we find an "intraTrinitarian kenosis" which demands that we re-interpret our understanding of the other transcendentals: being, truth, goodness, and beauty. It becomes clear that the key to understanding the true nature of these transcendentals, whether in God or as reflected in creatures, is to view them through the lens of "the transcendental par excellence," or love:

> Though perfect love also presupposes perfect knowledge, the Father's self-expropriation in favor of the Son, which thought cannot get behind [*unvordenklich*], owes itself to a love that, notionally, exceeds being and its self-knowledge, "Love is thus more

---

terms of the divine being, there is one thing we cannot do: ascribe the transcendentals simply to a divine being devoid of distinction. On the contrary, we have no choice but to anchor them in the process of the hypostases. Indeed, if we abstract from this process, we cannot even speak of a divine being or essence in the first place" (Balthasar, *Truth of God*, 178).

4. Ibid.

5. Ibid., 177–78.

comprehensive than being itself; it is the 'transcendental' par excellence that comprehends the reality of being, of truth, and of goodness."[6]

Only in light of the intraTrinitarian kenosis can this dynamic nature of reality be grasped. Bulgakov and Aquinas come together when the relation that is the divine essence is understood as the kenosis of the persons. The immanent kenosis of the persons is the divine essence; it is the source of both unity and difference between the persons. The difference between the divine persons is infinite and thus can also be the "space" or "source" of the difference between God and creatures that is also the foundation of their unity, or the basis for the analogy between them.

How can difference within God be the ground of difference between God and creatures? Recalling that Thomas differentiates between the divine persons with the opposition of relations in the divine essence as relation, Balthasar seems to follow Thomas in positing that the nature of the divine essence itself when considered as relation provides the foundation for understanding both unity and difference. Balthasar speaks of this triune unity and difference as follows:

> The Divine Persons are *themselves* only insofar as they go out to the Others (who are always other), the created essences too are *themselves* only insofar as they go beyond themselves and indicate their primal ground and their vocation of self-surrender.[7]

Personhood comprises the activity of relation or a self-surrender that makes the person himself the space for the indwelling of the other. Note that the divine essence, considered as relation, for Balthasar is inherently active. "We cannot avoid using the concept of 'process,' 'procession' in the context of the life of the Trinity to denote its constant vitality."[8] Immediately this brings up the question as to whether Balthasar is arguing that the relational nature of God entails development or change within the divine nature, or even a kind of "openness" to being genuinely changed by the creature. But, if we read Balthasar as someone who is working out of the context of both a Thomistic and a Bulgakovian Trinitarian setting, it becomes clear that Balthasar is describing a kind of active divine simplicity

---

6. Ibid., 176–77 quoting Gustav Siewerth, Metaphysik der Kindheit (Eisiedeln: Johannesverlag, 1957), 63.

7. Balthasar, *Final Act*, 76.

8. Ibid., 77.

that is possible only when we conceive of the divine essence as a relation of kenotic love. God's life is perfectly full, "perfect peace. Yet this peace, or rest, is not inert, but 'eternal movement,' since the divine processions that give rise to the fellowship of Persons are not subject to temporal limitation but are eternally operative."[9] The relation that is the divine essence is the activity of self-donation, and "this concept is the link between creature and Creator, between being and becoming."[10] Creaturely being is a participation, not in a kind of static being, but in the activity of self-offering.

> At first sight, these two differences seem to have no relationship to each other at all. The fact that the one essence of God lives in three hypostases has nothing to do with contingency; on the contrary, it is the supreme expression of the limitless plenitude of the divine being, a plenitude that could never be exhausted by one hypostasis but that requires the reciprocal ecstasy of the "Persons" in order to unfold itself as absolute love and, in doing so, as absolute truth.[11]

So, the vital point is that the triune life provides the basis for both unity and difference, both between the divine persons and creatures and Creator. The possibility for this lies in his taking from Aquinas the idea that the divine essence is a relation, and from Bulgakov that this relation is kenotic love. The great insight here, however, is the way that together these theses can posit a Trinitarian image in creation, a Trinitarian basis for creation, and a creaturely participation in the triune life that retains the distinction between God and creatures in being and freedom.

The foundation for genuine creaturely freedom in the image of the triune God lies in the fact of the divine relation as kenotic love. Though God is perfectly transparent to God's self, "he is also 'ever-greater' even to himself."[12] There is, in fact, a kind of surprise in the inner triune life, "so we can say that, if human love is enlivened by the element of surprise, something analogous to it cannot be excluded from divine love. It is as if the Son born of the Father 'from the outset surpasses the Father's wildest expectations.' 'God loves despite his omniscience, constantly allowing himself to be surpassed and surprised by the Beloved.'"[13] Love entails a genuine space for the other to be unique and free. It is an openness towards the positivity of

9. Ibid., 77–78.

10. Ibid., 77.

11. Balthasar, *Truth of God*, 179–80

12. Balthasar, *Final Act,* 78.

13. Ibid., 79.

the other. Whereas we will see in the following chapter, Bulgakov is forced by his sophiology to attribute the negative aspects of creaturely otherness to a kind of nothing or non-being, the concept of analogy allows Balthasar to maintain a positive ground for creaturely otherness in the relation between the divine persons itself. Absolute Being "expresses itself in perfect self-giving and reciprocal surrender."[14] In the divine life, the act of kenotic love is simple and dynamic. This act entails "identity, since the Lover gives all that he is and nothing else, and otherness, since otherwise the Lover would love only himself."[15]

The unity and difference in God has its analogy both in the unity and difference between God and creation and in the created world itself.[16] Balthasar is always careful to include the fact that "the gulf between Creator and creature, even when the latter receives grace and a 'share in the divine nature,' thus proves to be impassable. There is an 'ever greater dissimilitude' between God and the creature. Natural religion and mysticism are thwarted in their attempts to achieve identity with God."[17] Without this "ever great dissimilitude," creaturely freedom would be incapable of a genuine participation in the triune life. A true act of love, for Balthasar, entails a free self-surrender to an "other." It is only a Trinitarian theology of unity in the relation of kenotic love that preserves both the unity and the otherness in the divine persons as well as a positive and negative distance between God and creatures.[18]

14. Ibid., 82.

15. Ibid., 83.

16. "In the created order, by contrast, nonsubsistent being always infinitely overflows the finite essences, the vessels that receive it and bring it to subsistence. Each one of those receptacles, pondering its contingent existence, must leave room for an incalculable multitude of other actual and possible beings. The fundamental difference between esse and essentia in creatures thus seems to be caused primarily by the limitedness of the latter" (*Truth of God*, 180).

17. Ibid., 180.

18. Balthasar praises Thomas for grounding human finitude and participated freedom in divine infinitude and essential freedom, as expressions of creative love. "When God, in his knowing and omnipotent love, is seen as freely choosing to create, there can be no question of a restrictive fragmentation of being into finite essences. Esse can be suspended without confusion or limitation, in creaturely, free infinity and perfection, before the free God and only thus become the allusive likeness of the divine goodness. Thus and only thus is the creature liberated in the presence of God and in relation to God and can aspire with all its powers towards God and love him without having to comply with the perverse demand that it deny itself in its finite essence. . . . The metaphysics of Thomas is thus the philosophical reflection of the free glory of the living God of the

The "ever greater dissimilitude" between God and creatures, however, cannot be greater than the distance between the persons that allows for even a "surprise" in unity. There is no creaturely distance that cannot be "englobed" by the inner Trinitarian kenosis. The obvious proving ground for this idea would be in the creaturely rejection of God as the Good, True, Beautiful, or end of creaturely happiness and the effects of that rejection. The distance created by the act of rejection as they impact human relation with God must fit somewhere within God's own relation to God's self and to the world. We must even account for the "impersonal" effects of evil that inhere in the story of the world. If kenotic love is the transcendental par excellence, or the nature of the triune relation, then Balthasar must demonstrate that kenotic love can take the measure not only of the divine life as both unity and difference, but of the distance between God and creatures created by the total rejection by humankind of God's essential act. This is why the descent into hell is the ultimate statement of Balthasar's Trinitarian theology.[19]

By situating the analogy of being in terms of kenotic love as the transcendental par excellence, Balthasar is able to include within the analogy of being, not just the creature's positive relation to God in similitude, but also both the infinite distance between God and creatures as well as the negative distance between divine and creaturely reality caused by sin and corruption.[20]

Bible and in this way the interior completion of ancient (and thus human) philosophy. It is a celebration of the reality of the real, of that all-embracing mystery of being which surpasses the powers of human thought, a mystery pregnant with the very mystery of God, a mystery in which creatures have access to participation in the reality of God, a mystery which in its nothingness and non-subsistence is shot through with the light of the freedom of the creative principle of unfathomable love" (Balthasar, *Realm of Metaphysics in Antiquity,* 406–7).

19. "Nevertheless, the revelation of the Trinity throws an unexpected bridge across this (abiding) abyss. If, within God's identity, there is an Other, who at the same time is the image of the Father and thus the archetype of all that can be created; if, within this identity, there is a Spirit, who is the free, superabundant love of the 'One' and of the 'Other,' then both the otherness of creation, which is modeled on the archetypal otherness within God, and its sheer existence, which it owes to the intradivine liberality, are brought into a positive relationship to God" (Balthasar, *Truth of God,* 180–81).

20. "Divine and creaturely difference do enter after all, then, into a certain relation of comparability. The creature does not merely come 'from God' because its entire being (and this being's differences) is referred to him as its origin, conservation, and end. This reference extends just as expressly to the hypostases: primarily to the original archetype of all other images, the Son, who re-presents the Father to these images, as well as to the

Balthasar's Trinitarian theology maintains the fullness of divine simplicity while positing the completeness of God's self-revelation in Jesus Christ, particularly in his suffering and death. He is able to do this, not by positing an additional concept (Sophia) that somehow "bridges" the distance between God and creation, but rather by following a Thomistic understanding of relation where the single act that constitutes the divine essence is the basis both for absolute unity and infinite difference, and then by extending this notion of relation analogously to the Creator/creature relationship.

BULGAKOV'S INSIGHT IN A THOMISTIC FRAMEWORK

Balthasar appropriates Bulgakov's understanding of the triune life consisting of the mutual kenosis of the divine persons within the framework of a Thomistic Trinitarian theology as outlined above, where: 1) the divine essence *is* relation that is hypostatized by each of the persons in a unique manner of "being let-be,"[21] 2) the relation of the divine persons to the divine essence is characterized as a "real relation" distinguished by the "opposition of relations," and 3) the relation between God and creation can be described as a "logical relation" without compromising divine simplicity or the image of the Trinity in creation.

Balthasar resituates Bulgakov's thesis about the inner Trinitarian life being an act of kenotic love into a Thomistic understanding of the divine life as relation. Though this entails a conversion of both systems, he believes it retains the fundamental insights of both Thomas and Bulgakov as well as a consistency with the tradition. Neither the infinite distance between God and creation, nor the reality of the freedom entailed by human personhood need to be compromised within this paradigm.[22] This is because

---

Spirit, who is the 'personal' ground of the creative liberality of the triune God. This reference is based both on the primary diversity inherent in creaturely difference itself and on the fact that, absent this reference (which consists in creaturely difference begin different from God), creaturely difference would be unintelligible on its own terms. There can be no identity within the difference that cuts through the concrete finite being; this impossibility intrinsically presupposes a form of difference within the divine identity" (Balthasar, *Truth of God*, 181).

21. Nichols, *No Bloodless Myth*, 73.

22. "If we reflect once more on the intradivine processions, two approaches are barred us: the idea of a Father who generates the Son in order to come to know himself as God and the idea of a Father who, because he already knows himself perfectly, generates the

both creaturely participation in and difference from the divine life is given a foundation in the relation between the divine persons. What is more, this relation does not need to account for freedom and difference (and the negative realities that those entail in the creaturely world) by positing a *tertium datur* like Sophia, or providing a basis for sin and death in something outside of the divine relation. Balthasar is able to do this by following Bulgakov in defining suffering, death, absence, and difference as primarily positive analogies of the inner triune life, however, as realities which are only experienced by humans in a corrupt sense. However, he follows Thomas in situating the basis for these realities in the positive relation of the divine persons. Human freedom is not a reality in opposition to divine freedom, but rather a participation in divine freedom, a freedom that can only be understood within the context of kenotic love. "Love can thus be considered the supreme mode, and therein the 'truth,' of being, without, for all that, having to be transported beyond truth and being."[23] Creaturely reality is only fully itself when it engages in the activity of kenotic love, of absolute self-giving. This self-giving is both the "nature" and the "grace" of creaturely existence. It is the voice of the triune God calling out to his creation from within it. Creatures only truly receive the gift of themselves in returning themselves to God.[24]

The seeds of human personhood are found precisely in the possibility of self-offering. The same absolute openness to the other that characterizes the divine life is generative of a creaturely other who can receive the gift that is the indwelling of the Trinity. Balthasar develops the possibilities for the creaturely gift of self in the *triduum mortis*. Christ's self-offering in the Eucharist becomes humanity's participation in self-offering with Christ's death, descent, and resurrection. By making human helplessness and suffering his own, he englobes them within the triune relation, thereby enabling humanity to embody the divine life without somehow losing part of ourselves. Only in the Son's absolute openness to both human persons and the Father is human personhood given the possibility of "real" relation.[25]

Son. The first position would be Hegelianism, the second, thought through consistently, would be Arianism. For this reason, the immemorial priority of the self-surrender or self-expropriation thanks to which the Father is Father cannot be ascribed to knowledge but only to groundless love, which proves the identity of love as the 'transcendental par excellence'" Balthasar, *Truth of God*, 177.

23. Ibid., 178.

24. Balthasar, *Final Act*, 521.

25. I discuss the eucharistic and ethical implications of this thesis in the fifth chapter.

The love that both Balthasar and Bulgakov describe hinges on the Trinitarian thesis that the divine essence is kenotic love: "a boundless love where freedom and necessity coincide and where identity and otherness are one."[26] The difference between Balthasar and Bulgakov on this point will become clear in the next chapter.

OUSIA = RELATION = GLORY = SUFFERING

By defining the Thomistic notion of divine essence in terms of kenotic love, Balthasar provides a foundation for both positive and negative reality within the notion of personhood itself. He shows how the analogous nature of creaturely persons extends this to place both the difference between God and creation and the difference between human persons within the infinite distance entailed by the definition of personhood. Two important consequences of this formulation are: 1) the implication that it is in the deepest kenosis of the Son that the fullness of the divine essence will be revealed (I will discuss this thesis in the next chapter) and, 2) divine simplicity entails that if the divine essence is a relation of kenotic love, then divine glory, life, presence, freedom, and blessedness are identical with (but logically distinguishable from) kenosis, death, absence, necessity, and suffering. In the final chapter I will discuss the implications of this thesis for creaturely reality.

Just as Bulgakov believes divine simplicity entails that the divine essence is identical with kenotic love, and kenotic love with wisdom and glory, so Thomas believes that simplicity entails the divine essence be identical with relation. Though these concepts are logically distinguishable and certainly within creaturely reality, they do not have the same kind of interchangeability. For Balthasar, the fact of their unity in the divine life does have implications for the way we must understand the relationship of these characterizations of God's own being both within God and within the world.

> "I walk with the Lord toward the Cross and join him in bearing sin
> . . ." "So I feel my way toward the point where love and punishment
> form a single unity"; but this unity resides not in me: its origin
> lies in the Trinitarian relationship between Father and Son. Moses
> had to stand still before the Burning Bush: "Not until after the
> Son's Holy Saturday did it become possible for someone to entrust

26. Balthasar, *Final Act,* 83.

himself to God's fire and plunge into God. This is a Trinitarian mystery," whereby the Father gives permission to the Son so that he may allow himself to be consumed in the divine fire for mankind's sin. The Son "is the very fire he has come to cast upon the earth, but between heaven and earth this fire has undergone the transformation into suffering." "Because he himself is entirely pure and there is nothing in him to be consumed, he takes the world into himself as his fuel and consumes it in himself . . . suffering on account of each one of us."[27]

Love and punishment, the fire of divine love and suffering, helplessness and power, all of these paradoxes are united in the mystery of Christ and triune love. Balthasar does not collapse the polarities of the paradox, rather, his emphasis on the identity of suffering and love, helplessness and power highlights the mystery and uniqueness of the One in whom they come together.[28]

Ultimately, creatures cannot experience the simplicity or unity of suffering and love, power and helplessness, freedom and necessity etc. in any solely creaturely realm precisely because of our limitedness. However, we can experience this simultaneity within the simultaneity of the "creature's 'abiding in itself' and its 'abiding in God.'"[29] The fullness of this simultaneity is revealed in Christ (and the saints really), but is the true goal for all of creaturely life. "The miracle that transforms man's (relative) distance from God (particularly in his sinful existence) into 'nearness to God,' 'bestowing a more than earthly fullness upon earthly life,' is 'a life that comes from God and overflows on to man:' 'grace.'"[30]

CONCLUSION

As I have tried to demonstrate in this chapter, Balthasar's Trinitarian theology maintains the fullness of divine simplicity while positing the

27. Ibid., 367–68, quoting Adrienne von Speyr's *Objektive Mystik*, 368, 371, 317, 330.

28. It is beyond the scope of this book to discuss the full complexity of these paradoxes in Balthasar's thought. I only want to point out the fact, for Balthasar, of the unity between suffering and love, joy and helplessness, relation and ousia, and then to point out that this is inherently a result of his Trinitarian theology. I discuss the importance of these paradoxes and their Trinitarian basis for Balthasar's ethics in the final chapter of this dissertation.

29. Balthasar, *Final Act,* 83.

30. Ibid., 83, quoting Ph 52.

completeness of God's self-revelation in Jesus Christ, particularly in his suffering and death. He is able to do this, not by positing an additional concept such as Sophia that somehow "bridges" the distance between God and creation, but instead situating Bulgakov's Trinitarian insight within a Thomistic understanding of relation where the single act that constitutes the divine essence is the basis both for absolute unity and infinite difference, and then by extending this notion of relation analogously to the Creator/creature relationship.

The significance of Balthasar's employment and adaptation of both Aquinas and Bulgakov is clearest in the trajectory of his theology of the Christ's descent into hell. After examining this trajectory, two things will be clear: 1) Balthasar's use of Bulgakov's Trinitarian insight means that Christ's descent into hell is the fullest revelation of the triune God and the Creator/creature relation; the "God-abandonment" of the Son in hell is precisely the expression of the Son's divinity without somehow compromising divine impassibility; 2) Balthasar's use of Thomas's notion of relation allows him to say: a) that there is an infinite "distance/difference" between God and creation that is the very basis for a genuine relation between God and creatures, and b) that as a result of this difference humanity has a genuine freedom to reject relation with God. This rejection is the hell that the Son enters into and "englobes" in his relation to the Father, a rejection that he continues to carry in himself as the ongoing actual existence of sin and death in the history of the world.

4

Emptiness vs. Effigies
Christology and the Descent into Hell

INTRODUCTION

As we have seen for both Bulgakov and Balthasar, all creaturely reality is in the image of the Trinitarian life whether construed in terms of creaturely Sophia or an *analogia relationis*. However, both Bulgakov and Balthasar recognized the need to address the fact that some aspects of creaturely reality exist precisely as a rejection of the triune life, a self-centeredness which excludes the possibility of love. Both Bulgakov and Balthasar employ the Johannine idea that the ultimate revelation of God's glory, the pivotal intersection of the love of the triune God, with human rejection, is Christ's assumption of the entirety of human sin by his death on the cross and descent into hell.[1] For Balthasar in particular, Christ's descent into hell is the revelation of divine glory that shapes his Trinitarian theology, anthropology, and ethics.

---

1. "In the uttermost form of a slave, on the Cross, the Son's glory breaks through, inasmuch as it is then that he goes to the (divine) extreme in his loving, and in the revelation of that love" (Balthasar, *Mysterium Paschale*, 29). For Balthasar, the *triduum mortis* is a single event. The church's liturgical celebration of the *triduum* reflects this reality. We cannot truly grasp the meaning of the last supper until the resurrection, nor is the resurrection intelligble apart from Christ's descent to the dead.

In the first chapter of *Mysterium Paschale* Balthasar employs the kenotic Trinitarian theology of Sergei Bulgakov as he articulates the Trinitarian basis of the descent into hell. However, he does not adopt Bulgakov's Trinitarian theology *in toto*, but separates it from the sophiological context of Bulgakov's overall thought. Balthasar writes:

> It should be possible to divest Bulgakov's fundamental conviction of its sophiological presuppositions while preserving—and unfolding in its many facets—that basic idea of his which we agreed just now to give a central place high on our list of priorities. The ultimate presupposition of the kenosis is the "selflessness" of the Persons (when considered as pure relationships) in the inner-Trinitarian life of love.[2]

In chapter three we saw how Balthasar brackets sophiology from the kenosis of the persons by situating kenosis within a Thomistic Trinitarian notion of relational opposition. Whereas for Bulgakov, Sophia functions as an "ontological bridge" between Creator and creation as well as the divine and human natures in Christ, Balthasar "bridges" the Creator/creature difference without a sophiological framework. When we examine the two ways in which Balthasar brackets Bulgakov's sophiology with respect to the descent into hell, it is evident that he brackets Sophia because it depersonalizes the relationship between God and humanity.[3] Sophiology a) diminishes the genuinely "other" character of creatures with respect to their Creator, and b) eliminates the reality/consequences of human freedom in history. This collapses the infinite distance and thus eliminates the possibility of the act that constitutes personhood. These two negative connotations of Sophia become most evident in Bulgakov's account of the *triduum mortis*.

For both Bulgakov and Balthasar, Christ's suffering and death are the fullest revelation of the triune life. If Balthasar openly adopts Bulgakov's Trinitarian theology, and this theology has its clearest expression in its account of Christ's descent into hell, then Balthasar's particular understanding of this event will be visible in the ways he adopts and rejects Bulgakov. It is the concept of "personhood" rather than Sophia which structures the relationship between God and creation, a relationship which retains a genuine distinction between Creator and creature, as well as provides an ontological setting for the reality of human freedom and its consequences.

2. Ibid., 35.

3. He calls Sophia a supra-Christological structure that grounds the union of natures in Christ, which is both unnecessary and Gnostic. Ibid., 46.

The difference between Balthasar's descent into hell and Bulgakov's becomes significant only in light of their many similarities. The descent into hell is the ultimate expression, for both Bulgakov and Balthasar, of the Trinitarian kenosis. It is an event that encapsulates the whole of Christ's saving action.

> The descent goes from the act of incarnation right down to the "obedience unto death, death on a cross," and continues downward in the "descent into hell" in solidarity with all those who are lost to time. It goes farther: from the obedience of the cross to the atomizing of his bodily being, shared out in the Eucharist.[4]

An understanding of how that trajectory is shaped by Bulgakov's Trinitarian thesis is vital for grasping both the Trinitarian character of the descent as well as its ecclesial and moral implications. As I have shown in the first two chapters, Balthasar's appropriation of Bulgakov entails an awareness of Thomistic Trinitarian theology, not only interpreted well, but also the rather distorted reading that Bulgakov gives to it. By recognizing both the continuity and difference between Balthasar and Bulgakov, especially with regard to Sophia vs. relation, we can appreciate three vital theological and anthropological theses that guide Balthasar's descent theology: 1) The *triduum mortis* reveals that suffering = glory = relation in the triune life, both *ad intra* and in the economy; 2) In the *triduum mortis* we see a triune act that reveals the activity of personhood, a relation of infinite self-donation to the "other"; and 3) The revelation of God's life in the *triduum mortis* is a revelation about the relation that constitutes the divine essence. It is a revelation about the nature of personhood as an activity of absolute self-donation. In this way it is also a revelation of human personhood and the telos of human life. Ultimately, it reveals a call to communal participation in the activity of triune relation, a partaking in the absolute disappropriation of the Son, which has both ecclesial and ethical significance. I explore these implications further in chapter four.

First, however, how does a comparison of Bulgakov and Balthasar make these theses apparent? In this chapter I first outline five ways in which Balthasar's theology follows the trajectory set up by Bulgakov's thesis on inner-Trinitarian kenosis: a) the relationship between the kenosis of the divine persons and suffering, b) the relationship the economic self-offering of the Son as an expression of the immanent Trinitarian life and the nature

---

4. Balthasar, *Dramatis Personae: Man in God*, 411.

of divine simplicity, c) the notion of divine freedom within this paradigm, d) the notion that the kenosis of the Son in the incarnation entails an "inversion" in the inter-Trinitarian relations such that the Son experiences his relation to the Father through the Holy Spirit, and e) salvation is finally accomplished in the complete solidarity of the Son with sinful humanity in his death and resurrection. These five points demonstrate the way in which adopting Bulgakov's Trinitarian theology shapes Balthasar's entire trajectory of descent, a trajectory which is, at every point, Trinitarian. However, at each stage, from the inter-Trinitarian life to incarnation and death, Balthasar divests Bulgakov's Trinitarian structure of its "sophiological excesses."

In the second section of this chapter, I compare Bulgakov's notion of hell and Christ's descent into hell with Balthasar's. Balthasar's construal of the descent into hell diverges from Bulgakov in two ways: first, the Son does not "abandon his divinity" in his descent into death, and second, the sin assumed by the Son has a concrete reality in Balthasar's theology.

In the third section of this chapter I will look at the implications of a comparison between Bulgakov and Balthasar for addressing contemporary critiques of Balthasar's method and conclusion. In the first place we will see that, from beginning to end, Balthasar's exploration of the descent into hell is the ultimate exercise of his kenotic Trinitarian theology: only in hell can he verify whether this notion of love can maintain the full extent of divine impassibility, simplicity, and consistency as well as genuine human freedom and otherness. In the second place, I will show that Balthasar's adjustments to Bulgakov should alleviate the concerns of those who fear that the theology of descent makes God the only true agent in the salvation drama. On the contrary, Christ's descent, for Balthasar, provides the basis for an anthropology, ethics, and eschatology that maintain a sphere for genuine human activity, as well as addresses the misuse of human freedom, not just for the perpetrators of abuses, but also for their victims.

The theology of the descent into hell truly is one of the unique and most fascinating aspects of Balthasar's theological project. However, if one is to correctly situate this doctrine within the body of his work, the descent into hell must be understood, not as the formative notion governing his thought, but rather as the ultimate proving ground for his Trinitarian theology. A comparison with Bulgakov both situates the doctrine of descent as such a proving ground, as well as reveals Balthasar's theological and anthropological concern with personhood and the freedom it entails.

THE TRAJECTORY OF DESCENT

Balthasar's theology of the descent into hell is the result of his conviction that Christ's suffering and death are the fullest revelation of God's glory. In this way, like Bulgakov, he is following in the tradition of "kenotic theology," a nineteenth and twentieth-century movement that takes the Son's self-emptying as paradigmatic for the divine life. However, this tradition tended to privilege suffering at the expense of divine impassibility. These theologians take Christ's suffering and death as revelatory in the sense that creaturely reality conditions the divine life. In order to distance himself from these theologians, Balthasar surveys previous attempts to construct a kenotic theology before turning to Bulgakov's rendering of Trinitarian kenosis as both centered on Christ's passion as paradigmatically glorious as well as preserving a kind of divine impassibility.

The kenotic theologians of the nineteenth and twentieth centuries set out to take seriously the kenosis of the Son, his emptying to the point of suffering and death, using a Hegelian paradigm.[5] Balthasar critiques all of these methods for their setting kenosis only in terms of the divine nature or attributes rather than in terms of the Trinitarian life.[6] He concludes that "the *paradox* must be allowed to stand: in the undiminished humanity of Jesus, the whole power and glory of God are made present to us."[7]

Jürgen Moltmann, on the other hand, explicitly sets his kenotic theology in terms of the Trinity, and maintains that Jesus' humanity is in fact the full revelation of God. However, Moltmann fails to maintain the opposite side of the paradox. For Moltmann, in the cry of dereliction where God is abandoned by God, we see the very quality of Trinitarian love. "God is only revealed as 'God' in his opposite: godlessness and abandonment by God. In concrete terms, God is revealed in the Cross of Christ who was abandoned

---

5. Ibid. The German "kenoticist" Thomasius tries to explain the Son's kenosis by positing a scheme where God is able to maintain his intrinsic properties (love, goodness), while bracketing his relative properties (omniscience, omnipotence). Thus the Son can retain his intrinsic divine identity while relinquishing the divine attributes that would preclude his suffering as God. Gess, another German kenoticist, extends this bracketing of divinity to the point where the Son "loses himself" in the world process and thereby completes the divine life. The British kenoticists Gore and Weston also employ a Hegelian methodology. Gore does so by positing God's voluntary self-limitation in death as a revelation of God's true power, and Weston by uniting divinity with humanity through the consciousness of Christ, such that divinity experiences all that he suffers as a man.

6. Ibid., 32–33.

7. Ibid., 33 (emphasis his).

by God."[8] The triune God is able to voluntarily submit himself to being constituted eternally by the moment of suffering and abandonment that Christ experiences on the cross. The crucified God reveals and receives his identity as one who embraces human suffering and sin out of love. In fact, for Moltmann:

> The whole calamitous history of mankind is brought into the Trinitarian history of God himself, with its climax in the Cross and the dereliction of the "crucified God," so that it is primarily God—and only secondarily mankind—who "loads the world's sin" on Jesus. . . . For Moltmann, this kind of alienation within God is nothing other than the suffering of absolute love.[9]

Balthasar finds this thesis an improvement because it does deal in a Trinitarian dynamic. However, he ultimately finds it unsatisfactory because it posits a quality or created event (suffering) as more central than the perichoretic exchange of love between the persons. "For him, [Moltmann] the Cross is not the privileged (and ultimately the solely valid) locus of the Trinity's self-revelation. Rather, it is the locus of the Trinity's authentic actualization."[10]

In response to Moltmann, Balthasar expresses the need for a Trinitarian theology, which sees "the immanent Trinity as the ground of the world process (including the crucifixion) in such a way that it is neither a formal process of self-communication in God, as in Rahner, nor entangled in the world process, as in Moltmann."[11] Balthasar thus turns to Bulgakov, whose kenotic Trinitarian formula allows him to view Christ's death as the fullest revelation of divine glory while maintaining that God's inner life is determined solely by the activity of the divine persons, and in no way is it conditioned by creaturely reality.[12]

---

8. Balthasar, *Final Act,* 229 quoting Moltmann, *The Crucified God* (London: SCM, 1974) 27.

9. Balthasar, *Action,* 295 quoting Moltmann, *Grundzuge der Christolgie* (London: SCM, 1974) 183, 243.

10. Ibid., 321.

11. Ibid., 322–23.

12. Balthasar, *Epilogue,* 93. "This absolute *self-giving* can only be a "begetting" (within the divine identity). And its result can only be a total acceptance of, and a responding gift to, the origin. Thus the 'love' of giving back can never be less than that of the begetting. From this we conclude that the interpenetration of love elicits that identity of love, equally powerfully in all three Persons, which is both the fruit as well as the 'conclusive' manifestation of the absoluteness of divine love (once more, with all this taking place

Thus, Balthasar adopts what is the first and central point of correspondence between himself and Bulgakov: Bulgakov's "central conviction" that the substance of the divine nature is kenotic love. "The Father's
self-utterance in the generation of the Son is an initial 'kenosis' within the
Godhead that underpins all subsequent kenosis."[13] God is three persons
or hypostases in relation whose identity coincides with their particular
kenotic activity. For Bulgakov, this claim entails a further thesis: The divine
ousia, or nature, must also be conceived as Sophia.

A) Kenosis of the Persons Is Suffering, Suffering = Glory

Bulgakov's Trinitarian insight relies on a paradox: Christ's suffering, death,
and descent are unintelligible in terms of the triune life unless there is an
equivalence between suffering and glory within the divine nature itself.
As we saw in the previous chapter, Balthasar defines the relation that is
the divine essence in terms of an absolute self-donation. The kenosis is the
"selflessness" of the persons that entails a kind of eternal, divine "suffering."
What constitutes Father, Son, and Holy Spirit is precisely their self-abandonment to the "other" in the divine life. The Father gives himself entirely
to the Son. The Son does not hold onto his Godhood, but receives it from
the Father and returns it in full through absolute obedience. The Holy Spirit
is the bond of unity between them, who empties himself in uniting without
being either Father or Son. The inner triune kenosis is revealed to humanity
in the incarnation and passion of Jesus Christ.

> We shall show that to focus the Incarnation on the Passion enables
> both theories to reach a point where the mind is flooded by the
> same perfect thought: in serving, in washing the feet of his crea-
> tures, God reveals himself even in that which is most intimately
> divine in him, and manifests his supreme glory.[14]

Suffering and glory are identified at the source in the relation that is the
divine essence. Christ reveals their unity in his life, death, and resurrection,

---

within the divine identity). 'God is love' and nothing else; in this love lies every possible
form of self-expression, of truth, and of wisdom . . . In this 'life' all properties ascribable
to God are superseded: every power can be found in this beauty, especially at that moment when it is disarming every worldly power by becoming so nakedly and powerlessly
exposed to it."

13. Ibid.

14. Balthasar, *Mysterium Paschale*, 11.

not only in the divine life, but the possibility of their unity in creaturely life as well.[15]

Bulgakov, too, argues that each divine person's act of hypostatic love entails sacrifice or suffering. The Father gives himself in begetting. The Son only receives himself in obedience and in being begotten. The Holy Spirit is the joy of suffering overcome through sacrificial love, who ensures the all-blessedness of the divine life. These acts of suffering are acts of sacrificial love. However, they in no sense entail "the suffering of limitation," as that would be incompatible with the divine life.[16] (Human suffering always entails limitation and self-grasping. It is the refusal to allow one's self to be constituted entirely by the loving gift of God, and the impossibility of possessing any other kind of life as a genuine person). This inner-Trinitarian suffering is actualized in a different mode in the earthly passion of Christ.[17] Thus, impassibility, either with respect to the inner divine life, or with respect to economic activity, is an inaccurate abstraction. For, "in creating the world and providing for it, God interacts with the world and enters into a relation with the world process and with human freedom."[18] This relationship is both a product of the inner-Trinitarian love and also imposes a different *mode* of suffering upon that love with the incarnation.[19] The divine

---

15. "Creation, revelation, grace, and Incarnation are all God's humble act of adapting himself to the increasingly diminishing dimensions of the creature . . . This *humilitas Dei* is the most profound thing that God reveals of himself in his Incarnation and especially in his cross. The cross is absolutely the key to everything; *omnia in crucis manifestantur,* (quoting Bonaventure *De tripl. Via* 3.3 (VIII 14a); *cf.S.2 Parasc.* (IX265ab), not only sin not only man, but God himself. Thus it is in the humbling of self that the height of the imitation of God lies . . . None of this imitation surpasses God's humbling in Christ . . . But the path of descent and humbling of self is the bitter path of abandonment and betrayal" (Balthasar, *Studies in Theological Style: Clerical Styles,* 354).

16. "This suffering of sacrifice not only does not contradict the Divine all-blessedness, but, on the contrary, is its foundation, for this all-blessedness would be empty and unreal if it were not based on authentic sacrifice, on the reality of suffering. If God is love, he is also sacrifice, which manifests the victorious power of love and its joy only through suffering" (ibid., 99).

17. "One cannot admit an 'impassible' or indifferent relation to Christ's passion on the part of the hypostases that are not made incarnate, and first of all on the part of the Father, who sent his only begotten Son into the world . . . But this does not abolish that connection of love in the Holy Trinity in virtue of which the Golgotha mystery is accomplished in its special sense in heaven as well, in the Father's heart, which is the Holy Spirit" (ibid., 260).

18. Ibid., 261.

19. Balthasar, *Action,* 327–29.

suffering is a kind of "hypostatic dying" that results from the surrender of everything that the person possesses, even Godhood, to an "other." However, this suffering is always overcome with the blessedness and joy that results from receiving oneself from that "other" in return. The cross reveals this inner triune dynamic in its fullest expression.

In *Mysterium Paschale* Balthasar sets up Christ's descent into hell with precisely this Trinitarian theology. God is absolute love, "and his sovereignty manifests itself not in holding on to what is its own but in its abandonment."[20] Divine love entails kenosis, which has as its basis "the 'selflessness' of the Persons (when considered as pure relationships) in the inner-Trinitarian life of love."[21] The eternal, perichoretic, self-abandonment of the persons genuinely "costs" them something, both in the incarnation and in their eternal life,[22] and yet the price paid in suffering is also the glory of absolute love such that "on the cross, the Son's glory breaks through, inasmuch as he goes to the (divine) extreme in loving, and in the revelation of that love."[23] John Yocum critiques Balthasar on this point. He says that "a defect is imported into the Trinity, upon which, it seems, the divine love is dependent. The very intra-Trinitarian being is manifested and grounded in the requirement to suffer."[24] The intra-Trinitarian suffering that Balthasar is talking about, however, is not (like Moltmann) founded in the cross event. Rather, it is a characteristic of the eternal divine life irrespective of the incarnation. The kenotic love that constitutes the persons entails such an openness to the other, an absolute self-depletion into the other, that it cannot be characterized as "impassive." However, intra-divine suffering, as we have already seen, does not at all compromise divine blessedness within the particular kenotic theology of either Bulgakov or Balthasar. While Balthasar explicitly imports this idea that "suffering and death are the language of God's glory,"[25] from Bulgakov's kenotic Trinitarian theology, Thomas's notion of the divine essence as relation further anchors Balthasar's commitment to divine impassibility. Christ's suffering and death are the economic expression of his eternal immanent relation to the Father and Holy Spirit—the divine relation of kenotic self-abandonment

20. Balthasar, *Mysterium Paschale*, 28.

21. Ibid., 35.

22. Balthasar, *Dramatis Personae*, 188.

23. Balthasar, *Mysterium Paschale*, 29.

24. Yocum, "Cry of Dereliction," 74.

25. Balthasar, *Final Act*, 245.

that constitutes his very personhood. Christ's death on the cross is then a true revelation of divine glory and a revelation and recapitulation of human personhood as it participates through him in a relation with the Father and Holy Spirit.

The eternal selflessness that constitutes divine personhood is not an economic "adaptation." Nor is it the source of divine identity. Rather, the total self-abandonment (and in its triune context the God-abandonment) of the Son in the *triduum mortis* is the "blood circulation" of the triune life, and the cross is the place where that blood becomes available for human participation.[26] The cross is the "final word about God and man"[27] where "the appearing of beauty in what is nothing is here transfigured in the double mystery of Christ's humility and poverty."[28] Christ's humility, poverty, and suffering do not conceal the glory of God, but are the expression of love as beauty. This insight enables both Bulgakov and Balthasar to hold that Christ's suffering on the cross and descent into hell reveal the immanent triune life.

B) Divine Simplicity and Its Economic Expression

In the second shared presupposition, we find that the perichoretic self-giving that constitutes the divine life *ad intra* extends to the economic activity of God. Everything that God does with respect to creation is an expression of his own life. As such, there is a kind of necessity (for Bulgakov) or "fittingness" (for Balthasar) to the way in which God reveals himself, since economic activity is simply the immanent activity made present to creation in a new way. In creation, the Father "turns to the Son with the divine life." The Son as Word speaks that life into creation as an "other" in the image of the "otherness" between the triune persons. For both Bulgakov and Balthasar, this economic activity as extension of the triune kenosis has implications for human salvation, freedom, and ethics.

For Bulgakov, a triune God who is love "must" exteriorize himself into an "other" both in an act of creation and, since he creates free creatures, in an act of redemption when those creatures fail to respond to his offer of relationship. Bulgakov considers this necessity to be a necessity of love rather than of nature. I will explain this distinction in more detail in the

26. Ibid.

27. Balthasar, *Studies in Theological Style: Clerical Styles,* 356.

28. Ibid.

final section of this chapter. Though Balthasar agrees with Bulgakov that a triune God whose nature is kenotic love will create and redeem, he finds the sophiological implications of Bulgakov unacceptable, particularly as they shape the Creator/creature relationship.

For Bulgakov, creation is Sophia, not as she exists eternally hypostatized by the three persons, but in another mode.[29] Creaturely Sophia is the positing of divine Sophia into "becoming" or time. In eternity she is one and complete. In time she exists in multiplicity, though taken as a whole she is the precise image of divine Sophia. However, if the creaturely Sophia or world is an image of the divine world, then it must also have a hypostasis or hypostases to hypostatize it. The proper hypostases for creaturely Sophia are human persons who are distinct and yet, by *nature* united. Therefore, it is possible for the Son to become a hypostasis for creaturely Sophia, to, in a way, leave behind hypostatizing divine Sophia and enter into creation. The incarnation of the Son, his assumption of creaturely Sophia, entails a kind of inversion, or hierarchical shift, in the Trinitarian relations.

Salvation history, for Balthasar, is the unfolding of an interpersonal drama where human action is a participation in the triune life of God without collapsing the distinction between God and creatures. "God does not grow in himself, he grows in us."[30] For Balthasar as for Bulgakov, creation has its "ontic condition of possibility" in the kenotic nature of divine life, and the creation of free creatures already from eternity entails the incarnation. The inner self-abandonment of God is an "eternal exteriorization" or "tri-personal self-gift" which implies that the "created person, too, should no longer be described chiefly as subsisting in itself, but more profoundly . . . as a returning from exteriority to oneself and an 'emergence from oneself as an interiority that gives itself in self-expression.'"[31] For Balthasar,

---

29. Ibid., 220. "Everything in the divine and created world, in the divine and the created sophia, is one and identical in content (although not in being). A single Sophia is disclosed both in God and in the creation" (Bulgakov, *Bride*, 148). Mikhail Sergeev explains that "insofar as God differs from the creatures Sophia has two distinct aspects or centers, the divine and the creaturely, which correlate with the divine and created principles respectively. As Bulgakov points out, the doctrine of 'creation *ex nihilo* means nothing but the appearance of these two aspects in Sophia. The nothing (*nihilo*) as an *ouk on*—chaos or the absence (non-fullness) of being—in the process of creation is changed into a *meon*, or the potentiality of being. The appearance of the *meon* out of the *ouk on* is manifested in the split of the eternal Sophia and the origination of its temporal, created twin" ("Divine Wisdom," 577).

30. Balthasar, *Final Act*, 137.

31. Balthasar, *Mysterium Paschale*, 28–29

however, this exteriorization, or self-gift, is not a positing of the divine nature itself which the creature must return as a hypostasis of that nature in a "different mode." Balthasar explains that this would be equating the "divine foundation for the possibility of kenosis, and the kenosis itself."[32] Rather:

> The divine "power" is so ordered that it can make room for a possible self-exteriorization, like that found in the Incarnation and the Cross, and can maintain this exteriorization even to the utmost point. As between the form of God and the form of a servant there reigns, in the identity of the Person involved, an analogy of natures—according to the principle *maior dissimilitude in tanta simlitudine*.[33]

32. Ibid., 29.

33. Ibid., quoting *Enchiridion Symblorum*, ed. H. Denzinger, and A Schonmetzer (Freiburg: 1965) 806. Balthasar reads Bulgakov's Sophia as a kind of thing. The reification of the divine essence collapses that which for Balthasar makes a divine person: the total self-gift across an infinite distance which preserves the freedom of both giver and receiver. Sophia as a thing or a bridge creates a mechanistic system where both divine and human hypostases and their actions are determined by the content of divine Sophia.

Bulgakov himself seems to say conflicting things about the relationships between Sophia, the divine hypostases, and human freedom. On the one hand, there is a mechanistic determinism where both God and creation are locked in to the inevitable process of sophianization. On the other hand, the definition of Sophia as the activity of kenotic love that *is* only insofar as it is uniquely hypostatized by the three divine persons portrays a Sophia that exists as the openness of one person to the other. This openness is so complete that it produces a genuine contingent other, which also possesses the capacity to hypostatize Sophia through the activity of selfless love. Balthasar's construal emphasizes the activity of the persons in relation to the divine essence. However, we can see Balthasar setting up a possible redemption of sophiology when Sophia is read not so much as a thing or bridge, but as Balthasar describes God's essence: an infinite space across which the persons perichoretically communicate kenotic love. This space entails both a presence and an absence, or a "presence of the absence" in which the absolute self gift of the persons, one to another, provides an entelechy for the triune life and the cosmos while maintaining a kind of "space" for genuine otherness and the possibility of "surprise." But does naming this distance "Sophia" in fact fill it up and make it into a bridge? Does Balthasar, on the other hand, perhaps lose something of the unity of the ousia, and the imagedness of the creation as a unity in order to preserve the personhood and freedom of both God and humanity? Louis Marie Chauvet draws on Balthasar in order to describe a "Trinitarian metaphysics" of symbol. When Sophia is construed symbolically, the presence of the triune persons to each other entails an infinite distance or absence which preserves divine freedom. This same distance has its analog in the distance between God and creation. The otherness of creation from its Creator entails both the infinite distance and innermost presence of God to his creatures. The "bridge" across this distance always only exists as a personal act of self-gift which is only received when it is assimilated and returned.

The Person of the Son, rather than Sophia as divine nature and its self-positing into becoming, functions as the bridge between God and creatures. Just as the persons of the Trinity can maintain genuine "otherness" in the infinite distance of kenotic love, so between God and creatures there need not be a "natural/sophianic" or impersonal principle of correspondence.[34] When the divine essence is considered as relation, the infinite distance that is constitutive of divine personhood in the opposition of relations provides ample space for a participated human personhood. There is an analogously infinite distance inherent within human relation that entails a genuine correspondence between Image and image.

C) Divine Freedom as "Distance"

The third point of agreement between Balthasar and Bulgakov in the trajectory of descent is that, for both, freedom must be defined in terms of the kenosis of the divine persons in the triune life. Within this paradigm, the epitome of infinite freedom is revealed in the absolute self-donation of the Son. God possesses God's self most fully in God-abandonment. Human freedom has its foundation in the same paradox. We are most free when we are most actualizing the kenotic nature of our own personhood. Though both Bulgakov and Balthasar describe freedom in terms of the inner-Trinitarian kenosis as it is revealed in Christ's Passion, the different ways that they construe the relationship between the divine persons and divine nature produce very different notions of freedom particularly with respect to human freedom.

When the divine essence is considered in the Thomistic sense as relation, and the distinction of the divine persons as the opposition of relation, the very unity of the divine life entails a simultaneously infinite difference. Balthasar's thesis that the "blood circulation" of the triune life is the activity of relation, or infinite kenosis, implies that the notional activity of the divine persons is both an active self-giving, as well as a passive giving-over of self. Personhood entails a transparency to the other. The self-emptying of the persons into an "other" takes place across an infinite distance that grants a certain freedom to that "other."

> The Father must not be thought to exist "prior" to this self-surrender: he *is* this movement of self-giving that holds nothing back.

34. Balthasar, *Action,* 323.

> This divine act that brings forth the Son, that is, the second way of participating in (and of being) the identical Godhead, involves the positing of an absolute, infinite "distance" that can contain and embrace all the other distances that are possible within the world of finitude, including the distance of sin.[35]

For Balthasar, this dynamic of self-offering into the infinite distance constitutes personhood and the sharing in this activity is the divine essence that is relation. "This inseparability of Father and Son will be made clear to them at the moment when the separation of the two will apparently be total. This is the absolute paradox."[36] The activity of the persons constitutes divine freedom and the personhood of creatures is an image of that life and freedom. The notion of personhood alone is sufficient to describe both the divine life as well as creaturely existence as an image of and participation in that life. The distance, or absolute openness, between the divine persons is the basis for all otherness and personhood.

> It is the drama of the "emptying" of the Father's heart, in the generation of the Son, that contains and surpasses all possible drama between God and a world. For any world only has its place within that distinction between Father and Son that is maintained and bridged by the Holy Spirit.[37]

As we have seen, for Bulgakov, an additional concept, that of Sophia, is necessary to ground the unity of the divine persons, as well as construct an "ontological bridge" between Creator and creation. By setting up the personal or hypostatic triune life in terms of Sophia, Bulgakov dismantles the paradox of relation. Instead of unity and difference inherent within the same kenotic act, we have both hypostatic activity and the hypostatized content of that activity. Sophia as content, even an enacted or hypostatized content, entails a very different notion of freedom from that of Balthasar. Sophia as the content or world of the divine life sets a kind of limit on what

---

35. Ibid.

36. Balthasar, *Final Act*, 327–28. "The ultimate meaning of dying, as we see from the self-surrender of the Son at the absolute end. For he, bearing in himself the darkness of all false deaths and going beyond them, surrenders himself in this darkness into the hands—which he can now no longer feel—of the Father who sends him, the Father who, in doing so, surrenders himself . . . the finitude of this dying in forsakenness is 'pure, limitless revelation,' because 'in ultimate intensification, in this forsakenness,' it manifests 'the Father's infinity.' 'The Son's death is the exemplification of the supreme aliveness of triune love'" (326–27, quoting Adrienne Von Speyr's *Der Grensenlose Gott*, 63).

37. Ibid., 327.

the Father surrenders to the Son in his act of selfless donation. Balthasar's use of "surprise," or the opposition of relation that preserves an infinite mystery between one divine person and the others, situates both divine freedom and human freedom as a participation in terms of the activity of personhood (relation), rather than sophianization or actualization of a given content. For Bulgakov, in contrast, the relations between the divine persons occur in a given world or nature. Thus, the Father knows himself fully in his act of self-surrender to the Son, but what the Father knows is the "content" of the divine nature as kenotic love, or Sophia. In their kenoses as well, the Son and Holy Spirit can only hand over their hypostatizations of Sophia. There is no "surprise" possible within the divine life.

D) "Trinitarian Inversion"

We can see the relationship between personal activity and freedom play out in the fourth point of agreement along the trajectory into hell. Both Balthasar and Bulgakov agree that during Christ's incarnate life there takes place a kind of "Trinitarian inversion" where the Son's relation to the Father is "mediated" by the Holy Spirit. The Spirit presents the Son's prayers to the Father and the Father's will to the Son as a kind of law. The Son obeys what he receives from the Spirit. On the cross when the Son "gives up" the Spirit and dies, he enters into the deepest expression of his absolute obedience to the Father. He offers himself entirely, but as an expression of who he is from eternity. This is the clearest expression of the Son's eternal identity.

The incarnation of the Son, his assumption of creaturely Sophia, entails a kind of inversion, or hierarchical shift, in the Trinitarian relations. Bulgakov sets this inversion in terms of Sophia:

> In the Incarnation, the Son removes from Himself his divine glory, empties himself of his divinity, extinguishes it in himself, as it were. Therefore, the hierarchical place that is pre-eternally proper to him in the Holy Trinity and, in particular, his relation to the Father, takes on externally "subordinationalistic" traits. The relation becomes one of voluntary and absolute obedience. By his will the Father takes the place in the Son of the Son's own divinity, so to speak, which the Son, as it were, has abandoned.[38]

38. Bulgakov, *Lamb of God*, 305–6.

This shift in the Trinitarian relations also extends to the Son's relation to the Holy Spirit. Whereas in the inner-Trinitarian life the Holy Spirit occupies a sort of "third" place, in the incarnation the Holy Spirit presents the Father to the Son. Instead of reposing upon him "naturally," the "Son who humbles himself also no longer knows, *for himself*, this reposing of the Holy Spirit in which his divinity is realized for Him. In this sense the kenosis really signifies for the Son that in some sense he leaves the life of the holy Trinity, although his naturally essential presence in the Trinity is preserved."[39] In the incarnation, the Son experiences himself as human and experiences the Father in his human consciousness as mediated by the Holy Spirit. The Holy Spirit leads Jesus and presents the will of the Father to him as a man, albeit a man entirely conditioned by his relationship to the Father.[40] In this interim the Holy Spirit does not proceed through or to the Son, but rather reposes upon him. This "Trinitarian inversion" is one way in which we see the Son entering into a total solidarity with humankind. Even his relationship to the Father and Holy Spirit is conditioned to his humanity.

Whereas for Bulgakov, the Son's consciousness of the Father must be mediated by the Holy Spirit because of a "kenotic detachment from his divinity,"[41] Balthasar maintains a paradox: "In the undiminished humanity of Jesus, the whole power and glory of God are made present to us."[42] It is precisely because the Son maintains the fullness of his divinity that the incarnation must be a Trinitarian event, which, in a certain sense, "restructures" the Trinitarian relations for a time. Balthasar agrees then that Jesus experiences the Father through the Holy Spirit as "go-between."[43] The Spirit presents the Father's will to the Son as a rule he must obey unto death, which "reminds" both Father and Son what they agreed upon beforehand.[44]

39. Ibid., 307.

40. Ibid., 308.

41. Ibid., 265. Here, Bulgakov emphasizes that the cause of this "detachment" is only the total identification of the Son with the Father's will to send him into the world. The Son maintains the continuity of his identity, despite his "detachment" because he *is* the identical disposition of obedience in the immanent triune life that he demonstrates in the economy of salvation. This personal continuity, for Bulgakov, is based in the compatibility of hypostatic expression between divine and creaturely Sophia. Only the Son can express both, and he expresses both as the same person. For Balthasar's kenotic theology, Sophia is a superfluous concept here, and "detachment" is likewise unnecessary if divinity can be most perfectly revealed in suffering obedience.

42. Balthasar, *Mysterium Paschale*, 33.

43. Ibid., 30.

44. Jesus' self-consciousness, then, is completely occupied with the task given to him

The Holy Spirit "personifies" the shared will of Son and Father for the Son. He presents to him (and this is the fifth point) that Son's mission, established before the foundation of the world, is to "take on manhood" which means "to assume its concrete destiny with all that entails—suffering, death, hell—in solidarity with every human being."[45] The only difference between Balthasar and Bulgakov on this final point is what Christ's total solidarity with humankind entails.[46]

E) Solidarity and Salvation

The fifth point of agreement is that in order to save humanity the Son must enter into absolute solidarity with humanity. This includes an assumption of the fullness of human rejection of God.

Bulgakov emphasizes the importance of Christ's total solidarity with sinful humanity, even unto death. Christ must *voluntarily* assume everything human so that "the divine life in the God-Man is manifested as the triumph of the human essence, which turns out to be capable of obedience to the commands of the Divine Spirit of the Son, who does the will of the Father."[47] This entails an exhaustive obedience, or absolute openness, in the face of every human reality, including the realities of sin and death. Christ's experience of human reality is unique, not only because of his total obedience, but because: "In the New Adam this suffering had not a limited and quantitative character but a universal and all-human character, and this *universality* of the night of Gethsemane and of the feat of the cross is the mystery of the God-Man."[48] Christ not only undergoes the entirety of the human experience of suffering and sin, but he does this universally. He undergoes these things with and for all humanity. This solidarity extends beyond suffering on the cross and into death. "In death, he voluntarily made the measure of the fallen humanity his own measure."[49] Christ makes

by the Father, which is "expressing God's Fatherhood through his entire being, through his life and death in and for the world" (Balthasar, *Dramatis Personae*, 172. See also 183–88.

45. Balthasr, *Mysterium Paschale*, 20.

46. In *Final Act*, 313–14, Balthasar outlines Bulgakov's understanding of how Christ can be in solidarity with all of humanity and take on the sin of the whole world.

47. Bulgakov, *Lamb of God*, 310.

48. Ibid.

49. Ibid., 311.

human disobedience and rejection of God his own, entering fully into the consequences of that reality. He is able to do this because it is the will of the Father that he redeem humanity (and indeed his own will, inscribed into the foundations of creation), the fulfillment of which constitutes his very being, even as a man. Thus, in solidarity with humanity, the Son of God undergoes sin and death, and enters into hell.

Both theologians understand this assumption as a descent into hell, where the full use of human freedom to reject God is assumed and overcome in the Son's full use of his freedom to offer himself to God. His love for the Father is infinite and always reaches beyond the finite effects of human sin. The Father's love for the Son can always extend to receive the Son beyond those same effects. The Spirit who unites Father and Son is not exhausted in the break caused by the rejection. This dynamic is possible because the very act of divinity is a love that both forms the basis for and surpasses humanity's "No" to God.

> The world can only be created within the Son's "generation": the world belongs to him and has him as its goal; only in the Son can the world be "recapitulated." Accordingly, in whatever way the Son is sent into the world (*processio* here is seen to be *mission*, up to and including the Cross), it is an integral part of his "co-original" thanksgiving for the world. . . . Here, spanning the gulf of the Divine Persons' total distinctness, we have a correspondence between the Father's self-giving, expressed in generation, and the Son's thanksgiving and readiness (a readiness that goes to the limit of forgiveness).[50]

The self-giving love that constitutes the essence of God is life, thus the Son's death and assumption of human sin render death into eternal life.[51]

It is clear from the ways in which Balthasar's theology corresponds with and diverges from Bulgakov's on these points that, for Balthasar, Sophia is a distraction from the kenotic character of divine love. Sophia obscures the personal manner in which divine love empties itself, both within the triune life and in the acts of creation and incarnation. There is

---

50. Balthasar, *Action,* 328.

51. "It is easy for us to forget that a Divine Person, even in the Incarnation and in the vicissitudes of his human 'I,' is nevertheless pure relation and that God's blessedness consists in his *being* self-surrender. Bearing this in mind, we can draw the following conclusion: When the Son accepts dying in the agony of God-forsakenness, it is for him (and the other Divine Persons) not only an "external work" undertaken out of absolute love and joy but also the expression of his very own, his very specific life" (Balthasar, *Final Act,* 255.

no need for an "ontological bridge" between God and the world if the Son himself, who *is* complete obedience to the Father, and who thus shares in the infinite love of the Father and the Holy Spirit for humanity, has become man. Divine nature does not need to correspond to human nature in order for Christ to unite both in his person. If Trinitarian love extends across the eternal infinite distance between the divine persons, it can extend beyond the created (though still infinite) distance between God and man. It can "englobe" an "other" in the act of creation, and even encompass the negative distance created by that other's rejection.

> Everything turns on the inner-Trinitarian Love which alone explains that an act of obedience is not necessarily foreign to God himself. . . . Once we realized that even in the most extreme kenosis, inasmuch as it is a possibility in the eternal love of God, is englobed in that love which takes responsibility for it, then the opposition between a *theologia crucis* and a *theologia gloriae* is fundamentally overcome—even though those two may not dissolve into one another.[52]

Balthasar's paradigm accomplishes the "bridging" function in the person of Christ rather than in Sophia. This is particularly evident with the descent into hell.

BULGAKOV'S DESCENT INTO HELL

If the sophiological aspect of Bulgakov's thought causes him to, in a way, mitigate the Son's divinity in the incarnation, it should be no surprise that he would leave Christ's humanity to descend into hell on its own. The claim that the Son's divinity remains with the Father as he descends into hell is the first major difference between Bulgakov and Balthasar with respect to the descent. The second is the nature of the sin that Christ assumes. For Bulgakov, creaturely rejection of God can only result in nothingness. I will first explain why a sophiological rendering demands these two differences, and then in the next section show how Balthasar's descent illuminates and resolves the problems inherent in such a system.

For Bulgakov, creaturely Sophia has a dual foundation: divine nature and nothingness. "Becoming being is an alloy of the divine 'principle' with

---

52. Balthasar, *Mysterium Paschale*, 82.

nothing."[53] "Nothingness" is not co-eternal with God, but is rather created as the condition of creaturely freedom. Insofar as creatures reject the divine ground of their being creation deteriorates into a bad relation— it actualizes the "nothing" character of its existence rather than the divine. On the other hand, insofar as it exists, creation has a panentheistic character.[54] It is a "sophianic mirror" of the divine life.[55] Therefore, in order for the Son to assume the full consequences of human freedom and experience suffering to its full extent, he must not only become man, or even become a dead man. For there is nowhere in the creaturely realm as it exists for the Son to go where he could experience abandonment by God. So he must abandon his own Godhood and enter into the "nothing" produced by creaturely freedom in its rejection of God.

> In order to receive death God had to remove from himself his divinity; he had to stop being God, as it were. "My God, my God, why hast thou forsaken me?" (Matt. 27:46)—that is the cry on the cross of the dying God, of God forsaken by God. It is as if the Holy Spirit himself, the Giver of Life, had to "forsake" him, in order for this death to be "finished."[56]

The entry into this kind of "nothing" for Bulgakov is only through the grave.[57] In the grave "the greedy nothing out of which man is created, this nothing opened wide, because of sin, its yawning abyss and brought death into creation. . . . After the creation of the world, nothingness, the outer darkness, once again presented itself before God; and he illuminated this darkness with the light of his resurrection."[58] Bulgakov's description of

53. Bulgakov, *Bride*, 53.

54. "The world reposes not upon itself and not upon its creatureliness, but is affirmed in God, in whom 'we live, and move, and have our being'" (ibid., 228, citing Acts 17:28).

55. "God also has a relation to the world that issues not from divine eternity but from creaturely temporality . . . He himself lives in time with and for creation. For himself as well he posits becoming. Abiding in eternity and in the unchangeable fullness of being in himself, he lives in the life of creation and with creation. In himself, God is Absolute, supramundane being, but he is also God for the world. This means that he has a positive relation to the world; he interacts with the world; He establishes a 'synergism' with it" (ibid., 229).

56. Bulgakov, *Churchly Joy*, 117.

57. "To us, such as we are, to murderers of God, murderers of man, self-murderers, God came and experienced death on the cross for our sakes . . . This grave is a revelation of God's love for man; it is the gift of the insatiable sacrificiality of his love: to give all for love, so that nothing remains ungiven" (ibid., 106).

58. Ibid., 107. The sophianic paradigm is especially unclear with Christ's entry into

Christ's death focuses primarily on what it accomplishes, which is the destruction of the power of sin and death over humanity. Christ accomplishes this by entering into the nothing of God-abandonedness and the nothing produced by human sin. By entering into this nothing he fills it with his presence, which is love.

> Life in death is "hell," and the death of the God-Man was also a "descent into hell." But for him over whom death was deprived of power but permitted only by his voluntary acceptance, the descent into hell too was a continuation of his ministry . . . During the three-day sojourn in the grave, the Lord tastes death together with the human race. He shares it with the human race. And this death is not a sleep of passivity; it is a continuing ministry, uninterrupted obedience to the Father's will. *This death is love.* In Christ's grave, selfhood is annihilated, the sting of death is abolished, death dies.[59]

From this point on there is no longer a creaturely nothing lurking behind creation. The entire universe, all of humanity, all of history is filled with the light of Christ's love and, with Pentecost, becomes "panchristic and panpneumatic."[60] The descent into hell eliminates all creaturely opposition to sophianization and paves the way for the eventual hypostatization of creation in the triune life.

---

death and hell. Christ is able to hypostatize both human and divine natures properly, as his own. The different capacities of these natures imply that his hypostasis must undergo suffering and death, descent and nothingness differently in each nature, and, at times, it seems that the hypostasis of the Son must experience death, nothingness, and abandonment apart from his divine nature. His divine nature is consigned to the Father during his three days in the grave, and the whole Trinity suffers the separation of the hypostasis from his own divinity (Bulgakov, *Lamb of God*, 314). On the other hand, Bulgakov says quite clearly that the hypostasis of the Son cannot be separated from his divinity (ibid., 312). Another point of contradiction is Bulgakov's assertion that, for the Son, "death is not a sleep of passivity" (see full quote below), and also "The Son had brought his humiliation to the extreme of self-devastation, to death, the personality with its freedom no longer exists, but only receptive passivity remains" (ibid., 316). It is almost as if Balthasar's theology of the descent makes sense of Bulgakov's various ideas and systematizes them without the cumbersome presence of Sophia.

59. Bulgakov, *Churchly Joy*, 118.

60. Bulgakov, *Bride*, 261.

BALTHASAR'S "DESCENT"

Balthasar's theology of the descent, like Bulgakov's, is the extension and conclusion of his kenotic Trinitarian paradigm. We have already seen how Balthasar holds this paradigm together, not with Sophia, but with Christ's identity as the personal and embodied love of God.

> In the death and the dying away into silence of the Logos so become the centre of what he has to say of himself that we have to understand precisely his non-speaking as his final revelation, his utmost word: and this because, in the humility of his obedient self-lowering to the death of the Cross he is identical with the exalted Lord. What founds the continuity is the absolute love of God of man, manifesting itself actively on both sides of the hiatus (and so in the hiatus itself), and his triune Love in its own intrinsic reality as the condition of possibility for such a love for man.[61]

Christ himself, the God-Man, is the bridge over the "hiatus" of death and creaturely rejection that constitutes hell. There are two major differences in Balthasar's construal of hell which reveal the significance of having Christ's person, rather than Sophia, serve as the bridge between God and creation: Christ's descent into hell as the God-Man in the fullness of both divinity and humanity, and Christ's experience of human rejection as the concrete effects of sin rather than nothingness.

For Balthasar, Christ does not abandon his divinity in death. Rather, "hell is an event of the economic Trinity."[62] Christ is able to enter into creation in the incarnation as both God and man. His human life is a genuinely human experience even as he retains his full divinity. Though we have seen that, in the incarnation, the persons of the Trinity undergo a real "shift" in their relations, for Balthasar this does not entail a change or development in the divine nature. Rather, the essence of God, kenotic love, is simply more economically intense as the Son fulfills the will of the Father with an even deeper kenotic obedience. "In his self-emptying God does not divest himself of his Godhead, but rather does he give it precise confirmation."[63] This same dynamic is intensified with Christ's death and descent into hell. Divine love can enter into death as an even greater expression of what it is. What is more, divine love can enter into death in complete solidarity

---

61. Balthasar, *Mysterium Paschale*, 79.

62. Ibid., 175.

63. Ibid., 81.

with humanity without compromising its genuine creaturely "otherness." Bulgakov must somehow bracket out the divine nature from death in order for the hypostasis of the Son to experience God-abandonment because, for him, there never is a genuine creaturely otherness. There is only God, the image of God in becoming, and nothingness. Balthasar's Christ can descend into the fullness of creaturely rejection as God because Balthasar's God creates a true "other" with the freedom to reject God, a freedom so real that it can itself produce a negative creaturely reality. "By becoming man, he enters into what is alien to him and there remains at the same time true to himself."[64] Christ can enter into the full extent of human rejection and God-abandonment as God and man.

The possibility for Christ's simultaneous God-abandonment and full expression of divine life can be difficulty to understand. Matthew Levering, in *Scripture and Metaphysics*, claims that:

> For Balthasar, then, the Son's obedience on the Cross, in order to bear sin fully, must be characterized by two elements: absolute faithfulness, and absolute lack of grounding in knowledge.[65]

Levering concludes that Balthasar's analogy of the Trinity "overturns the principle of contradiction."[66] Either the Son receives everything from the Father, including knowledge, and the cross is a true revelation of both the Father's self-gift and the Son's reception and return of that gift in the Spirit, or there is a difference between the life of the Father as he possesses it for himself and the life he gives to the Son. Levering interprets Balthasar's statement that Jesus' mission "presupposes (right from the Incarnation) a certain veiling of his sight of the Father: he must leave it in abeyance, refrain from using it; this is possible because of the distance between Father and

---

64. Ibid.

65. "Jesus only moves to the pinnacle of obedience (the pinnacle of union with the Father's will) by simultaneously entering the abyss of not-knowing. The highest obedience—the highest charity—is that which obeys without (conscious) knowledge or hope. This highest charity expresses the self-abandoning that characterizes absolute Love, that is, the Trinity: 'This obedience alone exegetes God as absolute love, and that precisely by the Father's exposing his Son out of love for the world to the contradiction of the contradivine.' Complete self-abandoning to the 'other,' a self-abandonment made absolute by unknowing (so as to be willed as self-abandoning rather than as something else), serves as Balthasar's analog for the Trinity" (Matthew Levering, *Scripture and Metaphysics*, 131. Citing *Theologik* II, 331).

66. Ibid., 132.

Son in the Trinity"[67] to mean that Balthasar distinguishes between intellect and will in the triune life such that obedience is a matter of will that actually requires a total lack of knowledge. Levering notes earlier that, "because of 'the identity of unity and difference' in Jesus his metaphysical constitution already points to the unity and distinction of the divine Trinity. The suffering, death, and resurrection of the incarnate Son reveal analogously the eternal mutual kenosis of the Father and the Son in the *ecstasis* of love."[68]

Like Bulgakov, Levering seems to be assume that if love is primarily a matter of will and faith, and hope primarily acts of the intellect, then one could presumably have love without knowledge. Ironically, Levering accuses Balthasar of the same error that Bulgakov attributes to Aquinas: by positing a distinction between the intellect and will in the activity of the divine nature, they distort both the Trinitarian relations as well as the relation between God and creation. However, by following Thomas's Trinitarian theology where the divine activity is a personal relation (and therefore intrinsically involves the disposition of both intellect and will), Balthasar is not saying that in the paschal events the Son somehow possesses perfect unity in difference with the Father and Holy Spirit through obedient submission of his will while simultaneously entering into a "total lack of knowledge."

In order to interpret Balthasar correctly on this point we must return to both Bulgakov and Aquinas. The absolute selflessness of the divine persons constitutes the divine relation, which is the divine essence. This relation presupposes a unity in difference, a perfect possession in abandonment, and a perfect knowledge in "surprise." The persons only possess themselves as related to the "other." The opposition of relation in the triune life of kenotic love entails that knowledge of the "other" cannot be reduced (as Bulgakov attempts to do with Sophia) to a "content" that can be fully grasped. Rather, the very nature of personhood implies a "letting be" that entails "surprise" or an openness to the infinite mystery of the other. Levering recognizes the paradox of unity in difference that lies at the heart of Balthasar's theology, but fails to see how this extends to both knowledge in an openness to not knowing for oneself, and a love that bridges as it maintains an infinite distance.

The second point of difference between Balthasar's descent and Bulgakov's is that, for the former, Christ's experience in hell is not of the *meon* or

---

67. Levering, *Scripture and Metaphysics*, 128, quoting Balthasar, *Final Act*, 125.

68. Ibid., 123, quoting *Theologik* II, 117–18.

nothingness that is the potentiality of human freedom. Rather, Christ experiences the concrete reality of human sin. In Balthasar's understanding, humanity's rejection of God creates a negative distance between creature and Creator.

> The second death which, itself, is one with sheer sin as such, no longer sin as attaching to a particular human being, sin incarnate in living existences, but abstracted from that individuation, contemplated in its bare reality as such (for sin is a reality!) . . . Sin forms what one can call the second "chaos" (generated by human liberty) and that, in the separation between sin and the living man, is then precisely the product of the active suffering of the Cross.[69]

Christ experiences sin as a substantial reality generated by human freedom, or as the "effigies" of human actions gone wrong. For Balthasar, human freedom is not nothing. It is real and has real consequences. Significantly, these consequences can only be "measured" by God himself. Christ encompasses these depths of human sin, such that hell is a function of the Christ event.[70] It is his obedience—the obedience, which constitutes his identity as the Son—which "takes the existential measure of everything that is sheerly contrary to God, of the entire object of the divine eschatological judgment, which here is grasped in that event in which it is 'cast down.'"[71] The reality of human rejection that is measured and judged in Christ is hell. It is his obedient descent into the consequences of human freedom, which makes hell a reality for humanity, a reality which we only experience in and with Christ.[72]

Humans now experience the consequences of our freedom, not directly as hell, but in and with Christ as judgment and purgation. Purgatory begins in the event of Holy Saturday.[73] Now each person is confronted with their rejections of God in Jesus Christ "who is solidary with us."[74] This implies, first, that each person has a real capacity to reject God. Human freedom is not an illusive historical phenomenon. Sin generates a real consequence both in the person and in the world, and this consequence is assumed by Christ. Second, it implies that judgment and purgation are not

69. Ibid., 173. See also, *Truth of God*, 356.

70. Ibid., 172.

71. Ibid., 174.

72. Ibid., 178.

73. Ibid.

74. Ibid.

mechanistic functions of a "world process." Each person encounters their concrete sin and its consequences in Christ. "In purgatory he makes us to be fuel for the fire that consumes him."[75] There we are judged in Christ by our own works. "What becomes manifest here is not only the freedom of the Risen One to offer himself when and as he wills, but also a leaving free of man (this, too, is an aspect of Easter grace) to react just as *he* wills."[76] By rooting purgatory in Holy Saturday, Balthasar's theology of "descent" preserves the vital element of human freedom both to accept and reject God. It does this because forgiveness and purgation are intrinsic functions of Christ's voluntary kenotic love and human persons confronted with their own works in the face of that love.

Balthasar adapts Thomas's and Bulgakov's Trinitarian theology to posit creaturely participation in the divine life where freedom isn't based in a kind of nothingness that ultimately is overcome by the divine life. Nor does he situate negative creaturely reality in nothingness, or privation. In contrast, he is able to include all of the negative realities of the creaturely world within the triune life as relation. Hell itself is a Christological reality, and as such, a Trinitarian reality.

> For Balthasar, the descent "solves" the problem of theodicy, by showing us the conditions on which God accepted our foreknown abuse of freedom: namely, his own plan to take to himself our self-damnation in Hell. It also demonstrates the costliness of our redemption: the divine Son underwent the experience of Godlessness. Finally, it shows that the God revealed by the Redeemer is a Trinity. Only if the Spirit, as *vinculum amoris* between the Father and the Son, can re-relate Father and Son in their estrangement in the descent, can the unity of the Revealed and Revealer be maintained. In this final humiliation of the *forma servi*, the glorious *forma Dei* shines forth via its lowest pitch of self-giving love.[77]

By making himself the measure of human rejection of God, and as such, undergoing the full extent of God abandonment, the Son manifests the very character of the divine relation: self-giving love.

75. Balthasar, *Theo-Drama* vol. 5 quoting Adrienne Von Speyr's *Ojektive Mystik*, 383–84.

76. Balthasar, *Mysterium Paschale*, 252.

77. Nichols, "Introduction," *Mysterium Paschale*, 7.

Christ's descent into hell, his embodiment of God-abandonedness, not only reveals the divine relation, but also the potential of humanity to participate in that relation.

> The meaning of earthly life remains undecided and obscured, as long as life lasts. Only in death, through the divine judgment, does a man receive his definitive orientation. This is why Christ's redemption of mankind had its decisive completion not, strictly speaking, with the incarnation or in the continuity of his mortal life, but in the hiatus of death.[78]

Christ redeems humanity, not by dying in our place, but by opening death to eternal life, and earthly life to a "death to self." With his descent into finite suffering and death, Christ transforms these realities into participations in the eternal act of self-donation that is the life of God. Now humanity is able to "die with Christ" into the activity of self-offering that *is* eternal life.

> If God himself has lived out this ultimate experience of this world, a world which, through human freedom, has the possibility of withdrawing obedience from God and so of losing him, then he will no longer be a God who judges his creatures from above and from outside. Thanks to his intimate experience of the world, as the Incarnate one who knows experientially every dimension of the world's being down to the abyss of Hell, God now becomes the measure of man.[79]

Christ's descent into hell breaks open the false relation to self and others that has comprised humanity since Adam's fall. He reveals the truth of humanity's helplessness and limitation. He assumes the full effects of suffering and hate. Christ does this, not to judge us from without, but to break open the self-imposed limitation of relation that comes from denying our own finitude. By accepting the absolute helplessness and passivity of death as the "measure of man," humanity is, ironically, freed for participation in the infinite activity of loving relation.

PITSTICK'S CRITIQUE

For Balthasar, the descent into hell is not a theologically isolated event. What is, hopefully, evident from the above two sections is that for both

78. Balthasar, *Mysterium Paschale*, 13.

79. Ibid., 13–14.

Bulgakov and Balthasar the manner in which they conceive of the "descent" is a result of their Trinitarian theology. The concept of kenotic love consituting the triune life sets their theologies on a trajectory that leads straight to hell. Balthasar does not begin with a theology of "descent." It is the conclusion of his Trinitarian theology.

The "downward" direction of his Trinitarian trajectory could provide a response to a critique raised by Alyssa Pitstick. Pitstick has recently argued that Balthasar's doctrine of the descent into hell is, in fact, contrary to Catholic orthodoxy. She argues:

> The *unity of faith* and the *nexus mysteriorum* are just two ways to describe the fact that the mysteries of Christ's life, death, and resurrection are all knit together. The work of God in Christ is a seamless garment. To change the profession, formal or material, of one mystery will ultimately have a ripple effect through all. Balthasar's essentially new doctrine of Christ's descent raises the question whether one can still believe in the Christ professed by one's ecclesial community if one consciously rejects the descent it professes, just as the same question would be raised if one rejected Christ's resurrection, his incarnation, the Trinity, or any other article of the creed.[80]

Pitstick's intuition that Balthasar's theology of the descent is intimately connected to his Trinitarian and Christological theology is correct, but I would argue that the cause/effect relationship is reversed. The descent into hell is a result of his kenotic Trinitarian theology. Therefore, if one is going to object to theological speculation on any point it ought not be the "descent." The "descent" merely demonstrates most clearly (and Balthasar explicitly says this) the full extent of God's divine nature as kenotic love.

The points at issue in Balthasar's Trinitarian theology are precisely the points where Balthasar draws from Bulgakov. There are two misunderstandings that particularly demonstrate the importance of recognizing Bulgakov's influence on Balthasar. First, Pitstick argues that the "traditional" (Thomistic) doctrine of appropriation "suggest[s] a Trinitarian treatment of

---

80. Nichols et al., "Balthasar, Hell, and Heresy," 28. First, I would like to note Paul Griffiths's response to Pitstick's objection. He clearly explains the "traditional" Catholic distinction between three various levels of truth. He shows that theological speculation, even concerning truths at the highest level (though not, of course, speculation which calls into doubt their status as true), is acceptable within the Catholic system (Griffiths, "Doctrine?," 3).

the descent is irrelevant."[81] Second, she expresses difficulty with Balthasar's correlation between divine glory and God-abandonment.

Both misunderstandings result from a dichotomy between God's essence and the divine persons, where essence seems to be an impersonal set of properties such as immutability and omnipotence rather than relation. Within this paradigm, the glory of the divine essence would in fact preclude the possibility of God-abandonedness constituting the divine persons. However, a correct understanding of Thomas's doctrine of the divine person as subsistent relations, and the divine essence as relation, and the divine nature acting *simpliciter* both *ad intra* and *ad extra*, allows one to posit that whatever constitutes the act of relation within the triune life also constitutes the activity of God *ad extra*. If that act is in fact tri-personal self-gift, then all economic activity will be a tri-personal self-gift, and the self-offering of the Son on the cross can be understood as the revelation of God's eternal act which is the glory of self-abandonment to the other in love.

In the beginning of her section on the relationship between Balthasar's Trinitarian theology and his theology of the descent into hell, Pitstick points out that such a discussion should be unnecessary. The divine nature acts *ad extra*, simply, and only attributed to one divine person or another due to a likeness between the act and their particular personal property.[82] As I pointed out above, this statement presupposes that the divine activity *ad extra*, by virtue of its simplicity, must be impersonal (except perhaps in an abstract sense in which, for example, one might say that creation is appropriated to the Father from the likeness between his inner-Trinitarian relation as source and the act of creating). As we have seen, Bulgakov reads Thomas in the same way. He is perplexed by the bifurcation of the powers of the divine nature, intellect, and will, from the divine persons.

Once we recognize the inherently Trinitarian and personal nature of divine activity *ad extra*, the second difficulty is both clarified and intensified. How can the triune God be most clearly revealed in Christ's descent into hell? For Balthasar, the activity which constitutes the divine life is a kenotic love so absolute in its abandonment of self to the other that it is a death. However, it is precisely this kind of death that *is* eternal life. The "break" suffered in the divine relation is so profound that there is no finite break which is not encompassed by it. Yet, it is precisely this "break" in

81. Pitstick, *Light in Darkness*, 115.
82. Ibid.

relation that constitutes the divine relation. In God, love is "God-abandon-ment." And yet, in God this abandonment is glory. Pitstick asks, if suffering in God is an analogous term, then how can Balthasar talk of pain in God in opposition to pain in the world? Moreover, "pain and the overcoming of pain are *in fact* seen as opposites in the creaturely world, not analogues. The possible perfection is the approach to pain, not the pain itself."[83]

Balthasar's notion of divine suffering and glory requires two clarifica-tions: The first is that we cannot limit ourselves to such a narrow concept of creaturely pain and suffering, a concept that seems limited to the mere psycho-physical perception of pain, and explicitly excludes the subjects "approach to pain" as something entirely separate from the pain itself. This strict separation between suffering and the subjective appropriation of suf-fering is not a line that holds even within creaturely reality. The relationship between pain and joy, suffering and glory is not that distant. Childbirth, football, or writing are just some examples of situations where the brute fact of pain and suffering is assumed and transformed, not just after the fact of the pain, but in the act of suffering itself.

A second clarification is that we cannot limit analogical speech about God to positive creaturely realities. The analogical "distance" between di-vine and creaturely reality cannot be limited to a quantitative relation and exclude any qualitative difference. Analogous language is not limited to statements such as: God is good and powerful in the same way good and powerful creaturely realities are good and powerful, but more so. Pitstick wonders if suffering needs to be attributed to God, not merely as infinitely more than creaturely suffering, but "with a difference that cannot be defined positively (since to do so would require comprehending God's essence), one may legitimately ask what conceptual content *suffering*, *alteration*, and *obedience* have in regard to God if Balthasar denies all content pertaining to creaturely reality."[84] With respect to this question, Balthasar follows Bul-gakov in simply denying the aspects of suffering which are conditioned by the creaturely limitations of sin and finitude. Suffering in its primary, divine sense is an absolute openness to the other, an absolute pathos. Suffering in its creaturely sense is a deprivation of relation. As the first, Christ can fully inhabit the second. (I will explore this idea more in the following chapter.)

Both of Pitstick's difficulties with the issue of divine suffering relate to her starting point with respect to Balthasar's doctrine of the descent into

83. Ibid.,132.
84. Ibid.

hell. To properly understand Balthasar, one must begin with his understanding of the Trinity. The descent into hell is a revelation of the immanent divine life; it does not constitute that life. Pitstick seems to read Balthasar as though he thinks that God's life is freely and fundamentally conditioned by creaturely suffering. In fact, Balthasar follows Bulgakov by saying that creaturely suffering is a sinful distortion of the glory that is divine suffering. Referring back to our reading of Thomas where the divine essence is a relation, God acts *simpliciter* in his divine nature, both *ad intra* and *ad extra*, and this act, by virtue of its identity with the persons who are identical with the essence as relation distinguished only through opposition, is always a "personal" act. Thus, the cross is a revelation of God's personal life, the relation that constitutes the divine essence, and contains a "distance" which is itself the "opposition" of relations that constitutes the divine persons, and is also the basis for a creaturely other and the freedom of that other to reject its divine foundation.

DIVINE AND HUMAN FREEDOM

Another critique of Balthasar's Trinitarian theology is that there is no sphere for genuinely human activity. Sam Wells, in his work *Improvisation* articulates this critique saying that Balthasar is too "epic" in his understanding of the drama between God and humanity. He argues that within Balthasar's scheme "the drama isn't sufficiently about us."[85] Our analysis of the differences between Bulgakov and Balthasar on the descent into hell proves useful in addressing this critique as well. Wells's concerns about the "reality" of the consequences of human action in history would, I think, be legitimately raised with respect to Bulgakov's sophianization process. However, Balthasar's careful bracketing of this process from his appropriation of Bulgakov's Trinitarian theology has provided us with a very different picture of the relationship between human and divine freedom from his perspective. Balthasar's concept of human freedom is not so much sophianization as participation. Participation in the activity of relation keeps human/divine, time/eternity, virtue/grace simultaneously infinitely distant as well as united. From Balthasar's perspective, freedom is not either God's or humanity's. Genuinely free action is not a zero-sum game. The creaturely world is utterly contingent upon its participation in the divine. The nature

---

85. Samuel Wells, *Improvisation: The Drama of Christian Ethics* (Grand Rapids: Brazos, 2004), 50.

of divine freedom is thus the precise analogy of human freedom, in that both consist in an openness to relation with the "other." If God is free, we are free. The way in which God is free is the way in which we can be free. So, rather than wonder if Balthasar "may over-emphasize the degree to which the story is about the inner-Trinitarian relations,"[86] we see that the drama is a relation that intrinsically entails opposition (in the Thomistic sense of the opposition of relation) or mutuality.

When it comes to human freedom, Balthasar points to its source as the inner dynamic of the triune life. The same dynamic, where freedom is identical to obedience and surrender, operates analogously within human persons. The whole notion of personhood flows out of the possibility of absolute self-donation, which is kenotic love. Recalling that Thomas says it is not proper to say of the divine essence that it is a person, but rather relation, we see that personhood is rooted in the necessity of relation and the absolute openness that it requires.

> The exteriorization of God (in the Incarnation) has its ontic condition of possibility in the eternal exteriorization of God—that is, in his tripersonal self-gift. With that departure point, the created person, too, should no longer be described chiefly as subsisting in itself, but more profoundly (supposing that person to be actually created in God's image and likeness) as a "returning from exteriority to oneself" and an "emergence from oneself as an interiority that gives itself in self-expression."[87]

With the divine relation as loving self-donation comes the possibility of uniting such concepts as "poverty" and "riches," glory and suffering, life and death. However, the identity of these concepts depends on the fundamental unity of freedom and obedience as they are conceived within the "necessity of love."[88]

Both Bulgakov and Balthasar locate freedom within the immanent triune dynamic. For both, human freedom is a participation in this dynamic through Christ. However, Balthasar worries that Sophia "gums up the works," so to speak, of the "free decision" of self-offering that is the divine relation. Instead of being primarily oriented towards the divine inter-relation, the act of self-donation can be interpreted as "mediated" by

86. Ibid., 52.

87. Balthasar, *Mysterium Paschale*, 28.

88. Ibid., 35 citing Bulgakov, *Du Verbe Incarne: Agnus Dei* (Paris: Aubier, 1943), 281, 289, 305ff, 306.

the divine persons' hypostatizing of Sophia. (If the kenosis of the persons is the "blood circulation" of the triune life, then Sophia could be seen as a heart-lung bypass machine.) Thus, whereas for Balthasar freedom entails an openness or surprise, for Bulgakov, true freedom is fulfilling a given end or fully actualizing Sophia.

Balthasar's Trinitarian theology places openness or surprise within the concept of relation as such. The opposition of relation entails a total renunciation of self, a transparency to the other that is perfectly expressed in Jesus' "not my will but thine." The "content" of the relation that is the divine essence is, therefore, not "eternal humanity" (the "potency" for hypostatization by a contingent other in the self-donating act of the Son's hypostatization of divine Sophia). Rather, within Thomas's notion of relation Balthasar finds, not a given content, but an eternal act of donation that implies an infinite "content." The donation of the divine persons indicates an infinite fruitfulness, an ever-greater "surprise" which preserves the "otherness" between divine persons, as well as provides a foundation for a finite participation in both the impersonal "content" as well as the personal activity of relation that constitutes the life of God. The "necessity of love" in this understanding of kenotic love is therefore grounded in the definition of relation itself. Thus freedom, necessity, obedience, suffering, dying, life, and glory are all descriptive of the act of kenotic love that is the relation that is the divine life.

We must ask, however, if the unity brought about by human participation in the infinite kenosis of the Son entails somehow subsuming human freedom into divine freedom. Does Christ override the free choice of humanity to reject his love? Again, this is a point where Balthasar's bracketing of Sophia is vitally important. Human sin, our rejection of God and of the kenotic act that constitutes our real selves, exists precisely as a rejection of the relation that makes us what we truly are. While both Bulgakov and Balthasar describe Christ's passion and death as a complete solidarity with the human condition, Bulgakov has no place within reality (as it is entirely situated within Sophia as the divine life) for human sin except as a kind of denial of being. Insofar as creaturely reality *is* it is the actualization of creaturely Sophia as a participation in the divine. Thus, Christ's solidarity with humanity is a "panchristism, and panpneumatism" that, as it were, plugs up the holes into nothingness created by human sin.

Balthasar, however, recognizes that Bulgakov's kenotic Trinitarian theology does not require Sophia in order to deal with creaturely freedom.

Even the "necessity of love" takes on a different character for Balthasar. The very nature of God's self as a relation of kenotic love, as it is revealed in Christ's paschal mystery, contains a place for the free "action" of the human drama in history.

> All the contingent "abasements" of God in the economy of salva-
> tion are forever included and outstripped in the eternal even of
> Love. And so what, in the temporal economy, appears as the (most
> real) suffering of the cross is only the manifestation of the (Trini-
> tarian) Eucharist of the Son: he will be forever the slain Lamb,
> on the throne of the Father's glory, and his Eucharist—the body
> shared out, the Blood poured forth—will never be abolished, since
> the Eucharist it is which must gather all creation into his body.
> What the Father has given, he will never take back.[89]

There are two ways that this can be construed. First, with Moltmann, we could say that God takes his identity, the nature of his divine life, from the suffering he experiences on the cross. God suffers with and in humanity, always in the hope that love and the glory of the resurrection will overcome hatred and death.

The second possibility is the opposite: on the cross God as man reveals the true character of both suffering and glory. Balthasar (and Bulgakov) is keenly aware of those, such as Hegel or Moltmann, who would place Christ's suffering and death as a Trinitarian *response to* the world. Balthasar and Bulgakov, in direct contrast to this thesis, place human freedom as a participation in the eternal act of the Son's self-offering to the Father. An important distinction must be made here between various proponents of this kind of kenotic Trinitarian theology. For Moltmann, the triune God most fully *becomes* himself in the event of the cross. "Where God represents and reveals himself, he also identifies and defines himself."[90] For Balthasar, in contrast:

> What is provocative in Jesus' message is that he manifests the glory
> of divine power in lowliness, defenselessness and a self-surrender
> that goes to the lengths of the Eucharistic cross. This unveils a to-
> tally unexpected picture of God's internal, Trinitarian defenseless-
> ness: the wisdom of God that is folly yet wiser than the wisdom of
> men. Only thus can the Son really reveal the Father; only thus can
> the Spirit who proceeds from both be the revelation of their loving

89. Balthasar, *Mysterium Paschale*, ix.

90. Moltmann, *Crucified God*, 179.

fellowship. Truth, at its origin, is unreserved self-surrender and hence the opening-up of the depths of the Father.[91]

Within the eternal divine relation, helplessness is power and suffering is glory. Thus, humanity is freed from the limitations of finite suffering and death, and opened through Christ's making of hell a Christological reality into the possibility of participation in an infinite relation of kenotic love. Within this relation, finite suffering and helplessness can be real participations in infinite life.

The very fact that there is a paradox involved in uniting concepts like freedom and necessity, glory and suffering, life and death implies that the experience of relation that constitutes creaturely personhood has been distorted. Christ's life, death, and resurrection reveal the fact that the very nature of love unites suffering and glory, death and life, helplessness and power. Similarly, it is the necessity of love, whereby the Son must surrender himself to the Father that reveals the true nature of freedom:

> The gospel of John is also dominated by this "must," which at the same time is sovereign freedom. But here the journey and the goal (the latter being passage to the Father in the unity of death and resurrection) are so integrated that Jesus' Passion can be interpreted as the personal consecration of Jesus for the men whom God has given him, and as the proof of supreme love for his friends. This love asks as its return not only the same lying down our lives for the brethren, but also the joyous self-abandonment whereby the beloved Lord was drawn into that death which brought him back to the Father.[92]

Joyous self-abandonment, the necessary act of love, defines both divine and creaturely freedom. By locating freedom in the activity of "letting be" or joyous self-abandonment, Balthasar eliminates any possibility of setting up freedom as a limited resource. The freedom of one person does not set a limit on the freedom of the other. Instead, the perfect freedom of one relation towards the other is the very basis of the freedom of the "other." Creaturely freedom is a participation in the freedom of God, and the sovereign freedom of the divine life, far from being limited by human rejection, is in fact the source of creaturely freedom even in its negativity. "The creature's

---

91. Balthasar, *Action*, 450.

92. Balthasar, *Mysterium Paschale*, 19.

No, its wanting to be autonomous without acknowledging its origin, must be located within the Son's all-embracing Yes to the Father, in the Spirit."[93]

The possibility for this interplay of divine and freedom lies in the Son's solidarity with humanity and his restoration of human nature. According to Balthasar, this happens when the God-forsakenness incurred by human rejection of relation is englobed by the God-abandonedness of the Son that is a result of his own eternal relation to the Father.

> These two forms of timelessness—the God-forsakenness of the damned and the God-forsakenness of the Son on the Cross—are not simply unrelated. The latter is because of the former. . . . The damned . . . does not want to accept the bitter consequences of sin. He does not want to follow to the end that leads him away from God. In his obedience, by contrast, the Son has followed his path to the very end; and this very path has brought him to an encounter with man who is pursuing his path, having turned away from God and "willfully adopted a new standpoint that (he imagines) puts him out of range of God's intervention. But the Son has placed himself in man's way: even if man has turned his back on God, he still finds the Son in front of him and must go toward him. Thus the sinner can move toward God, albeit unawares or reluctantly."[94]

The infinite distance between the persons that is the basis for the incorporation of negative reality is also the basis for the overcoming of this negativity by love. Love as such always entails a free donation across infinite distance.

> Man's refusal was possible because of the Trinitarian "recklessness" of divine love, which, in its self-giving, observed no limits and had no regard for itself. In this, it showed both its power and its powerlessness and fundamental vulnerability (the two are inseparable). So we must say both things at once: within God's own self-for where else is the creature to be found?—and in the defenselessness of absolute love, God endures the refusal of this love; and, on the other hand, in the omnipotence of the same love, he cannot and will not suffer it.[95]

In his discussion of freedom, Balthasar continually refers us back to the triune life as the source of freedom. The absolute selflessness of the divine

---

93. Balthasar, *Action*, 329.

94. Balthasar, *Final Act*, 312.

95. Balthasar, *Action*, 329.

persons in their eternal relation of kenotic love, which constitutes both unity and difference between them makes it possible to speak of freedom and necessity, omnipotence and powerlessness as inherent within the same relation. When human freedom is considered within this paradigm, the basis for both creaturely rejection of God as well as the adoption of creaturely persons as sons is located as a participation within the same divine relation.

We can see Christ's perfect display of not only divine freedom, but human as well in his suffering and death on the cross. He demonstrates that true freedom is self-abandonment to the other in love. It is the opposite of demanding an autonomous self. Instead, we must receive ourselves completely as the free gift of God. In his death, Christ not only exhibits what true freedom means, he presents himself as the source of that freedom. We can either take up our cross and follow him into the perfectly free relation of the divine life, or hold onto our "selves" in isolation from the activity of love that is the source and summit of human life.

> "Becoming flesh," since it involves "not being received," is for that reason a crushing of the self. It is dying into the earth, disappearing, yet being "lifted up" in death-and-resurrection like the serpent in which all poison at once gathered and met its antidote. For this is the one who, light of heart, was sacrificed for the multitude—and for more, indeed, than his murderers thought—as the bread of life which vanishes in the mouth of the traitor, and the light which shines in the darkness that does not comprehend it and therefore cannot extinguish it. If he who is subsistent judgment itself does not judge of himself, nevertheless, by his existence as love he necessarily causes an inexorable division, a crisis.[96]

Christ's power is revealed not as domination or even an extrinsic judgment. Rather, the power of God is revealed in Christ as a crisis of self-identification. The No of humanity meets the inexhaustible Yes of the divine relation. We can hold on to what is "our own," but in that very act we negate our

---

96. Balthasar, *Mysterium Paschale*, 19. In a different discussion on the nature of human freedom, Balthasar refers to Thomas in order to support his claim that "Our freedom is laid up in God's Word; thus, so is our true 'I.' If our ultimate freedom is laid up in our idea, there are necessarily two sides to it: one side concerns the Idea in God, who waits for us to be fully realized in him. The other side concerns the structure of the created spirit: Thomas terms this the *syneidesis* or *synteresis*, which infallibly cleaves to the Good, however much we may fall away in sin; it alone, in fact, makes it possible for us consciously to turn away from the Good" (Balthasar, *Final Act*, 389 quoting Aquinas, *ST*, Ia. 89. 12).

selves. Or, we can die with Christ to self and into the helplessness of receiving ourselves entirely from God. However, the very power to reject God is grounded in our capacity for relation to him. Thus, the striving for power and freedom from suffering is the real source of suffering and helplessness in the world. Whereas surrender and obedience render us transparent to the very power and glory of God. Balthasar's approach to human freedom in its ultimate sense preserves both the unity and difference, or the relation between God and creation that is the basis for human freedom.

CONCLUSION

This chapter examined the ways in which Balthasar's theology both depends upon and differs from Bulgakov's with respect to Christology and the descent into hell. We have seen two important differences: First, the nature of both divine and human personhood with the notion of imagedness connecting them. Second, the nature of human freedom and sin, including what is necessary to overcome it.

Comparing Balthasar's doctrine of the descent into hell with Bulgakov's is a vital exercise for understanding why the descent into hell is necessary for Balthasar. This comparison also provides helpful insights into his theology, which can address recent critiques to his theology of the descent, such as those advanced by Alyssa Pitstick. In particular, this comparison reveals the importance, for Balthasar, of Christ assuming the reality of human sin, both individual and social. By bracketing Sophia, Balthasar is able to retain a space for genuine human freedom and all of its consequences.

This will serve as a preparation for a deeper treatment of the nature of the good revealed in the paschal mystery as well as how the freedom that results from personhood leads to a sacramental ethics, which I will address in the next chapter. Balthasar believes that Sophia collapses the distance necessary for genuine human freedom. The logical structure of Balthasar's Trinitarian theology that we find in the descent into hell carries with it a distinct notion of glory and goodness for both divine and human persons. Christ's suffering and death both reveals and restores true human nature and is the basis for sacramental participation in the triune life. This is the foundation of a Trinitarian sacramental ethics that, I argue, not only has a place for genuine human action, but requires a historical and corporal response to evil and injustice in the world as a part of the participation in the kenotic love that is the basis for human personhood.

5

Ethics as Participation in Relation

INTRODUCTION

In *The Systematic Thought of Hans Urs Von Balthasar*, Kevin Mongrain discusses the "organic" and "personal" connection between Balthasar's aesthetics and ethics. The logical and instrumental binding between God and humanity, between contemplation and ethics, is the personal dynamic of the triune life and creaturely participation in that dynamic:

> Contemplating the Christ form gives birth to a praxis that undergoes a highly personal guidance and development under pedagogical guidance by the Trinity. . . . This education into one's finite freedom by the Spirit, means that one is given a unique role to play on the stage of history . . . The more one cooperates with Christ in this mission, the more one is drawn back to contemplation of him as the primary and central historical agent of the Father's plan. As one is drawn to ever-deeper levels of contemplation, one is educated into ever deeper levels of freedom and ever-more profound missions of love in the overall plan of salvation history.[1]

1. Mongrain, 191–92. In this quote Mongrain's description of the dynamic between contemplation and praxis flows out of his thesis that Balthasar retrieves the Irenaean pedagogical vision of history that lays out a vision of human salvation as a participation or enactment of the *corpus triforme* within history. Mongrain's emphasis on the pedagogical aspect of history could be problematic if contemplation and praxis are considered merely as extrinsic reactions. The language of cooperation and education, in order to

What Mongrain points out here is how the relation that constitutes the Trinitarian life and the basis of human participation in the Trinitarian life connects contemplation and ethics. Aiden Nichols also points to the paschal event as the pivot between the aesthetic and ethical or between glory and the good.

> The dialectic of disclosure and concealment in the appearing of the divine Glory was resolved in favor of its positive pole only with the Cross and Descent into Hell, as became clear in the resurrection. The self-emptying divine Love, which is what the Glory of the Trinity turns out to be, thus manifests itself as judgment on human lovelessness and the re-orientation of human nature, at least in principle, to its true transcendent end . . . just as among the transcendentals, the beautiful and the good as also the true are co-constituting, for no one of these is a manifestation of being without reference to the others, so also in the ambit of revelation the aesthetics cannot be separated from a dramatics, if it is to have maximum force . . . aesthetics and dramatics are inter-related essentially, not accidentally—not contingently, but of their very nature.[2]

I want to explore this Trinitarian pivot between contemplation and ethics particularly in light of the work I have done in the first four chapters. How does Balthasar's Trinitarian theology in its starkest form—the triune relations in the descent into hell—inform an anthropology and ethics as the good that is the form and telos of human nature?

An awareness of both Bulgakovian and Thomistic influences, particularly with respect to the idea of God-abandonedness that we see in the descent, will be essential for understanding Balthasar's notion of the good. Only with this background can we understand how hell, or God-abandonedness, can be the revelation of God; how a man suffering and dying on a cross can reveal the personal act that constitutes the telos of humanity; what it means to say that suffering is glory, death is life, and that the most free act of self-positing takes place in complete obedience and passivity. These are the questions that an understanding of Balthasar's Trinitarian theology as it adopts and adjusts the Trinitarian theologies of Aquinas and Bulgakov is prepared to answer. And, as I will discuss in this

---

accurately describe Balthasar's thought (and in my opinion, reality), need to be set within a context of participation and realization. I discuss this in more detail below.

2. Nichols, *No Bloodless Myth*, 4.

chapter, these are the questions that we really need to ask in pursuit of a sacramental vision of the ethical life.

In this chapter I look at the implications of Balthasar's Trinitarian theology for the realities of human life in the world. In the first section, I look at the "good" as it is revealed by Christ's suffering, death, descent, and resurrection.[3] Here we must re-envision the good by taking Christ's death and descent as a revelation and recapitulation of human nature and human happiness. This is not a "merely moral" construction, but relies entirely on the structure of Balthasar's Trinitarian conception of personhood, relation, and kenosis. As we will see, misunderstanding the Trinitarian concept of

---

3. There are two ways that the "good" is used in this chapter. The first is as the "first good" or the life of God as the source and term of all that is. "God is the supreme good simply, and not only as existing in any genus or order of things. For good is attributed to God, as was said in the preceding article, inasmuch as all desired perfections flow from Him as from the first cause. They do not, however, flow from Him as from a univocal agent, as shown above; but as from an agent which does not agree with its effects either in species or genus. Now the likeness of an effect in the univocal cause is found uniformly; but in the equivocal cause it is found more excellently, as, heat is in the sun more excellently than it is in fire. Therefore as good is in God as in the first, but not the univocal, cause of all things, it must be in Him in a most excellent way; and therefore He is called the supreme good. The supreme good does not add to good any absolute thing, but only a relation. Now a relation of God to creatures, is not a reality in God, but in the creature; for it is in God in our idea only: as, what is knowable is so called with relation to knowledge, not that it depends on knowledge, but because knowledge depends on it. Thus it is not necessary that there should be composition in the supreme good, but only that other things are deficient in comparison with it" (Aquinas, *ST*, Ia.6.2). In this first sense, the good describes the perfection of the divine nature. In the second sense, the "good" as I discuss it in this chapter is simply the end or term of human nature as a participation in the good that is the divine Life. A sacramental ethics of participation in the Trinitarian kenosis requires that we look at the good both from the perspective of human flourishing as well as from the perspective of the first good. Balthasar's Trinitarian thesis provides a place marker for the first good, or the participated source and term of human flourishing, as well as sets the parameters for the way in which humans, as relational creatures, enact that good in a finite and participated manner. The mechanism of participation comes from Thomas's notion of the way good is diffused from the first good and truly possessed and enacted in finite ways by creatures. "The very nature of good is that something flows from it, but not that it flows from something else. Since, therefore, good has the nature of end, and the first good is the last end, this argument does not prove that there is no last end; but that from the end, already supposed, we may proceed downwards indefinitely towards those things that are ordained to the end" (ibid., Ia.IIae. 1.4). The key point of connection between the first good and participated goods is the notion of relation. Within the divine life, the good consists in the relation of kenotic love that *is* the divine essence. The creature participates in this relation, both as the basis of its own nature and its fulfillment.

the good where suffering = glory, and power = loving-surrender is disastrous for our understanding of ethics.

The second section of this chapter explores the mechanism of participation as the ethical extension of Balthasar's Trinitarian theology. Human participation in Christ's act of redemption is the summit and source of the ethical life. The third section of this chapter looks at the sacraments as they make present in the world the self-offering of the Son to the Father through the self-offering of the church. As such, the sacraments are the paradigmatic means of human participation in the self-offering of Christ that constitute an extension of Christ's mission in history through his body the church. Next, I test this ethical extrapolation in response to a critique of Balthasar's own ethics as to whether it provides a sufficient basis for addressing oppression and the plight of the sinned-against.

I argue that an ethic of sacramental participation based in Balthasar's Trinitarian theology retains a genuine sphere for human agency and precludes resignation and apathy in the face of oppression and injustice. The active resistance to injustice in the world that arises out of a Christian sacramental ethic is corporate, corporal, and "consubstantial." In other words, it is a social reality, the reality of the church as the body of Christ as a tangible alternative to the oppressing body of the state and a healing vessel for the fragmented bodies of the oppressed. The sacraments incorporate humanity into the activity of the triune life, making the power of kenotic self-abandonment physically present in history to stand against injustice, suffering, isolation, and violence. A full participation in the life of God is a full participation in the suffering of my brothers and sisters, a full participation in the redemption and forgiveness of my oppressors. It is the reality of a new creation.

THE IMAGE OF THE TRINITY AS BASIS FOR HUMAN PARTICIPATION IN THE GOOD

As we saw in chapter three, Balthasar brackets Bulgakov's sophiology from his Trinitarian insight in order to preserve both divine and human freedom. The reasons for this are most evident in his theology of the descent into hell. Similarly, the Trinitarian theses that he adopts from both Bulgakov and Thomas are most clearly at work in the descent. What the descent reveals about freedom is that, for Balthasar, divine freedom is based in the infinite distance, which constitutes both the unity and difference between the persons in the opposition of their relations. Human freedom is a participation in divine freedom made possible by human participation in Christ's total solidarity with humanity and absolute obedience to the Father. Whereas Bulgakov believes that Aquinas's distinction between nature and essence results in a reification of the divine life where the image of God in creation would be essentially impersonal and abstract, Balthasar employs Aquinas's Trinitarian theology to ground unity and difference both within the divine life and between God and creation. Balthasar recognizes that Bulgakov's sophiology can easily be read as promulgating the same error that Bulgakov sees in Aquinas; it collapses the dynamic nature of the triune life as kenotic love into a static set of content which eliminates the possibility for both a real exchange between God and creatures as well as genuine freedom for either.

Chapter two demonstrates that Balthasar brings together Bulgakov's Trinitarian insight that the divine persons simply *are* self-gifts of kenotic love and Thomas's understanding of the divine essence as relation and the persons as opposition of relations to establish the act of self-donation rather than Sophia as that which constitutes the life of God. From this perspective, then, freedom is the "space" inherent within the opposition of relations, and not the actualization or hypostatization of a given nature.[4] The Son is free precisely in his absolute obedience and transparency to the Father.

> He can, so to say, let himself renounce his glory. He is so divinely free that he can bind himself to the obedience of a slave. In this reciprocal detachment of two images of God, the self-emptying Son stands opposed, for a moment, to God the Father who is still in some way depicted in the colors of the Old Testament palette. But theological reflection at once opens out this difference: it is in fact the Father himself who "does not believe it necessary to hold on to this Son," but "delivers him over," as indeed the Spirit is continuously described as the "Gift" of them both.[5]

---

4. Though it is far beyond the scope of this book to prove it, I would argue that Balthasar's understanding of freedom here could be a consistent interpretation of Bulgakov's intent. Sophia, I believe, is a far better fit within Bulgakov's own system when it is read in continuity with Balthasar's use of relation. Bulgakov is constantly distancing himself from Sophia considered as a thing or abstract nature. His use of terms like "non-hypostatic love," and "impersonal life" reflect his reliance on German idealism, Schelling in particular, to express the relation between hypostasis and nature.

5. Balthasar, *Mysterium Paschale*, 28.

The Father and the Holy Spirit are likewise free in their openness and transparency vis-á-vis the other divine persons. This dynamic is constitutive of the divine life, not only in its economic revelation, but as the act of relation that is the eternal divine essence itself. Thus, the nature of divine freedom is located within the concept of divine personhood as a relation of kenotic love.

For Balthasar, the triune God most fully *reveals* himself in Jesus Christ's physical and historical self-offering to the Father on the cross. The Son's temporal sacrifice does not constitute the inner life of the Trinity, but is the earthly mission that makes the procession of the Son present in a new way within creation. In "The Sophiology of Father Sergius Bulgakov and Contemporary Western Theology" Antoine Arjakovsky points to the endebtedness of this aspect of Balthasar's Trinitarian theology to that of Bulgakov's fundamental idea that "the apocalyptic vision of the Lamb immolated [before the creation of the world] signifies not that a blood bath inaugurated the world but that inter-Trinitarian love is the common foundation of both the creation and the Incarnation." Here he quotes Balthasar: "To grasp that is impossible for me, except if one dares to speak with Bulgakov of the first inter-Trinitarian kenosis."[6]

In the third chapter I gave a detailed analysis of Balthasar's descent theology as it adapts Bulgakov's Trinitarian thesis. It became clear that Balthasar's correction of Bulgakov was primarily a correction of the way in which humanity possesses the divine image and participates in the divine act of kenotic love. In other words, the point at which Balthasar adapts the Trinitarian thesis is the point where contemplation of the divine essence or God's Glory intersects with the act of participation. The Trinitarian logic of the descent is the pivot between Balthasar's aesthetics and ethics. Thus, Balthasar's decision to bracket Bulgakov's sophiological appropriation of the divine life provides an essential tool for understanding Balthasar's dramatic vision of human participation in the divine act of self-abandoning love. The act of self-offering to an "other" constitutes personhood both in God and in creatures, and freedom is a function of personhood, both human and divine. Balthasar's Trinitarian theology of the descent into hell gives rise to his dramatic ethical paradigm where both divine and human action takes place in the personal space or opposition of relations that constitutes both unity and difference between the divine persons when the divine essence is considered as the relation of absolute self-donation.

6. Balthasar, *Truth of God*, 177–78.

It is this relation of self-donation that Balthasar considers to be a "good" that can serve as the end for both God and creation—not an end "in which both the triune God and the personal creature lose all definition, but on the basis of a definition that is appropriate to both God and the creature."[7] The act of absolute self-donation to the other *is* the divine life and the truth of human nature with respect to both natural and supernatural ends. As such: "Everything that, in the created world, appears shot through with potentiality is found positively in God."[8]

As human nature finds its end in the act of participating in God's own act, and its freedom as a participation in God's freedom, so, just as in Christ *processio* and *missio* are united, our mission is an expression of our procession from or relation to the triune God. Our mission is found in "the economy of Christ's redemptive Body."[9] Our mission flows out of Christ's own mission of glorifying the Father and as such allows human mission to "flow out of his own center."[10] In other words, the human mission is an expression of human nature as a participation in the self-offering love of the triune God. The "good" for humanity lies in fully expressing the divine idea of ourselves or freely entering into the particular act of self-offering that is our own embodiment of Christ's love.

The theme of the *Theo-Drama* is precisely this extension of Christ's mission from the Father through humanity. In the *Theo-Drama*, Balthasar, according to Kevin Mongrain, retrieves the Irenaean pedagogical vision of history with humanity.[11] Mongrain contrasts this with epic or Gnostic

7. Balthasar, *Final Act*, 389.

8. Ibid., 389–91. I think that this statement could serve as Balthasar's "reconstruction" of Bulgakov's sophiology. Ironically, he uses Thomas's notion of participation to do for Bulgakov's Trinitarian thesis what sophiology could not do: it provides a way to ground creation in the activity of the divine nature that serves to both unite and distinguish between God and creation.

9. Ibid. quoting *Dramatis Personae*, 263–71.

10. Ibid., 393. Stephen Wigley summarizes this dynamic saying: "In von Balthasar's theodramatic theory, a Trinitarian and soteriological dimension is introduced to this process, in which the Son as 'actor' places himself at the disposal of the Father, the 'author' of this saving drama, subject to the direction of the Holy Spirit" (Wigley, 79).

11. Mongrain argues that Balthasar lays out a vision of human salvation as a participation or enactment of the *corpus triforme* within history. "In being led by the Spirit into contemplation of the entire *corpus triforme*, believers are thereby led into the paschal mystery, where they learn that creation has been redeemed from the 'pitiless destiny' of fate, and they are now free to live in the 'acting area' within history opened by Christ." (Mongrain, 201.)

renderings of human salvation that seek to spiritualize the work of human salvation. "Thus he [Balthasar] characterizes the 'theodrama' of salvation history in terms of a 'Yes or No to the Incarnation of the Son of the Father.' A yes or no to the mystery of Christ and its power to draw persons into active lives of discipleship."[12]

To summarize: Balthasar's moral theology is an extension of his Trinitarian theology, particularly as it appears in the descent into hell. The "good" for humanity is the actualization of our nature as persons in a relation of self-surrender to the Father as a participation in the Son's own self-offering.[13] The "goodness" of this activity, for Balthasar, is a sacramental simultaneity between body and spirit, time and eternity, God and creation. Christ's mission and our participation in it is transformative in such a way that "the world, *in spite of and because of* its being genuinely created, and created in freedom, cannot be 'outside' God. . . . On the contrary the world must have its locus within the Trinitarian relations."[14] The goal of this activity is an "ultimate, though unimaginable, state 'with' God. This state is reached via a transformatory death that both concentrates its temporal duration into a summary unity and hands it over, in its totality, to its origin—which has now become its goal."[15] All of creation, through human activity, must enter into Christ's self-offering and make of it our own self-offering to the Father as Christ makes of us *his* own self-offering to the Father. This is the source and summit of creaturely existence, a state of full participation in Christ's body. What kind of ethics arises out of a sacramental embodiment of Christ's self-offering to the Father?

---

12. Ibid., 43 quoting Balthasar, *Action,* 181.

13. Humans do not participate in the triune life as substantial relations, but as "members" of the Son's relation. The unity implied here is possible because of the nature of personhood as precisely the activity of self-offering in relation. The difference between Creator and creatures on this point lies in the fact of participation. The relation within which creatures live is only logical, not a real relation in the Thomistic sense. Another way to describe the dynamic would be to say that, while the mutual self-offering of the triune persons constitutes the divine identity, creaturely self-offering is always a finite response to a gift already given. While that response does constitute our identity, it doesn't constitute God's identity.

14. Balthasar, *Final Act,* 395.

15. Ibid., 394.

THE GOOD REVEALED BY CHRIST

It is difficult to come up with ideas that are more abstract than the ideas of the "eternal blood circulation" of the immanent triune life or the sophianization of the cosmos. Though there might be some application of these theologies for a hiker contemplating the beauty of the Caucus Mountains or an artist pondering the ever-deeper mystery within the manifestation of a tree, it is fair to ask what, if any, relevance a kenotic Trinitarian theology or the descent into hell might have for daily Christian life.

Bulgakov writes about Christ's overcoming of the world that is already present in history, and in fact, he describes the whole of history as involved in the process of becoming Christoform. Rather than dismissing Bulgakov's final major work as a poetical rambling of apocalyptic escapism, or setting aside Balthasar's dramatic rendering of divine-human interaction and its ultimate manifestation in his imaginative construal of Christ's descent into hell, I propose that the kenotic Trinitarian theology and its ecclesial application which lies at the heart of these projects is in fact vitally relevant for some of the most pressing social and theological issues confronting us today. Far from irrelevant, the thesis that the divine life is the absolute selfless donation of the persons, and that this life has been fully revealed in Christ and the *mysterium paschale*, is in fact the deepest relevance that Christianity has for the suffering in the world.

As we saw in the last chapter, Balthasar's Trinitarian theology driven by the thesis that the inner triune life consists of the utter selflessness of the divine persons is both stretched to the limits and confirmed with his theology of the descent into hell. We have already looked at the logic that would allow Balthasar to say that Christ makes of hell a Christological reality. Now I want to look at the quality of that reality. What does the descent into hell as the fullest revelation of the divine life reveal about the Good, not only for God, but especially the good as it relates to human happiness and flourishing?

I will start with the conclusion: Balthasar follows Bulgakov in asserting that the good of the Trinitarian life and the entelic good of human life consists in a self-abandonment or suffering that is actually perfect blessedness or glory. The poles of suffering and glory, abandonment and perfect communion, are held together within the dynamic of inter-personal love. Love between persons entails a kind of suffering and even death in the very act of opening up to the "other" as "not I." It requires an abandonment of control, knowledge, and self-possession in order to allow the other to be who they are, to preserve their incomprehensible mystery. Only with this "loss" am I able to receive the "other." And in this reception, this openness to losing myself, both "I" and "Thou" enter into a relation that gives us back to ourselves. There is a constant dynamic of loss and gain, suffering and joy, appropriation and disappropriation, which is the mutual self-abandonment that constitutes our communion.

Within this understanding of the nature of both abandonment and communion we can say that Christ enters into God-abandonment in perfect solidarity with humanity as well as in a perfect expression of his immanent triune relation with Father and Holy Spirit. Christ's self-offering on the cross reveals the eternal nature of the divine life, a life so open to the act of the other that even total abandonment and separation cannot annihilate the relation, but rather confirm it. Christ's self-offering also reveals the brokenness of human nature as it seeks to make for itself an identity and a happiness apart from its true end. Christ transforms the creaturely "No" by affirming it as his own and allowing it to carry him into and beyond any one "No," and beyond every concrete consequence of these refusals that litter the history of the world. He is able to transform them precisely because he is the Father's "Yes" to humanity, to history, and to his own life as a pure response to, and expression of, the Father. This is all possible because the act that constitutes the divine nature is the act of kenotic love, and the infinite distance of self-donation is the fullness of the divine communion. The Trinitarian theology undergirding Balthasar's descent theology allows for a "re-mapping of the cognitive landscape."[16] The "good" as revealed by this

16. Here I am making use of an article by Robert Masson, "Reframing the Fields," *Zygon*, vol. 39, no. 1 (March 2004). In this article Masson describes a phenomenon he refers to as a "tectonic shift" in meanings. This involves an analogy between two concepts which seems "uncalled-for" given the landscape of meaning. "What most distinguishes such uncalled-for analogies is the disruptive effect on the fields of meaning associated with them. The force of the analogies does not simply add new information to the world of physics and astronomy, expanding knowledge the way the discovery of a new planet or a new mechanical law might. Nor does it clarify the given world of meanings, the way affirming an apt analogy between something known and something unknown might. In Newton's day, for example, Galileo's understanding of the heavens and Kepler's understanding of mechanics were already known. The uncalled-for analogies had a more tectonic effect because they forced a reframing in the until-then accepted fields of meanings. The result was reconfigured fields of meanings that constituted a better understanding of reality. In that sense, the result was a new world of meanings. Moreover, such shifts in fields of meanings typically make available a new logic and understanding of what is reasonable" (Masson, 51). The tectonic shift I am identifying in Balthasar's work arises from his adaptation of Bulgakov's Trinitarian theology that allows him to posit the identity in the divine life of glory and suffering.

relation is simultaneously the suffering of utter loss of self and the glorious joy of receiving one's self entirely as a gift from the "other."

If Christ's death and descent into hell reveal the nature of God's goodness, they also reveal the nature of the good for humanity. Any misconception of what is taking place on the cross can lead to serious distortions of what the church is called to be and what kinds of actions are totally incompatible with the Christian life, or, for that matter, any notion of human flourishing. The first contribution that Balthasar's Trinitarian theology as a background to an ethics of sacramental participation in the triune kenotic relation makes to a "practical" moral vision is the remapping of what constitutes human flourishing and happiness. To give an example of the power of this shift we need only to think of our own goals for happiness. They probably involve some amount of material success—a place to live, decent clothes, good food—as well as relationships with pleasant people, a sense of meaning or purpose, and a lack of pain, illness, and loss. There is of course nothing wrong or false about these notions of flourishing. However, when we look at someone like Mother Theresa who voluntarily endures life in a community, taking care of diseased and ignorant people, loneliness, poverty, depression, and pain, we are forced to ask what she was getting out of it. Or take the example of Francis of Assisi who considered it a blessing to be with lepers and experience Christ's wounds. Why would these people, and so many others famous and unknown, pursue lives so contrary to our normal understanding of human happiness? On the one hand, a background of Balthasar's Trinitarian theology and his claim that human flourishing entails a participation in Christ's own mission provides a context for understanding (at least theoretically) and perhaps even acquiring some of the joy experienced by saints and martyrs in their suffering. On the other hand, it provides a correction to our tendency to distort secondary goods and make them ultimate. In particular, the goods of glory and power are placed in the context of love.

One could say that misunderstanding the meanings of power and glory are basic to the human condition. Adam and Eve disobeyed and took in order to be like God. The crowd urged Jesus to prove he was the Son of God by coming down from the cross. It seems that humanity is easily able to grasp the idea that God's life is characterized by glory, majesty, power, and blessedness. The God who thunders from Sinai and tramples out the grapes of wrath is a God we can worship, and most importantly, imitate. Such a God can be employed as the "muscle" behind social projects and moral positions both good and bad. An ethic that arises out of Balthasar's adaptation of Bulgakov's thesis that the life of God consists of the absolute selflessness of the divine persons would require a vastly different concept of power, glory, as well as imitation. Within this vision:

> The Cross or, better, the Crucified, is, therefore, the term to which all human existence, whether personal or social, tends . . . not only is the world enabled by God to reach its goal, but God himself, in the moment of the world's very perdition, attains his own most authentic revelation and glorification.[17]

The way in which Christianity conceives of Christ's power and glory and reconciles these with Christ's suffering is pivotal for constructing a Christian understanding of morality. In some cases, ethical atrocities result from defective Christology. Kelly Brown Douglas, in her book *The Black Christ*, ponders how a "Christian" society such as the antebellum south could have maintained the institution of slavery. She concludes that, far from indicting the slaveholders for their injustice, Christianity was actually used as a justification for the institution of slavery. The God behind this justification revealed himself as "the white Christ."

> The white Christ is grounded in an understanding of Christianity suggesting that Jesus of Nazareth was Christ . . . because God was made flesh in him. . . . It is God's act that is important to who Jesus is. What Jesus did on earth has little if anything to do with what it means for him to be Christ. His ministry to the poor and oppressed is virtually inconsequential to this interpretation of Christianity. . . . Christians are the passive recipients of God's grace. . . . To believe God's act in Jesus is to become convinced and through that act salvation has been secured. With salvation guaranteed through belief, White people could be slaveholders *and* Christian without guilt or fear about the state of their soul.[18]

This distorted picture of the God who reveals himself in Jesus is also the object of worship in the following prayer used at induction ceremonies for the Ku Klux Klan:

> God of our fathers, we thank thee for these tall, sun-crowned men who are about to become knights of the Ku Klux Klan! May they so live as Klansmen as to always be an honor to their God,

17. Balthasar, *Mysterium Paschale*, 14.
18. Brown Douglas, *Black Christ*, 13.

country and fellow knights! These favors we ask in the name of Jesus Christ, the Klansman's true criterion of character. Amen![19]

I include the above quotes, not merely to illustrate the negative possibilities of faulty Christology, but to demonstrate the vital importance of Balthasar's Christology, as well as the Trinitarian theology that is its source and the anthropology that is its conclusion as a resource for ethics. While I do not imagine that many Christians would ever espouse the Christ who is the "true criterion of character" for the Klan, we still experience a reluctance in recognizing Christ's helplessness and suffering as *essential* (and I mean this in the sense of *essentia*), to the divine nature, the descent into hell as revelatory of God's glory. However, this reluctance leaves us without a sufficient Christological or anthropological objection to alternative ethical visions where power, health, autonomy, control, and pleasure are the central goods. This kind of moral vision in a Christian context not only misconstrues the nature of glory, but also brackets Christ from a robust Trinitarian theology. Christ's relation to the Father and to the Holy Spirit is essential for understanding his "character," and as such, self-abandonment and obedience are the foundation of his identity. If Christ's suffering is simply a manifestation of his human nature and the descent into hell is a demonstration of the triumph of divine power over death, then we must look elsewhere for grounds to discount such a distorted "Christian" ethics.

The Trinitarian theology that Balthasar adopts from Bulgakov allows him to posit the simultaneity between glory and suffering, power and helplessness, not merely in an abstract sense, but as constitutive of the divine essence itself. Balthasar's Trinitarian theology serves to ground an ethics that is capable of proposing an alternative to the ethic of the "white Christ" precisely by re-envisioning the "good" of human nature.

> Thus Christian ethics takes on the form of the cross: though both vertical and horizontal, this "form" can never be isolated from its concrete content, that is, from Jesus who was crucified and lifted up between God and men. He makes himself present as the only norm in every situation.[20]

---

19. Kennedy, *Klan Unmasked*, 49.

20. Balthasar, "Nine Theses in Christian Ethics," 195. Balthasar's elaboration on this point: "All things are lawful for me if I only remember that I owe my liberty to my belonging to Christ" (ibid.) is similar to St. Augustine's "Love and do what you like." Both indicate that perfect conformity to the Christ who reveals his divine glory and love in the paschal mystery entails perfect freedom. This is the perfection of human nature.

Humanity, as revealed by Christ, is a personal identity and activity in relation to God and other humans. The entelechy of this identity, the strength and glory it contains, is revealed by Christ's passion. From this theological starting point Christ can never be used as a figurehead for hate or oppression because:

> God is not, in the first place, "absolute power," but "absolute love," and his sovereignty manifests itself not in holding on to what is its own but in its abandonment—all this in such a way that this sovereignty displays itself in transcending the opposition, known to us from the world, between power and impotence.[21]

The reality of Christ's self-surrender, not only as a man, but as the Son of God to the Father, not only on the cross, but in his eternal act of relation in the triune life, calls for a "tectonic shift" in the way we conceive of the good and seek to participate in it. The "white Christ," and any subtle version of it, is an illusion, an idol extracted from reality that can only maintain itself by ignoring the truth of our own humanity and rejecting a relationship with God and other humans. Power, glory, happiness, and life are fragmented illusions unless they are embedded in the perichoretic act of self-surrender in relation. On the flip side, suffering, death, and solitude are equally fragmented and distorted outside loving relation. The truth about human nature and human good lies in the God-man's relationship to his Father, and to his fellow humans. Christ not only commands self-surrender, but also embodies it in his own self-offering.

> But the self-surrender is, on the one hand, obedience to the Father, and, on the other, a decision in favor of defenselessness—renunciation of the "twelve legions of angels." . . . Here now is the only valid and obligatory image of what the sin of the world is like for the heart of God, made visible in "the" man. In the image of the complete Kenosis, there shines "the light of the knowledge of the glory of God in the face of Jesus Christ."[22]

True power is the power of love. It is absolute helplessness and transparency with respect to the other, even to the point of being totally rejected. As such, Jesus' cry "Why have you forsaken me?" is the ultimate prayer of intimate union between Father and Son. The Son's openness to being rejected and abandoned out of obedient love and the Father's validation

21. Balthasar, *Mysterium Paschale*, 28.
22. Ibid., 117–18.

and acceptance of the Son's willingness entailed in turning his face away is in fact the very bond of love that unites them. This is the Spirit who allows himself, as the bond of love between Father and Son, to be the presence of one to the other only as an absence.

With the Trinitarian theology of glory and suffering that Balthasar adapts from Bulgakov we can recognize Christ's action as the basis for participation in the divine life in a way that counteracts an anthropology of power and consumption. However, Christ is never just an example to interpret. Rather he is God's presence to us—an invitation into the relation that comprises our every good. As such, Christ requires a holistic response, and our response to him as the presence of the triune relation *is* our very self, our personal life:

> I only appreciate fully that God is my "highest good" when I learn (in the Son) that I am a "good" to him, affirmed by him; this is what guarantees my being and my freedom. And it is only when I learn that I represent a "good" and a "thou" to God that I can fully trust in the imparted gift of being and freedom and so, affirmed from and by eternity, really affirm myself too.[23]

Our self-affirmation consists in the acceptance of ourselves as a gift from God, and in participation in Christ's self-offering to the Father through our own self-offering to God and one another. Our affirmation of self comes not through self-grasping or self-aggrandizing; "It is the realization, by the finite 'copy' of the definitive model exhibited by the infinite prototype."[24]

A Christian ethics of sacramental participation in the triune kenotic life reconfigures our understanding of power and glory. It presents to the world an understanding of human flourishing and an accompanying ethic that is in tune with the reality of human frailty, dependence, and suffering without glorifying these conditions. Rather, it emphasizes the meaning of our limitations and the possibility of transforming them. It refuses to justify the power of some to force "sacrifice" onto others. It refuses to attribute

---

23. Balthasar, *Dramatis Personae: Man in God,* 287. John Laurance explains this dynamic in terms of how we receive ourselves as God's self-gift: "As God's creation, we are actually God's gift of himself to us in grace, 'our whole existence [consists in] the acceptance or rejection of the mystery which we are.' Therefore, we can become what we were created to be — God's self-gift—only by opening ourselves to God in all the actions of our lives, that is, to fully accept ourselves as God's self-gift," (Laurance, SJ, "Configured Into Christ's Body," quoting Karl Rahner, "On the Theology of the Incarnation," *Theological Investigations* IV, trans. Kevin Smyth (Baltimore: Helicon Press, 1966), 108.

24. Balthasar, *Dramatis Personae: Man in God,* 291.

glory to those who attain success through exploitation. These are not mere proclamations; they are principles intrinsic to human nature and its telos of participation in the triune relation. God does not ask a sacrifice from us that is not first his own sacrifice. He does not even ask of us a sacrifice that is independent of his own offering. The sacrifice that God asks is the ratification and affirmation of our own human nature as an acceptance of and participation in his loving relation.

Our relation with Christ is a participation in the triune relation that is the divine life. Our relation with the world we live in, or our ethical life, is a participation in and an extension of Christ's mission, as the appropriation of our own identity and mission. As we enter into the current of Christ's mission, the spark within us, the kindling that is our nature as persons in relation, ignites and we become "all flame."[25]

PARTICIPATION AS THE MEANS OF ACTUALIZATION

In order to continue to develop an ethical vision from Balthasar's Trinitarian theology, I want to integrate a Thomistic account of participation as the means of actualizing the *imago trinitatis*, which is both the source of human goodness and its full realization. Such an account of participation relies on the Trinitarian theology of relation already laid out in chapter two. It also serves as a foundation for discussing the sacramental nature of an ethics arising from Balthasar's Trinitarian theology. In this first section I will explore the dynamic of participation that implicitly connects the dynamic of relation to sacramental and ethical expression.[26] Relation is the basis for both unity and difference both in the triune life and, in another way, between God and humanity. Human nature in the image of God is able to participate in the divine relation, and thus in the unity of the divine life, while still maintaining the integrity between God and humanity as well as individual humans. This is possible because the basis for participation is the personal self-offering of each to the others as an expression of their own "I." In this section I want to employ Thomas's moral theology as a

25. "Abba Lot went to see Abba Joseph and said to him, 'Abba, as far as I can I say my little office, I fast a little, I pray and meditate, I live in peace and as far as I can, I purify my thoughts. What else can I do?' Then the old man stood up and stretched his hands towards heaven. His fingers became like ten lamps of fire and he said to him, 'If you will, you can become all flame'" (Ward, *Desert Fathers*, 103).

26. It is for this reason Balthasar says that "liturgy cannot be separated from moral life" (Balthasar, "Nine Theses in Christian Ethics," 192).

tool for exploring the way in which concrete human acts can be means of participation in the triune life of kenotic love.[27] If the previous section highlighted the quality of the act in which we participate, this section looks at human disposition and behavior as means and indications of participation.

In the previous section we looked at the quality of the good with respect to the activity of relation that constitutes human personhood. The good for relation is an openness or self-surrender to the "other" which is both an imitation of and a participation in Christ's own relation to the Father. The dynamic of participation is the appropriation of Christ's own mission as our own. In this way we both participate in the triune life and sacramentally extend that life and light into the world. Just as the glory of God that Christ reveals can only be properly understood and imitated as the revelation and invitation of the divine essence as relation, so human participation in the good, or actualization of our humanity, takes place only as our whole life "catches flame" with the fire of divine kenotic love. This is an interpersonal igniting where we appropriate the divine life by offering ourselves entirely to God paradigmatically in the symbolic self-offering in the eucharistic celebration, and by confirming that self-offering through a disposition of disappropriation throughout our lives. There are two components to this discussion: First, there is the way in which human actions partake of the good in any sense, and the way in which this participation unites us to Christ. Second, there is the presence of Christ in the world through human actions that is properly sacramental; Christ's self-offering to the Father is embodied and enacted in history.

The basis for human participation in the divine life is both revealed and made available in the paschal mystery. If humans are made "in the image and likeness of God," then we attain that likeness by conforming to/participating in the triune dynamic—where God-abandonedness is the relation of kenotic love that is the divine essence. We partake of that life by entering into the dynamic of "appropriation as expropriation."

27. Balthasar's moral theology clearly relies on a system of participation, however it always also makes the connection between participation and the sacramental life. "As created beings we remain 'heteron' but we are also given the capacity to unfold our personal and free activity by virtue of God's strength (the 'drink becomes in us a 'spring' or 'well' [John 4:13ff; 7:38]. This strength comes to us from the Eucharist of his Son through our being reborn with him for the Father and through the gift of their Spirit. Since God in bestowing his grace works gratuitously and since we likewise should act gratuitously when we love, the 'great reward in heaven' can therefore be nothing else but Love itself. Thus in God's eternal plan the last end coincides with the first movement of our freedom" (ibid.).

> It is not therefore possible to take God to oneself through an act of appropriating him, because God is personified handing-over, and one "knows" him and "possesses" him only when one is oneself expropriated and handed over. It is precisely thus that the creature can be fully affirmed by his creator.[28]

This simply means that, just as Christ's identity as the Son of God is wholly constituted by his self-abandonment to the Father and accepting himself wholly as the Father's gift, we receive ourselves as persons in relation to God (and other human persons) by expropriating or offering ourselves completely to the other.

> It is not possible to be indifferent in the face of this action, because man cannot adopt a position of indifference *vis-à-vis* his own true being. But in the act of one's fellow man Christ—if this act is affirmed in faith to be what it portrays itself to be—there lies an act of the total self-expropriation of the love of God, the deepest aim of which is to give man the gift of the same love.[29]

The Trinitarian relation of kenotic love is the act that constitutes the divine life and the act of relation that humans are called into as the fulfillment of our human nature.

Humans participate in Christ's self-offering in a human manner. In other words, participation as a metaphysical concept requires that the participator enact the *actus essendi* (for our purposes the act of expropriation as appropriation) of the one in whom he participates according to the capacities of his own essence.[30] The Thomistic structure of participation is present in Thomas's structure of virtue as actualization of the "good" both as a properly human good and as the transformation of human good through grace into *caritas*. If the essential act of God is self-disappropriation in relation, then human perfection would be an appropriation of

---

28. Balthasar, *Theology: the New Covenant,* 400.

29. Ibid., 402.

30. "Thomas develops his own original notion of participation based on the notion of *esse* as *actus essendi.* He does this by taking the general definition of participation, which is sharing in or taking part in something in a partial manner that belongs to another fully and placing it within an Aristotelian framework that emphasizes that act is a perfection. For example, humans are perfected by the act of *esse* that takes part in the *esse* of God. Yet even here Thomas goes beyond Aristotle by seeing potency as the capacity to receive perfection and seeing act as the perfection of *esse.* Thus, in Thomistic thought, participation is a sharing in the essential act of another, which is limited by the potency of the participating subject" (Rziha, *Perfecting Human Actions,* 10).

that disappropriation to the extent that the act of disappropriation is an extension of the presence of Christ's own identifying act that has become the identity of the human person. Thomas says, "Perfection of form can be looked at in two ways: first, from the viewpoint of form itself; second, from the viewpoint of the subject's participation in the form."[31] The perfect good of personhood in itself lies in God, but that form can be participated in to a greater or lesser degree as it informs any human activity. The good for human nature is not qualitatively different from the good that is the divine life. Nor does the increasing actualization of the good in a human person entail the addition of substantially different forms to their human nature. Thomas describes the dynamic of participation with the analogy of heat increasing in an object:

> Therefore such an increase of habits and other forms is not caused by the addition of a form to a form, but by the subject's participating more or less perfectly in one and the same form. And just as, through an agent which is in act, something is made actually hot, beginning anew, as it were, to participate in that form—not that a new form is caused . . . so by an intense action of the agent it is made more hot, as though it were participating more perfectly in the form, not as though something were added to the form.[32]

Thus, the form of the virtue increases when "the subject participates more perfectly in a form already existing, or it makes the form extend further."[33] The heat of perfection, or realization of the form, increases, not by adding something like lighter fluid from the outside, but by the increasing participation by the person in the personal act of the divine life, by the increasing appropriation of the Son's mission of expropriation. The activity of expropriation, or kenotic love, is the act of embracing transparency to the flame of divine love.[34] Personal participation in the divine life entails an actual engagement with God in the activity that is the divine relation. This is only possible through grace.

---

31. Aquinas, *ST*, IaIIae.5.5.

32. Ibid., 52.2.

33. Ibid.

34. "Since the substance of God is his action, the greatest likeness of man to God is in respect to some operation. Therefore, as we have said, happiness or beatitude, by which man most of all is conformed to God and which is the end of human life, consists in an operation" (ibid., 55.2).

Thomas describes grace in three ways: as love, as gift, or as gratitude for that gift.[35] The grace that humans receive is a gift or expression of God's love. Human reception of the gift entails using the gift and being thankful for it. Since the "gift" is the divine life itself, or participation in the relation of kenotic love that is the divine essence, reception of and gratitude for the gift are not mere mental dispositions, but rather entail acts of self-disappropriation that come to constitute our own relation to God and to others. God gives grace both in a general or "natural" way, and in a particular or supernatural way to human beings. In the first sense he gives it when "he gives all things their natural being. But the second is a special love, by which he draws the rational creature above the condition of its nature to a participation of the divine good . . . it is by this love that God absolutely wishes the eternal good, which is himself, for the creature."[36] God gives himself as relation to one capable of receiving him by giving herself in return. This mutual act of self-offering constitutes the identity of the person.[37] Supernatural grace is a gift that acts upon the soul to give it a different character or quality.[38] A person given the gift of grace has "what is substantially in God"[39] in their own soul through participation in the divine goodness. That character or quality enables the person to be an expression of divine goodness themselves to the extent in which they participate in God by making Christ's mission of expropriation their own identity and the formative principle for their actions in the world.[40]

Human actions that proceed from a person wholly embodying Christ's mission in the world are still internal principles of activity, but do not have

35. Ibid., 110.1.

36. Ibid.

37. It is important to recall here that God's act of self-offering, while genuinely engaged with the creature, is not constituted by its relation to a creaturely person. Rather, God's eternal act of self-offering is complete in the triune life, made available to the creature in a new way in the created person's apprehension of it.

38. "Grace as a quality is said to act upon the soul not after the manner of an efficient cause, but after the manner of a formal cause, as whiteness makes a thing white and justice just" (ibid., 110.2).

39. Ibid.

40. "What is substantially in God becomes accidental in the soul participating the divine goodness, as it is clear from the case of knowledge. And thus because the soul participates in the divine goodness imperfectly, the participation of the divine goodness which is grace has its being in the soul in a less perfect way than the soul subsists in itself. Nevertheless, insofar as it is the expression or participation of the divine goodness, it is nobler than the nature of the soul, though not in its mode of being" (ibid.).

their source in human nature as such. Rather, these actions that proceed from the flames of *caritas* arise in a different kind of participation, namely grace. "But if we are speaking of a higher nature, of which man can be a participator (2 Pet. 1:4 'that we may become partakers of the divine nature') nothing prevents a habit, namely grace, from being in the essence of the soul as in a subject."[41] Grace is the cause of supernatural virtues as principles informing human activity. When human actions are so informed, it is divine goodness at work in the person and in the world; it is the personal presence of the triune God as relation now "relating" in and through the life of the human person. For Thomas, Christ is the image imprinted on human nature by the Holy Spirit, and the infused virtues of faith, hope, and charity are in themselves a participation in him.[42] Thomas quotes 2 Peter 1:4 and says by Christ we are made partakers of the divine nature.

> A nature can be attributed to a thing in two ways. First, essentially, and thus these theological virtues exceed human nature. Second, participatively, for example, as ignited wood participates in the nature of fire, and thus, after a fashion, man partakes of the divine nature, as we have explained. And so these virtues belong to man as he is made a participant of a nature.[43]

41. Ibid., IaIIae.50.2.

42. If the theological virtues are habitual participations in God, what can we make of the fact that, for Thomas, Christ himself possesses *caritas* perfectly, but does not have either faith or hope? The idea that Jesus would possess *caritas* perfectly is not difficult since his whole person is an expression of the divine love both as it relates to the inner triune life and especially God's perfect love for humanity. But if faith and hope are supernatural participations in God, what is the significance of his lack of these virtues? (see *ST* IIIa.3–4.) Faith and hope are eschatological virtues. Where *caritas is* the life, the *essencia* that constitutes God and our participation in him, faith and hope and the means of participation for human intellect and will in history. They are both a participation in God already and the necessary awareness that our participation is not yet complete. In love we partake of God's fullness now, the fullness, which he has made available in history in Jesus Christ mediated sacramentally. Christ possessed that love fully and directly, but even for the disciples faith and hope were necessary to recognize and receive the *res in sacramentum.*

43. Ibid., 62.1. Thomas uses two analogies with respect to participation: heat, and flame. With respect to natural participation a thing increases in heat, but supernatural participation or deification increases the principle of heat to an extent that the nature in which the heat inheres is so infused that it catches flame. It is not just like the fire insofar as it is hot, but rather it becomes fire itself insofar as it takes its identity from the fire with nothing remaining untransformed. (Always this identity is participated because were the thing removed from the fire it would cease to be fire, whereas Christ cannot cease to be what he is in his divine nature even when he united a human nature to himself.)

In Christ, human virtue or activity comes to participate, not just in God as its natural perfection, but also in the divine life/nature as a supernatural gift. "The light of glory, by which God is seen, is in God perfectly and naturally, whereas it is in any creature imperfectly and by likeness or participation."[44] Through the Person of Christ intrinsic principles of human action are transformed from mere *means* of participation into the thing itself. This is especially apparent with the theological virtue of *caritas* where:

> The divine essence itself is caritas, even as it is wisdom, and good-
> ness. Therefore just as we are said to be good with the goodness
> which is God, and wise with the wisdom which is in God (since
> the goodness by which we are formally good is a participation of
> divine goodness, and the wisdom by which we are formally wise is
> a share of divine wisdom), so too, the caritas by which formally we
> love our neighbor is a participation of divine caritas.[45]

True *caritas* is always a supernatural participation, above our natural human capacity precisely because it is a personal participation in the life of God, a "supernatural fellowship."[46] The supernatural fellowship of the triune life is present in and through the human person aflame with divine love. The "good" we discussed in the first section—power as obedience, glory as suffering, life as dying to self—is perfected in the "caritas by which formally we love our neighbor." When human action is "on fire" with *caritas* it is a pure appropriation of the disappropriation that is the divine relation. It is, in fact, the presence of God in the world.

However, in both the case of heat and flame the source of warmth remains the same: it is the divine nature, in which participation is grace—always mediated by Christ—that makes us both an expression of the divine likeness as we participate in being with all other created things and an expression of the divine life itself insofar as we are members of Christ. What Christ mediates to humanity is "the sonship of adoption" which "is a participated likeness of natural sonship." Adoption best describes the goal of participation insofar as it is a sharing in the triune life. As such, it is accomplished as an act of the Trinity through Christ in the Holy Spirit. Christ is our perfect mediator precisely where he offers himself on our behalf. As such, he *is* the perfect revelation of both God and humanity and unites both in his one act of self-offering.

44. Ibid., IaIIae.5.7.

45. Ibid., IIaIIae.23.2.

46. Ibid., IIaIIae, 24.2. "Caritas is in us . . . by the infusion of the Holy Spirit, who is the love of the Father and the Son, and the participation of whom in us is caused caritas."

SACRAMENTAL ETHICS

An ethics that grows out of Balthasar's Trinitarian theology allows us to posit a concept of human perfection as a participation in Christ's self-offering. This idea of human perfection redefines glory as suffering love, power as obedience, life as death to self, and wealth as poverty and humility. When we realize that the telos of human nature is rooted in the *imago trinitatis* and that human perfection entails participation in the divine act of expropriation as appropriation, we can begin to see how concrete human acts lead to greater or lesser actualization of nature through their greater or lesser embodiment of Christ's own mission of self-offering. An ethics of participation brings these ideas together such that human perfection is the appropriation of loving disappropriation, or the presence of the divine life in and through human persons in the *caritas* by which we love our neighbor. In this section I discuss the inherent sacramentality of this Trinitarian ethical paradigm.

When we talk about participation in terms of circulating kenotic love, it becomes obvious that there is no independent or impersonal access to the divine life. Being made in the image of God entails an inherently relational existence—we cannot somehow separate ourselves from the social and historical reality we inhabit in order to escape to a realm of spiritual self-abandonment. Included within our social and historical setting is the fact that we only have access to the divine relation through Christ's historical and social gift of himself.

> When he [Christ] talks about discipleship, he speaks of the Cross as the fundamental form and synthesis of self-renunciation. It consists in drinking the cup that he must drink, and being baptized with the baptism with which he must be baptized. He himself longs for this ending, just as he longs for the supper where he will be able at last to distribute his immolated flesh and poured out blood. Despite the divine "must" which determines his journey, all of this takes place in perfect freedom, in a sovereign disposition of self.[47]

The "form and synthesis of self-renunciation" for human beings is a truly human appropriation of God's loving disappropriation. It is a physical and social self-offering through the tangible acts of everyday life. Primarily, we enter into the relation that constitutes our personhood through the

---

47. Balthasar, *Mysterium Paschale*, 18.

sacramental acts of baptism and Eucharist. Sacramental incorporation is, like Christ's act into which we enter, both a historical and an eternal reality. If God enters into history to transform it by bringing it into God's eternal relation, then our participation in that act will have both a physical/historical as well as a spiritual and eternal aspect. Thus sacramental ethics cannot be one or the other, but must be both. The personal and social identity of the communicant is either constituted in the relation, which the sacraments enact such that the person actually "is what they eat," or the very act of "communion" becomes a self-incrimination a rejection of the relation it represents.

A sacramental Trinitarian ethics forces us to attend to both spiritual and physical, historical and eternal aspects of human participation in the triune life, particularly as they are embodied and enacted in the sacraments.[48] When Christ's paschal sacrifice becomes the pivot between the revelation of God's glory and the appropriation of Christ's mission by redeemed humanity the remembering of the paschal event in the church's eucharistic offering becomes the locus for eschatological hope and temporal transformation. In the Eucharist, the Son's relation to the Father, and human participation in that relation are made present in the world. Vitally, the presence of Christ's mission and the church's identity is not a mere object on the altar, but an *activity*. The eucharistic sacrifice is the continued act of self-offering in and through the Son that is the presence of Christ's body—a living, moving, ethically relevant body in the world. As such, the church's sacramental life provides a way for humanity to freely enter into the triune life, not just in an ultimate metaphysical sense, but also in a present ethical and communal sense. The liturgical act of Eucharist is truly eschatological in uniting both heaven and earth, humanity and God in the perichoretic activity of kenotic love. In the Eucharist we can truly give back to God what he has given to us in Christ.[49]

48. Again, Balthasar's decision to bracket Sophia from Bulgakov's Trinitarian thesis is of importance. For Bulgakov, it is the identity between divine and creaturely Sophia that brings all of creation into the body of Christ. Yes, Sophia is the ecclesia, but there is that sophianic distance between the personal ethical activity of humans and our union with God. Similarly, he can be read as proposing a sophianic mediation between the kenotic activity of the divine persons and their union. Establishing both unity and difference in the activity of relation rather than Sophia continues to be vitally important as we examine the ethical ramifications of this Trinitarian theology.

49. "Christian existence is a 'reflection' of the form of Christ: as one has died for all so, at the deepest level, all have died (II Cor. 5:14). Faith must ratify this truth (Romans 6:33ff); life must manifest it (II Cor. 4:10). And if this death happened out of love 'for

The Eucharist is a truly relational reality where thanksgiving is an appropriation of disappropriation, the embodiment of personal participation in the triune relation. It is the participation in the One who reveals and recapitulates human perfection in his act of total obedience and self-offering. He shows us the true meaning of the human "good" and allows us to partake of it there. It is essential to our appropriation of Christ's sacrifice that we recognize the relational nature of sacramental activity and the ratification such a relation requires.

In the work of Louis Marie Chauvet we see the contrast between the sacraments as relational act and the sacraments as reified bits of grace. A preoccupation with the real or true as physical and historically comprehensible demands that "sign" be reduced to a veil under which realities are hidden. These realities are tangible causes of grace, produced and producing what they signify. If the eucharistic host is a sign veiling Christ, its effects do not follow from what it is. Rather, the sign is an instrumental cause of grace. The result is an understanding of the church as neither sufficiently united to nor distinguished from Christ as her head. In the first case, the Eucharist infuses the church with grace, but grace, as instrument, is not identified with Christ or the Holy Spirit as relation; it is a causal power. Thus, its effects are not personal participation or metaphysical identification between the church and Christ. Instead the church becomes another instrument of grace, her true reality veiled by accidents, which can be taken as accidental.

In the second case, if the sacrament is a cause of grace that confers an identity then the church can, and has, insufficiently distinguished between herself and Christ as her head. There is a danger that the church will claim to wield Christ's glory and power as an effect of the sacrament, forgetting the fact that what we primarily participate in is Christ's total self-offering, his absolute self-negation on the cross.

> It is neither a matter of pure presence in language, nor of the "reification" of Christ's bodiliness, but of the indivisible unity of his self-gift "for the multitude"—and this gift is not just an "attitude" but an integrally human enactment carried out precisely by virtue of the bodiliness which discloses in a deeper way the identity between the person of Jesus and his soteriological function. In that function, he is at once a disposer (as institutor of the Eucharist,

me' (Gal. 2:20), then my response must be a 'faith' which consists in total self-gift to this divine destiny. In this way, scandal and persecution become titles of glory for the Christian (Gal. 5:11; 6:12–14)" (Balthasar, *Mysterium Paschale*, 17).

the new covenant in his blood) and the disposed of (in obedience to the hour, when, at the Father's disposition, he will be handed over).[50]

Balthasar's Trinitarian theology and the Thomistic ethics of participation are vital resources for a sacramental and ethical theology that seeks to overcome distortions such as those listed above. The glory and power that Christ extends to us as we participate in the Eucharist are the glory and power of self-offering love. Far from a mere means of mechanistic grace, the sacraments in this paradigm are participations in Christ's own self-offering that can only be truly received in a holistic self-offering in thanksgiving. In the sacraments, Christ's self-offering in the divine relation is made available to humanity as the presence of God's self-gift, the relation that constitutes the identity and mission of the church.

The basis for a sacramental appropriation of the Son's relation to the Father lies in the fact that Christ is the one who perfectly mediates grace to us because he is the thing he is mediating, the gift of perfect *caritas*. Since Christ is both man and God he can mediate between God and man, communicating the relation of kenotic love that is the divine life to humanity.[51] In this role he is the high priest of humankind, as well as the gift being offered.[52]

If the Christian mode of appropriation is expropriation, and this is a participation in the triune relation, then this points to the eucharistic liturgy as a kind of active metonymic elision where the church both participates in the triune life of God as well as makes that life present to the world.[53] In the first case, the church becomes the body of Christ by entering into his story as her own. The paschal mystery begins with Christ's offering himself to the disciples in the bread and wine of the last supper. The meaning of

50. Ibid., 97.

51. "What belongs to the divine nature is predicated of the human nature—not, indeed, as it belongs essentially to the divine nature, but as it is participated in by the human nature. Hence, whatever cannot be participated in by human nature (as to be uncreated and omnipotent), is in no way predicated of the human nature. But the divine nature received nothing by participation from the human nature" (ibid., III.16.6).

52. Christ's priesthood can be considered with respect both to the offering he made and the participation in that offering. In the first respect his priesthood is more like the Levitical priesthood, but in the second sense more like that of Melchisedech "who offered bread and wine, signifying ecclesial unity, which is established by our taking part in the sacrifice of Christ. Therefore also in the New Law the sacrifice of Christ is presented to the faithful under the form of bread and wine" (ibid., III.22.6).

53. Laurance, "Christ's Body."

this act is fulfilled in his offering of himself to the Father on the cross. This self-offering reveals the eternal dynamic of the triune life. The Father gives himself eternally to the Son, who can only receive himself by returning the gift to the Father. The Holy Spirit is the one who unites Father and Son without collapsing one into the other or himself. Christ's resurrection is the Father's acceptance of his offering and his gracious return of the gift by giving himself back to the Son. The risen Christ lives entirely for another, and human salvation consists in appropriating his life for ourselves.

The ethical dimension of the liturgy entails the church's self-gift in and with Christ as living entirely for God. This implies that the eucharistic offering is not merely a matter of the elements on the altar. It extends to the lives of those gathered to celebrate. Thus the offering we offer is not simply Christ's action, but our own reception of and return of that action through the ways we live in the world.

The sacramental ethic that arises from Balthasar's Trinitarian theology is corporate. It is a social ethics that is based in the notion of participation in relation. First, it is the participation in the divine relation of kenotic love that is the divine essence. However, this primary participation intrinsically extends to the human community where those who receive themselves in relation to God now possess their lives only by losing them—offering them as a sacrifice of love in thanksgiving to the Father with the Son in the Holy Spirit. This corporate reality is shared in a concentrated symbolic sense in the sacramental life of the church. Here we see the continued corporality or embodiment of God's relation primarily in the Eucharist where, as a community the church offers herself on the altar and receives herself as the body of Christ in and for the world. As such, it is a consubstantial ethics where participants are able to "fill up in [their] flesh what is still lacking in regard to Christ's afflictions, for the sake of his body, which is the church" (Col. 1:24). In this way humans are able to "catch fire" and serve as a light of truth because the good that is the perfection of human life *is* the relation that constitutes the lives of those who receive it. We see this in Jesus admonition of John 15 to "Remain in me, as I also remain in you. . . . If you remain in me and I in you, you will bear much fruit; apart from me you can do nothing."

The cross makes conversion possible because it opens up the possibility for humanity to participate in the divine life of *kenotic* love. "Therefore, it is impossible to separate the divine *kenosis* from the one that must be carried out in ourselves: our corporality is charged with becoming the place for this *kenosis*."[54] If we recall that participation entails that the "participator enact the *actus essendi* of the one in whom he participates according to the capacities of his own essence," then the corporality of the sacraments and human participation in the sacraments makes sense. Among human capacities for enacting the relation of kenotic love are social and physical capacities. Sacramental self-offering entails the participation of the whole human person, and its implications and effects extend to the full spectrum of human actions.[55] In particular, Christ's mission of expropriation extends to the social and physical *interactions* that characterize our relations to one another:

> "In the history of which we are a part, freedom and justice" can only come about "through the representative suffering of Jesus Christ, and through our discipleship of him, acting in solidarity with those who suffer." Thus "the anticipation of Christian hope is vital and effective only when we act on behalf of those who have no future." When believers, "the first fruits of the new creation . . . take up their cross, they anticipate the future of redemption." Thus the eschatology of the future and the theology of the cross are interwoven.[56]

If the Eucharist constitutes the identity of the church, "it is only a point of passage, but it is fully that."[57] In our physical, social lives the church lives out her identity as the body of Christ. We offer together with Christ the gifts he has given us. In this offering we confess our radical dependence upon Christ. But the Eucharist "has neither its origin nor its end within itself."[58] Since it is only a point of passage it cannot be a closed event, but must open out into the ethical life:

> For the resurrection of Jesus and the gift of the Spirit specify corporality as the eschatological place of God. God wants to assume flesh, the flesh of the Christ, by the Spirit. For us, this is the theological import of an ethics lived as the prime place of a liturgy pleasing to God. The body is henceforth, through the Spirit, the

54. Chauvet, *Symbol and Sacrament*, 509.

55. "The believer and the Church must not turn away from the world and yearn to take refuge in an already fulfilled 'above,' thus neglecting and betraying their mission to the world . . . nor should they resign themselves to the condition of the world and put up with personal and social sin and injustice, and with death" (Balthasar, *Final Act,* 170).

56. Ibid., 171.

57. Ibid., 281.

58. Ibid., 282.

living letter where the risen Christ eschatologically takes on flesh and manifests himself to all people.[59]

The sacraments are constitutive of ecclesial life insofar as they unite us to Christ as members of his body. But our participation in him is genuine insofar as it extends to our whole lives, as we participate in him ethically as well as liturgically.

The Christian life is a participation in the life of God already in this world, and if the sacraments are constitutive of that participation, if it is to be genuine, they cannot be the exhaustive means of participation. There is a mutual informing between sacraments and the ethical life. In both, humans become what they are called most deeply to be. In the ethical life we participate in God by giving ourselves to others as an expression of the sacramental life where we are given in Christ's own self-offering to the Father. Just as in the triune life, the Father and Son are entirely other and entirely one, held in unity and difference in the self-kenosis of the Holy Spirit; humanity is brought into the triune dynamic as wholly other and wholly loved in the Son. The Holy Spirit who is the love of the Father and the Son imprints us with *caritas* such that we really express the life of God.[60]

> The church's sacrifice is, therefore, at once distinct from that of Christ and identical with his, since it consists in a consenting to the sacrifice of Christ (and to all the consequences that flow therefrom for the Church). Christ's kenotic condition—as bread to be "eaten" and wine poured out—appears to confer on the table-guests an active and absorbing role; but "when I am weak, then am I strong" and "the weakness of God is stronger than men," precisely in the Eucharist. There Christ actively incorporates the participants into his mystical body.[61]

59. Ibid., 264.

60. "Fire, which no one can seize without being consumed, is the symbol of the absolute otherness of God, whom no one can see without dying (Exod. 33:20). This is why it is 'from the midst of the fire' that God speaks to God's people at Sinai, just as it is 'out of the bush' that God reveals God's name to Moses (Exod. 3). But if this fire keeps God apart, it is also the place from which God communicates with humankind. Fire is thus a particularly expressive symbol for the paradoxical twofold function of the Holy Spirit: it is simultaneously the agent of God's recession from the world in God's absolute holiness, and of God's procession into the world through the communication of God's holiness to humans . . . [The Spirit is] God as ex-static opening who is in God's self only by moving out of God's self and who creates human respondents in God's own image- also ex-static—who do not find themselves except by losing themselves" (ibid., 513–14).

61. Balthasar, *Mysterium Paschale*, 99–100. Cavanaugh describes the same dynamic:

The Eucharist as symbol is as real as the triune life. The church, by engaging in this relational reality, partakes of salvation, achieved in Christ's self-offering to the Father (in itself constitutive of the perichoretic kenosis of the triune life) precisely in offering ourselves with and in him. Christ's offering is a gift of his whole self, and he enables us to receive his self-gift in the activity of offering ourselves together with him. We receive Christ by conforming to his total self-abandonment to God. Our self-offering is our participation in the triune life. We experience this in every aspect of our lives, but primarily in the sacraments. The liturgical expression of this reality is a unique intensification of the dynamic that structures all of human life. In baptism we die with Christ; we are conformed to his death and resurrection. In the Eucharist, we offer our whole lives together with others; in and with Christ we present ourselves as "a living sacrifice, holy and pleasing to God" (Rom. 12:1). Thus, liturgically, we are incorporated into the *totus Christus* as we unite our offering to Christ's in thanksgiving. This offering is constitutive of Christian identity in Christ as a symbol which effects the reality it represents.

These symbolic connections between the Eucharist as Christ's physical body and the church united to that body emphasize the relationship between what we do and who we are. In the Eucharist we participate in the activity that symbolizes who we are, the offering of ourselves in Christ. This offering establishes our identity to the extent that even outside the eucharistic liturgy we remain the body of Christ. Ethics cannot be separated from the Eucharist because Christians cannot be separated from Christ as his body. A Trinitarian sacramental ethics points out the connection between our activity and the degree to which we participate in God. However, it is the point in which our self-offering, our obedience, our virtue is united with Christ's as the *totus Christus* that human nature partakes of divinity, that heat becomes flame.

What this Trinitarian sacramental ethics of participation shows us is that each of us has already begun the process, which we see fulfilled in the

---

"A true sacrifice does not subtract something from us, but unties us to God in holy Fellowship by reference to our eternal end. A human being can become a sacrifice, therefore, by dying to the world and rising with Christ . . . Christ adopted the form of a servant. His self-gift to humanity, his complete kenosis, is such that he gives over his very identity to the community of his followers, who thereby become in history his true body, which in turn takes the form of a servant. The Christian sacrifice unites us both to each other and to God in the body of Christ, so that we become what is offered on the altar. This, says Augustine, is the import of the Eucharist" (Cavanaugh, *Torture and Eucharist*, 230).

saints and the martyrs. Our very being is a gift and our every good act a ratification and acceptance of that gift and an embodiment of Christ's own mission, handed over to the church in the paschal event. The Eucharist is the activity where the divine image, our kenotic identity, is most fully realized. In sacramental participation we offer our whole selves and we receive Christ: body, soul, and divinity. To quote *Sacrosanctum Concilium*, the Eucharist "draws the faithful into the compelling love of Christ and sets them afire."[62]

My task has been to show how this ethical paradigm can be developed on the basis of Balthasar's Trinitarian theology. Personhood consists in absolute selflessness—an abandonment that goes to the infinite lengths of the opposition of relation. The distance of relation is sufficient to hold together life and death, joy and pain, suffering and glory, power and helplessness. It is also sufficient to englobe not only positive reality, but the consequences of human sin. With his descent into hell "the Son brings his mission to a close at the point where everything enters into the triune life."[63] Nothing can go beyond the love of the Father for the Son (not even nothing).[64] The proof of this thesis for Balthasar lies in the beauty of the saints. In their self-offering God reveals his presence, the power of the Son to make their sacrifice a perfect participation in the Son.

> What does God gain from the world? An additional gift, given to the Son by the Father, but equally a gift made by the Son to the Father, and by the Spirit to both. It is a gift because, through the distinct operations of each of the three Persons, the world acquires an inward share in the divine exchange of life; as a result the world is able to take the divine things it has received from God together with the gift of being created, and return them to God as a divine gift.[65]

62. *Sacrosanctum Concilium*, paragraph 149.

63. Balthasar, *Final Act,* 521.

64. As I discussed in chapter three, Balthasar allows for a certain reality to evil. Christ assumes the real consequences of humanity's "No" to God in his descent into hell. Mongrain discusses a difference between Balthasar and Barth on this subject: "The gist of von Balthasar's argument is that Barth interprets the demonic as 'nothingness' (following Hegel's thesis that the demonic is 'negativity') because he does not take seriously a theology of the created order in which genuinely free creatures (angels, demons, or humans) can exist as ontologically other than God. In other words, von Balthasar contends that there are no real demons in Barth's theology because he reduces all reality to a Christological monism" (Mongrain, 166 quoting Balthasar, *Final Act,* 480 and 207).

65. Balthasar, *Final Act,* 521.

The corporate, corporal, consubstantial sacramental ethics that arises from Balthasar's Trinitarian theology does not flinch away from the negative human realities that Christ encounters and transforms with his death and descent into hell. Balthasar's belief that the whole of the *triduum mortis* is a sacramental event which we can embody now through participation in Christ is in fact inherently ordered towards confronting injustice, suffering, and death as both historical human realities as well as cosmic eschatological obstacles. In the final section of this chapter I address the question of whether this ethics places far too much emphasis on the eternal and spiritual aspects of human existence to the exclusion of the social and historical. To this end, I want to turn to the implications of a sacramental Trinitarian ethics for the suffering of the "sinned-against."

THE SINNED-AGAINST

One criticism that may arise with an ethics that takes the paschal event as paradigmatic for both theology and anthropology is that the emphasis on Christ's passivity and obedience in his suffering and death could glorify passiveness and "weakness" which, in turn, can be employed by oppressors as a weapon against the suffering oppressed. Does a notion of suffering as glory and a focus on the cross as a revelation of God's power in some way empower or even justify oppression? I suggest that a sacramental ethics rooted in kenotic Trinitarian theology can address human suffering, oppression, and injustice in several ways: First, by attending to the realities of sin both as a defect or distortion in the human person's response to God, *and* as the consequences of these distorted actions that cause suffering for others. Second, participation in the life of Christ, especially in the Eucharist, is an eternal and temporal, spiritual and physical activity that depends for its authenticity on the transformation of the entire social and ethical lives of the participants. *Caro factum est* is only a fact insofar as it is a mission, and this is an extension of the Trinitarian reality of the Son. Third, this ethics requires us to reformulate our understanding of the good, power, and triumph in light of the nature of Christ's triumph over death and evil through loving self-surrender. Such a conceptual conversion leads to a fourth contribution, namely that the broken bodies and stifled voices of the "sinned-against" become central to understanding and enacting the kingdom of God in history. Far from setting aside the "sinned-against" as a byproduct of Christ's finished action, this ethical paradigm situates their suffering as a critical point of Christ's ongoing presence in the world. Before turning to the positive contributions of this ethic, I want to clarify the problem.

The Problem of Involuntary "Pointless" Suffering

Steffen Lösel, in his article "A Plain Account of Christian Salvation?" poses the question as to whether a Trinitarian theology that emphasizes suffering and passivity has anything to offer for those who experience suffering and passivity, not as a voluntary solidarity with Christ, but as an involuntary and inescapable force that defines their whole lives.[66] As discussed in chapter three, according to Balthasar, Christ assumes the actual consequences of sin. Lösel critiques Balthasar for not adequately accounting for the suffering of the "sinned-against" in terms of their passive suffering, and focusing instead on Christ's assumption of the sins as defects in those who commit them. Lösel argues that "theirs [the sinned-against] is neither the death of sin nor the death of love."[67] He says that we must, unlike Balthasar, interpret the Christ event as "the radical outcome of God's solidarity with the too often seemingly god-forsaken sinned-against."[68]

If human perfection consists in the participation in the relation of kenotic love revealed in Christ, then the way in which Christ encounters concrete human sin and rejection in hell is an important parallel for human participation in his loving relation to the Father and to the world. If it is true that Christ's assumption of human sin is limited to inner dispositions of sinners and does not address the consequences of those sins in the "sinned-against" in history or in the environment, then the re-membering of Christ's saving act in the Eucharist would be a matter merely of a spiritual and personal conversion, and not a matter of social and historical import.[69]

---

66. Lösel, "A Plain Account," 152, referring to Balthasar's *Truth of God*, 356.

67. Ibid.

68. Ibid.

69. In *Torture and Eucharist*, William Cavanaugh describes the effects of this precise Christological and sacramental error in the Chilean Church during the Pinochet regime. The church had to overcome a theology that separated out the spiritual and historical/political planes. The church at first understood itself in an organic relationship with the state as twin guardians, one of the soul the other of the body. Cavanaugh argues that this concept of church/state relations eliminates the church's visible, social body and leaves it without a way to combat the fragmentation described above. The church had to become incarnate to oppose the state. The church becomes incarnate through the liturgy which

A sacramental ethics of participation that draws on Balthasar's Trinitarian theology looks to the pivot of Christ's paschal self-offering to interpret suffering in the context of human nature as relation. This eliminates a false distinction between physical and spiritual, eternal and temporal, and instead focuses on the continuity of relation as a participation and suffering as the consequences of the distortion of that relation.

A Christological Account of Suffering

The first contribution that a sacramental ethics of participation growing out of Balthasar's Trinitarian theology can make to a discussion of the suffering of the oppressed is to provide a holistic account of human action based in the notion of human nature as a participation in the Trinitarian relation of kenotic love. Within this account of human action, sin and the experience of oppression are taken to be relational realities that are taken up and transformed in Christ's paschal self-offering. As such, "effigies" of sin that Christ assumes in the descent into hell cannot be isolated from their source and effects in the distortions of relation caused by sin. I think a more accurate reading of "effigies" would be to understand them not only as constituted by individual sin and rejection of God, but also as the historical effects of societal, structural sin throughout history.[70] The dramatic character of the relation between God and humanity is based in the *imago*

---

both constitutes her participation in the body of Christ as well as constitutes her as a social/physical body. With the Eucharist as the "incorporating" activity Cavanaugh argues that Jesus' life and cause are given "their form" (61). "The imitation of Christ is not reducible to some principle such as 'love,' but is rather a highly skilled performance learned in a disciplined community of virtue by careful attention to the concrete contours of the Christian life and death as borne out by Jesus and the saints" (62).

70. This would only be possible if we, like Balthasar, assume that Christ assumes all of human nature as a concrete universal, and that this assumption is at once universal and personal. Balthasar already assumes Christ's solidarity with concrete, historical humanity in its every instance. Recalling Balthasar's divergence from Bulgakov on this point—that Christ assumes, not a "nothingness," but the actual historical facts of sin—we see a concern for human freedom and its consequences. For Balthasar, personal distance rather than Sophia as constituting the opposition of relation in the triune life provides a way to talk about both a genuinely "other" foundation for creaturely existence without falling into dualism. (Since the basis for that "otherness" is the same distance which is the basis for the infinite "otherness" of the divine persons.) Here again we see that his use of "distance" rather than Sophia also situates human freedom such that, not only the particular acts as they effect the agent, but the historical effects of those acts in the creaturely sphere are assumed and redeemed in Christ's descent into hell.

trinitatis, or the activity of relation that constitutes personhood. The Son's assumption of human sin is not an external or merely forensic assumption, but a full entering into the absence of relation, the self-negation, which is a consequence of distorted human freedom.[71] Only as such can the Son's saving act preserve the relational character of human persons and bring them into the divine relation. If the Son truly enters into the full abyss of human sin, then no aspect of the reality of that sin, whether personal evil or the historical consequences of sin, can be excluded from the Son's experience of God-abandonedness.

There are two implications that arise out of the Trinitarian context of Christ's mission and our human participation in it: First, passive or unwilling suffering is also a participation in Christ's active overcoming of sin and isolation. Suffering has a redemptive value because it is a participation in and extension of Christ's self-offering to the Father.[72] Second, and equally important, is the active component of our participation in Christ's self-offering which means that:

> Christian hope, theological hope, goes beyond this world, but it does not pass it by: rather, it takes the world with it on its way to God, who has graciously prepared a dwelling in himself for us and for the world. This implies that the Christian in the world is meant to awaken hope, particularly among the most hopeless; and this in turn means that he must create such humane conditions as will actually allow the poor and oppressed to have hope.[73]

An emphasis on the triune nature of Christ's redemptive act and the passivity of Christ with respect to the Father should not lead us to conclude

---

71. "It is sin, and not just the consequences of sin, that the Suffering Servant takes upon himself. The Russian Orthodox dogmatician Sergei Bulgakov and the French Catholic exegete Andre Feuillet enable Balthasar to edge nearer still to the most dramatic truth of all. In Bulgakov's *Agnets Bozhii,* the Christological volume of his so-called 'great trilogy,' the suffering of Christ on Calvary is in its supra-temporal intensity—a divine person undergoes it, albeit humanly—the 'equivalent' of that due to sinners . . . the consenting self-surrender of the Son; his changing place representatively with sinners; man's consequent liberation and initiation into the Trinitarian life, which (finally) shows the whole of the foregoing to be a divine love-story—achieve satisfactory integration only when they are set within a *theodramatic* context" (Nichols, *No Bloodless Myth,* 164).

72. "Recognizing our suffering as Christ's, and as a grace, [we] can enjoy the Christian hope that—in however hidden a manner—this suffering, in union with Christ's, will promote the salvation of the world" (Balthasar, *Final Act,* 177).

73. Ibid., 176.

that Christoformity on the part of Christians entails apathy or a rosy-eyed displacement of responsibility towards some eschatological resolution. In fact, Christ's assumption of all human suffering and his rendering it a Christological—and therefore Trinitarian—reality, means that "our earthly life, in heaven" will be "not a mere memory but a real present," and the statement that "God will wipe away all tears" "does not exclude the fact that the blessing hidden in earthly tears will remain simultaneously, as it were, 'bodily' present."

> And if it is true that the suffering of the Crucified One can trans-
> form even worldy pain, unintelligible to itself, into a co-redemptive
> suffering, then the most unbelievable, most cruel tortures, prisons,
> concentration camps, and whatever other horrors there may be
> can be seen in close proximity to the Cross, to that utter night,
> interrupted only by the unfathomable cry of "Why?"[74]

Far from an eschatological escapism, this Trinitarian theology brings human suffering, even the most senseless and brutal, into eternal life as a "present" reality. As a product of our human capacity for genuine action, and as such, for genuine relation, sin and suffering can be redeemed, but cannot be negated. In the drama between divine and human persons, "What the Son experiences on the Cross as total night is in God's sight the Son's ultimate obedience and hence his highest glory. In the Crucified, this glory is reflected solely in his letting-be, that is, in the fulfillment of his mission."[75] The unique dignity of humanity is our capacity to participate in the Son's mission, and thus, in the Son's ability to transform suffering into glory through loving self-surrender.

Eucharist as Mission

As I discussed earlier in this chapter, an ethics that takes its starting point in a kenotic Trinitarian theology and assumes that human good entails participation in the divine activity of self-surrender requires a genuinely human means for receiving and extending that mission in the present. In the Eucharist, the church has been given a physical, spiritual, historical, temporal means for enacting her own identity as the body of Christ. When

74. Ibid., 501.
75. Ibid., 502.

we realize the Eucharist as an extension of Christ's mission of self-offering to the Father then:

> The church can never be restricted to a sphere of the personal and the spiritual because human life is social, and the religious lives of people are interwoven with the political, economic, and cultural processes of society. "entrusted by Christ not with 'souls' but with 'men' nothing human can be alien to (the church)."[76]

The many ways that Christians extend Christ's mission of self-offering love are thus rooted in Christ's own suffering. In the eucharistic celebration Christ gives himself entirely to us and we perform the Eucharist by becoming his body and giving ourselves away in turn. We offer our sacrifice together with his sacrifice as we are made his body. As such, the church participates already in the divine life because "a true sacrifice does not subtract something from us, but unites us to God in holy fellowship by reference to our eternal end."[77] At the same time the church makes the divine relation present in history and transforms it. The "Eucharist effects the body of Christ, a body marked by resistance to worldy power. Torture creates victims; the Eucharist creates martyrs, witnesses. Isolation is overcome in the Eucharist by the building of a communal body which resists the state's attempts to disappear it."[78] The relation that eucharistic participation makes present is an activity. It is the activity appropriation of disappropriation, receiving one's self through self-abandonment, the *caritas* by which one acts with respect to the neighbor. Sacramental participation makes the communicants a living and active body in the world who are called together to live out their identity as Christ's body now. Thus, though suffering and death are certainly inevitable and "the poor are always with us," the ratification of the relation that is our identity requires—in fact consists in—whatever we have done to the least of these. Apathy and indifference are like arterial plaque in the blood circulation that is the human participation in the divine life.

---

76. Cavanaugh, *Torture and Eucharist*, 109 quoting address by Fr Azocar.

77. Ibid., 229.

78. Ibid., 206.

Consequences of Reformulating the Notion of the "Good"

Christ reveals that divine power is absolute obedience and openness. Self-abandoning love is the presence of the omnipotent God in the world. Therefore, as the church lives out her eucharistic identity as the body of Christ through participation in the goods of human perfection that Christ reveals and extends in his Passion she embodies the power of God to transform and redeem the world.

Earlier in this chapter I referred to the distorted theology that gave rise to "the white Christ" which has been used to justify so much evil and oppression in American history. A sacramental Trinitarian ethic could be applied to this concrete instance of oppression and injustice. It is an ethic that begins with the triune life as self-abandoning relation. It defines personhood, not as what we hold for ourselves, but as what we receive and give away in relation. It demonstrates that power and glory are found in self-abandoning love. It requires a "tectonic shift" where the relation that is the divine essence is revealed in a man suffering and dying on a cross. As James Cone says:

> One has to have a powerful religious imagination to see redemption in the cross, to discover life in death and hope in tragedy. "Christianity," Reinhold Niebuhr wrote, "is a faith which takes us through tragedy to beyond tragedy, by way of the cross to victory in the cross."[79]

Through the window of the cross as a revelation of the triune life, the tables are turned. The mockers' cries to "save yourself if you are the Son of God" are no longer directed from a position of power to the one who is helpless. Instead, Christ reveals the power of self-offering love to go beyond and englobe every rejection, to take up and heal even the wounds of death. He reveals the absolute impotence of hatred in the face of love and forgiveness.[80]

79. James Cone, "Strange Fruit: The Cross and the Lynching Tree," 53.

80. Balthasar specifically addresses the issue of how the victory of the cross is meant to apply to social justice. He asks whether the "cross of Christ can be changed into a 'tactical' instrument in issues that are purely this-worldly? Can the agape that suffers and endures al things provide a technique for the attainment of political goals? Is this not the attempt to take 'divine virtue'—that is, something that is and remains God's own possession—and manipulate it on the human stage?" (*Action*, 484). The issue Balthasar addresses with these questions is different from what I am describing above. Here, Balthasar is concerned with the use of Christ's passion as a means or a tool for political change. The transformative power of Christ's passion that I am discussing above is not a tool, but a relation. The divine virtue of *caritas*, that is the divine relation, is participated

If the good for human nature is really the participation in the triune relation of self-surrender in both a temporal and historical way, and the good and glory that fulfill our humanity is the joy of self-abandoning love, then how should we understand the role of temporal suffering? Is it a good to be actively sought, and should we tell those who suffer that they are blessed to do so? Again, we must take our answer from the Trinitarian relation. In the first place, there is a "positive" aspect of temporal suffering. Balthasar describes this positive aspect of suffering in terms of the Son's paschal offering:

> Might it not be, in the end, that this baffling weight of suffering in the world is a feature of transcendence (of which we are largely unconscious), a way of training us for the great act of self-surrender that concludes our temporal life? Might it not be that all the blood spilled in vain has something to do, after all, with that "precious blood" with which we have been bought and washed? Can the many tears that human beings shed, unfruitfully, on their own behalf or because of a friend's sufferings, be transformed into something that is fruitful for eternity?[81]

Rather than assume that Balthasar is glorifying human suffering here, it is helpful to recognize that, no matter how much we want to advocate for justice and equality in the world, no matter how much we actively seek to alleviate pain and suffering around us, the immensity of suffering in the world is unfathomable and insurmountable apart from its englobing in the life of God. A kenotic Trinitarian theology addresses the inevitable and insurmountable fact of human suffering by empowering humanity to make of our own suffering a participation in the eucharistic self-offering of the Son, and as such, a fulfillment (rather than the destruction) of our human nature as a participation in the triune relation.

In the second place, the good of self-offering and surrender that we enact in the Eucharist and extend in a eucharistic life in the world has an active aspect with respect to injustice and suffering in the world.

> It is not a question of glorifying earthly suffering (often the result of worldly injustice, persecution and abuse, which could be morally

---

in and embodied in the lives of those who appropriate this relation as their own through disappropriation. Thus, the power of the cross is never directly applied to a social injustice, which would be impersonal and, as such, a distortion. Instead it is mediated through the persons who embody it both individually and corporately as the church.

81. Balthasar, *Final Act,* 499.

doubtful) but of whether we are open or closed to the fundamental values of the kingdom of God. Such openness can prove itself through action, even through militancy, just as much as through endurance. There are enough places in the New Testament that summon us to God's call-to-arms and challenge us to seize the "sword" brought by Jesus; there seems to be nothing against a just defense, even the armed protection, of earthly goods that we hold to be willed and given by God. It is surely right, while eschewing avarice and egoism, to take action to preserve earthly goods that, while they are transitory, nonetheless have a rightful place in the will and rule of God.[82]

In this second sense, we can affirm the very good goods of temporal life and seek to protect and promote them as part of our participation in the triune life.

The Embodiment of Christ in the Sinned-Against

A further resource that a sacramental ethic based in Balthasar's Trinitarian theology brings to the situation of the "sinned-against" is its emphasis

---

82. Ibid., 500–501. This quote supports the notion that Balthasar's critiques of liberation theology should not be taken as opposition to the motive of liberation theology so much as the method. Liberation, both spiritual and political, is a positive good. However, Balthasar believes that the starting place for defining liberation as well as achieving it must be Christ. Kevin Mongrain outlines two basic deficiencies in liberation theology with respect to Balthasar's Christological vision of liberation. "The first deficiency is the lack of an authentically theological aesthetic perspective; the second deficiency is liberation theology's chronic naïveté about Christianity's agonistic historical context and about the exact nature and strategies of the Gnostic antagonist" (Kevin Mongrain, *The Systematic Thought of Hans Urs Von Balthasar* (New York: Herder and Herder, 2002), 43 quoting Balthasar's *Action*, 32). Mongrain believes that the most accurate characterization of Balthasar's opposition to liberation theology is that he "finds liberation theology guilty of only naïveté about its historical context, a misidentification of Christianity's true enemies, and, consequently, a theologically imprudent and uncritical appropriation of Gnostic modes of reflection" (ibid., 167). Mongrain proposes that Balthasar's interpretation of *Gaudium et Spes* provides the hermeneutical key for his interpretation of liberation theology. "Like *Gaudium et Spes* Balthasar finds liberation theology too simplistic in its analysis of socio-economic issues and too ready to make alliances with those who advocate seemingly neutral notions of progress . . . Balthasar things liberation theology's appeal to praxis is inherently Christian, and hence it requires special emphasis. Thus he lauds liberation theology for calling Christians to engage in a 'world-transforming cooperation' with Christ's mission, explaining that this call expresses 'the heart of Christianity, and it reveals the dramatic situation of the Christian in this world as perhaps nothing else does'" (ibid., 171 quoting Balthasar's *Action*, 482).

on embodiment. The concrete physical act of Christ offering his body and blood to the disciples in the Last Supper and then offering his body on the cross as an expression of his identity in relation to humanity and the Father points to the nature of human participation in Christ's self-offering. Not only is human participation in the triune life necessarily embodied in its eucharistic nature, but also the bodies of the sinned-against continue to be a locus for Christ's presence on earth, a living expression of the cross.

> To understand what the cross means in America, we need to take a good long look at the lynching tree in this nation's history—"the bulging eyes and twisted mouth," that "strange fruit" that Billie Holiday sang about, "blood on the leaves and blood at the root." The lynched black victim experienced the same fate as the crucified Christ.

> The cross and the lynching tree interpret each other. Both were public spectacles, usually reserved for hardened criminals, rebellious slaves, and rebels against the Roman state and falsely accused militant blacks who were often called "black beasts" and "monsters in human form" for their audacity to challenge white supremacy in America. Any genuine theology and any genuine preaching must be measured against the test of the scandal of the cross and the lynching tree.[83]

Both Cone and Balthasar's theologies of the cross share in common that they begin with the truth about the personhood of the one hanging on the tree and the nature of the power each person possesses with their capacity to participate in and embody the divine relation of love. However, with Cone we may ask, "What kind of salvation is that?" Ultimately, we are driven to ask again whether this vision of the cross as a means of participating in the divine life and as a revelation of divine glory has anything to say about the suffering of the sinned-against. And, ultimately, we are driven back to the eucharistic nature of our ethical life as constitutive of our participation in God and the fulfillment of human nature; it is a historical as well as eschatological participation that cannot be extracted from human embodiment in history and in community. In this way, at least in the American context:

> The cross and the lynching tree need each other: the lynching tree can liberate the cross from the false pieties of well-meaning Christians. The crucifixion was a first-century lynching. The cross can

83. Cone, "Strange Fruit," 53.

redeem the lynching tree, and thereby bestow upon lynched black bodies an eschatological meaning for their ultimate existence.[84]

In the context of a sacramental Trinitarian ethics, the suffering bodies of the lynched, the sick, the abused, the drug-addicted, the homeless become an interpretive lens for understanding ourselves, our God, and the meaning of our sacramental incorporation in Christ and in one another. Their suffering, and our own, are no longer obstacles to be overcome but invitations to participate in Christ's power in helplessness, relation in God-abandonedness, and glory in suffering.

A sacramental ethics that arises out of a Trinitarian kenotic theology is oriented by the human telos of participation in the kenotic divine relation. It takes as its starting point the definition of personhood as a self-offering relation of love. This ethic is able to contribute to a notion of justice for the sinned-against by emphasizing four areas: the reality of sin and suffering in its human and Christological context, the nature of the Eucharist as an extension of Christ's mission in the world, the reformulation of the good in light of the cross, and the embodiment of Christ in the sinned-against and in those who enter into solidarity with their suffering.

This ethic combats the suffering of the sinned-against in two ways: First, by recognizing the inevitability of human suffering and the experience of unwanted oppression, and by reconceiving of power and human flourishing, not as freedom from these things, but as the capacity to transform them through a participation in Christ's own self-offering to the Father. Second, this ethic requires a historical, social, embodied response to suffering and injustice as an extension and validation of the church's eucharistic practice.

Within this ethics it is vital to recall that action which is not participation is an engagement on the level of power and autonomy. It is not possible to somehow "independently" embody Christ's mission or to divorce that mission from its Trinitarian context. Christian ethics begins and ends as a participation in the triune life of self-offering love. In particular, it is an ecclesial embodiment of Christ's love as offered in the Eucharist. The connection between Trinity, participation in the sacramental life, and ethics forces us to examine our "idols" of God that we use to justify areas in our own lives: where we either oppress or ignore oppression, where we either actively or by omission create another effigy of the sinned-against.

84. Ibid.

Social and political agendas, individual benefits, visions and projects for human salvation, and even/particularly ecclesial mechanisms cannot stand alone or apart from the unity of the last supper, Christ's sacrifice on the cross, and the Christian "in-corporation" of Christ in the Eucharist. These human projects, insofar as they promote genuine human good, are participations in the triune relation of kenotic love.[85] However, there are implications in the opposite direction as well; sacramental participation in the triune life is at best vacuous, if not vicious if it does not have physical, historical, and social ramifications. The relation into which we are sacramentally incorporated is one of service, humility, and self-gift. Jesus himself lays out the situation clearly when he says, "Inasmuch as you have done to the least of these, you have done it to me."

Sacramental participation is verified throughout our lives as we enter deeper and deeper into the mystery of Christ through our own self-offering in and for others. It is important to recall that self-offering and a life of obedient service are not supposed to make us miserable. The relation of self-offering in which we participate is the true good of human nature. It is the telos for human happiness. As such, the Eucharist is simultaneously a participation in the mission self-abandonment and in the joy of love. At the heart of Christ's self-offering and the Trinitarian kenosis is a joyful thanksgiving. The expropriation that we appropriate is not primarily a solemn acceptance of the inevitability of suffering, but rather self-abandonment in love that inherently involves thankfulness, even in suffering. There is a kind of relief and levity involved in the constant reception of one's self as a gift from God. The Apostle Paul, when he admonishes Christians to conform to Christ, repeatedly includes thankfulness as an essential aspect of what it means to receive him as Lord.[86] Our self-offering, then, is always a receiving of Christ's prior self-offering. Our sacrifice is always a participation in his sacrifice. "God as ex-static opening who is in God's self only by moving out of God's self and who creates human respondents in God's own image— also ex-static—who do not find themselves except by losing themselves."[87]

---

85. "There ceases to be any 'either/or' as between body-and-blood in their literal pertinence, and spirit-and-life as their inner kernel of meaning, since the two pairs coincide perfectly in the Eucharist. The Son thanks the Father (*eucharistein, eulogein*) for having allowed him to be so disposed of that there comes about, at one and the same time, the supreme revelation of the divine love (its glorification) and the salvation of humankind" (Balthasar, *Mysterium Paschale*, 99).

86. E.g., Eph 5:4, 19–20, Phil 4:4–7, Col 3:12–17.

87. Chauvet, *Symbol and Sacrament*, 514.

We find ourselves by losing ourselves, and this is always accompanied by, or ratified in, thanksgiving. Thus:

> The task of the church in the temporal is to embody what Christ has already accomplished in history by re-membering his broken and victorious body. Christ's victory is already won, and the Kingdom is to have transformative effects on Christian practice in history. The task of the church is to live as if this is the case, until Christ comes again and fully consummates his reign.[88]

There is a mutual informing between sacraments and the ethical life that forces us to not only acknowledge injustice and oppression, but recognize in the sinned-against and oppressed our Savior and the means of our participation in our salvation. In doing so, humans become what they are called most deeply to be. In the ethical life we participate in God by giving ourselves to others as an expression of the sacramental life where we are given in Christ's own self-offering to the Father.

CONCLUSION

Throughout this work I have been arguing for the necessity of the correct interpretation of Balthasar in terms of his appropriation of Bulgakov. It is with this insight that one is been able to extrapolate upon Balthasar's Trinitarian theology in the direction of a sacramental ethics that maintains the practical import of systematic Trinitarian doctrine. Balthasar's Trinitarian theology sets Bulgakov's thesis in the center of his understanding of God, and of humanity as partakers of God's life. Christ's revelation that, in God, power and helplessness, suffering and glory, life and death are simultaneously descriptive of the nature of divine personhood invites us to reconsider what discipleship looks like and reconfigure our lives as a participation in Christ's self-offering.

Christ gives himself to the church in the Eucharist as a relationship of self-offering love. The church becomes herself as she re-members Christ's body in the world in her enactment of the Eucharist. As a true incorporation of the body of Christ, the Eucharist demands that the church extend his glory in suffering, his power in helplessness and obedience, and life in death to the ethical life. In this way the members of Christ offer themselves

---

88. Cavanaugh, *Torture and Eucharist*, 185.

with Christ and through the church the love of God overcomes the "No" of sin and death.

> For the church, together with the Father, Son, and Spirit, has a role in the administration of death. Since the whole world is involved in the Son's Trinitarian movement, in the Spirit, to the Father, death in its entirety belongs to the past. For it is only he who does not love who remains in death. . . . Love by contrast, is the constant transformation from death into life.[89]

An ethical paradigm where the church participates in the Son's self-offering to the Father flows directly from kenotic Trinitarian theology. Real personhood consists in absolute selflessness, an abandonment that goes to the infinite lengths of relation. For humanity this entails rejoicing "inasmuch as you participate in the sufferings of Christ, so that you may be overjoyed when his glory is revealed," (1 Peter 4:13) and casting our whole selves—physical, spiritual, and social into the abyss of love. Only there, precisely in the act of self-offering, can we receive ourselves.

89. Balthasar, *Final Act,* 141 quoting 1 John 3:14.

Conclusion

Balthasar summarizes the whole of his work as an exploration of relation between infinite and finite, between God and humanity. My project in this book has been to look at the relation between God and creatures in terms of the triune life as revealed in Jesus Christ as an eternal relation of self-offering love, demonstrating the importance of Sergei Bulgakov's Trinitarian theology and Thomas Aquinas's notion of relation in the triune life for Balthasar's theological project. It is the notion of personhood as self-offering in relation that forms the analogical "bridge" between God and creation for Balthasar—a bridge that allows for a simultaneous infinite distance and participated union between divine and creaturely persons.

Only with an accurate grasp of his kenotic Trinitarian theology can one adequately interpret difficult aspects of Balthasar's work such as the descent into hell, the idea that "God-forsakenness" is constitutive of the divine relation, the notion of "surprise" between the divine persons, and his understanding of the relation between divine and human freedom as "openness" to the other in relation. Each of these concepts arises directly from the fundamental Trinitarian dynamic of relation as kenotic self-offering in relation.

The anthropological implications of Balthasar's notion of personhood lead to a notion of the good for human persons that entails imitation and participation in Christ's own self-offering to the Father both sacramentally and ethically. First, this Trinitarian theology and a sacramental ethics that emphasizes participation as the appropriation of Christ's self-offering to the Father in love has vital implications for the formation of an ethical community as it presents an understanding of the good. If power is exemplified in obedience, and glory in humility, then the ethical imagination of the community can undergo a drastic shift. Value must be reassigned and priorities reassessed. This concept of the good is the theological and anthropological framework for principles of Catholic social teaching such as a preferential option for the poor and the solidarity of persons. The plight of the poor and vulnerable in human society is not merely an extrinsic moral obligation, but an indication of the actualization of human persons in relation.

Second, It gives us a framework for confronting impotence and tragedy. Rather than describing ethical "problems" like injustice or dishonesty or cowardliness in terms of individual failure and seeking solutions, we are brought back to the complexity of relation. Sin, vice, mediocrity, and death are human problems. They are problems of persons in vast sets of relations. This is not to say that there are not often concrete resolutions to problems, but to acknowledge that often there are not. We cannot cure many diseases, end government corruption, bring back extinct species, win the war on drugs, or even heal the wounds in our own families. What we need in these cases is the miracle of faith and love and hope that comes only through the grace of participation in Christ's loving act of entering so deeply and help-lessly into all of these tragedies that no matter how deeply we are mired, or how much we share in suffering, he's already transformed those depths into a revelation of love.[1] As human persons participate in Christ's act of self-offering love, tragedies and failure are transformed by grace into deeper acts of self-surrender, or a greater saturation in the triune act of love.

The third contribution Balthasar's Trinitarian theology can bring to the ethical life is in its ability to address suffering in the forms of injustice and oppression. Again, this is a relational transformation that takes place, not through a moral example (which certainly informs it) nor through a social program (though that could emerge), but primarily through relation within a human community as a partaking in the divine community of self-offering love. This type of community, like a burning bush that is not consumed, makes Christ present both through sacramental participation and through the necessary self-emptying and communal incorporation that occurs as a genuine appropriation of the sacramental act. This

---

1. "The ecstatic love which is enkindled by the forms of expression of the self-sacrificing love of God penetrates through to the ultimate source from which all beauty in its appearing flows. The name of this source and centre is without qualification, love, in its incomprehensible passing over from itself into what is other than itself: love as the eternal generation of the Son from the Father, as God's act of creation directed into the nothingness—a passing over that reveals at one and the same time the absolute power and fruitfulness of God and his disposition of poverty, which wishes to have and hold on to nothing for itself. This disposition becomes visible in creation, and fully in redemption, as a descent into nothingness and fruitlessness" (Balthasar, *Studies in Theological Style: Clerical Styles,* 359 quoting cf. de sex alis seraphim ch. 3, 4: viii, 136–40).

community simultaneously recognizes itself as physical and spiritual, historical and eternal, genuinely human inasmuch as it enters into relationship with the divine. As such, it is able to be an eschatological community that embodies or makes present the gospel message of "God's liberation in an unredeemed and tortured world."[2] The message and *practice* of the gospel must be formed by the cross, which is:

> The most empowering symbol of God's loving solidarity with the "least of these," the unwanted in society who suffer daily from great injustices. We must face this cross as the terrible tragedy it was and discover in it, through faith and repentance, God's suffering solidarity with today's crucified people, which bestows on them the power to resist the daily crosses of injustice in their lives.[3]

In this quote Cone refers to the cross as a tragedy that holds a greater, transformative meaning. I think that Balthasar's Trinitarian theology intensifies this claim by saying that the cross reveals not only God's love and solidarity with humanity, but God's eternal love for God's self. Thus, the tragedy of abandonment and suffering is englobed within the eternal act of self-offering love of one divine person to the others. Only in this way can suffering and tragedy be truly transformed into a Eucharist, the thankful self-gift that constitutes relation. The relation of kenotic love between God and humanity and among human communities is the real source and summit of human dignity and the common good that we seek in social and historical transformation. It is the realized *imago trinitatis*.

This is a key point for recognizing the importance that Balthasar assigns to bracketing Sophia: social transformation is a historical, embodied, and *personal* participation in Christ's self-offering. On the one hand it is not mechanistic, programmatic, or primarily political.[4] If it were, it would

---

2. Cone, "Strange Fruit," 51.

3. Ibid., 52.

4. The political follows from the personal as the social promotion of human dignity. The relation between personal and social good can be negotiated in terms of the principles of solidarity and subsidiarity. Subsidiarity would indicate that personhood is promoted through participation in society at the most immediate level possible. People have a right and a duty to participate in society, seeking together the common good and well-being of all. There must always also be a recognition of the universal human nature, or the solidarity among persons. This entails a belief that the person is sacred and social. How we organize our society directly affects human dignity and the capacity of individuals to grow in community. Thus, the care for society extends also extends beyond our immediate world to the political sphere.

not be personal and so it could not be the presence of the triune life, and thus not a real conversion to the good. On the other hand it is not purely spiritual, pious, or otherworldly, emphasizing "Christian values" at the cost of human persons. If it were, it would not be sacramental, and would be divorced from both human and divine reality. Instead, Christ's self-offering in the paschal mystery reveals that the gospel is both a transcendent reality of the eternal relation in which Christ enables us to participate, as well as an immanent reality. Our embodied and communal participation in Christ's self-offering "is a powerful liberating presence among the poor right *now*."[5]

The fourth point that I will mention is an extension of the rest: Balthasar's Trinitarian theology and the human good that it envisions opens our eyes to the recognizing beauty and the image of God in the created world, in the suffering of ourselves and others.[6] It allows us to recognize the solidarity between ourselves and the broken bodies of the tortured, starved, or lonely especially as we identify ourselves with Christ's broken and tortured body offered up for the world. It also empowers those who suffer to have a special place in embodying God's love in and for the world, and an essential, if quiet, voice to which we must attend. It entails the transformation of suffering through participation in Christ's resurrection that is made present sacramentally and ethically in the world.

In conclusion, Balthasar's Trinitarian theology relies on the Trinitarian insights of Bulgakov and Aquinas to posit the divine life as a relation of kenotic love that is perfectly revealed by Christ in his passion and death. His understanding of the triune dynamic entails that we look to the divine life for a true picture of suffering, death, and helplessness. In the perichoretic relation of self-donating love these concepts are revealed to be glory, joy, power, and life. The triune life is not a mere theoretical construct or eschatological destination. It is the foundation of creation, the image of human

---

5. Cone, "Strange Fruit," 51.

6. Cone expresses the importance of recognizing Christ in the suffering and oppressed, not only in order to prevent or oppose injustice, but to transform the experience of suffering into beauty. "Through the experience of being lynched by white mobs, blacks transcended their time and place and found themselves existentially and symbolically at the foot of Jesus' cross, experiencing his fate. If blacks could identify with Jesus suffering on his cross, Jesus also could *not only* identify with hanging and burning black bodies on the lynching tree, but also redeem black suffering and make beautiful what white supremacy made ugly. . . . The gospel of Jesus is not a beautiful Hollywood story. It is an ugly story, the story of God snatching victory out of defeat, finding life in death, transforming burning black bodies into transcendent windows for seeing the love and beauty of God" (ibid., 54).

life, and the good in which we live and move and have our being. Christ has restored humanity's capacity for participation in the divine relation by enabling us to appropriate his self-abandonment to the Father through the sacraments and through our ethical life. The vision of the human ethical response that emerges is entirely a matter of "catching flame" with the very substance of the divine life that is the relation of self-abandoning love.

Bibliography

Aquinas, Thomas. *Summa Theologica*. Translated by Fathers of the English Dominican Province New York: Benziger, 1947.

Arjakovsky, Antoine. "The Sophiology of Father Sergius Bulgakov and Contemporary Western Theology." *St. Vladimir's Theological Quarterly* 49 (2005) 219–35.

Balthasar, Hans Urs von. *The Action*. Vol. 4 of *Theo-Drama: Theological Dramatic Theory*. Translated by Graham Harrison. San Francisco: Ignatius, 1994.

———. *Cosmic Liturgy: the Universe According to Maximus the Confessor*. Translated by Brian E. Daley. San Francisco: Ignatius, 2003.

———. *Creator Spirit*. Vol. 3 of *Explorations in Theology*. Translated by Brian McNeil. San Francisco: Ignatius, 1993.

———. *Dare We Hope, "That All Men Be Saved"?* Translated by David Kipp and Lothar Krauth. San Francisco: Ignatius, 1988.

———. *Dramatis Personae: Man in God*. Vol. 2 of *Theo-Drama: Theological Dramatic Theory*. Translated by Graham Harrison. San Francisco: Ignatius, 1990.

———. *Dramatis Personae: Persons in Christ*. Vol. 3 of *Theo-Drama: Theological Dramatic Theory*. Translated by Graham Harrison. San Francisco: Ignatius, 1992.

———. *Epilogue*. Translated by Edward T. Oakes. San Francisco: Ignatius, 1987.

———. *The Final Act*. Vol. 5 of *Theo-Drama: Theological Dramatic Theory*. Translated by Graham Harrison. San Francisco: Ignatius, 1998.

———. *Love Alone: the Way of Revelation*. New York: Herder & Herder, 1969.

———. *Mysterium Paschale*. Translated by Aidan Nichols. San Francisco: Ignatius, 2000.

———. "Nine Theses in Christian Ethics." In *The Distinctiveness of Christian Ethics*, edited by Charles E. Curran and Richard A. McCormick, 190–207. Readings in Moral Theology 2. New York: Paulist, 1980.

———. *The Realm of Metaphysics in Antiquity*. Vol. 4 of *The Glory of the Lord: A Theological Aesthetics*. Translated by Brian McNeil et al. Edited by John Riches. San Francisco: Ignatius, 1989.

———. "A Résumé of My Thought." *Communio* 15 (1988) 468–73.

———. *Seeing the Form*. Vol. 1 of *Glory of the Lord: A Theological Aesthetics*. Translated by Erasmo Leiva-Merikakis. San Francisco: Ignatius, 1982.

———. *Spirit and Institution*. Vol. 4 of *Explorations in Theology*. Translated by Edward T. Oakes. San Francisco: Ignatius, 1995.

———. *The Spirit of Truth*. Vol. 3 of *Theo-Logic*. Translated by Graham Harrison. San Francisco: Ignatius, 2005.

Bibliography

──────. *Studies in Theological Style: Clerical Styles.* Vol. 2 of *The Glory of the Lord: A Theological Aesthetics.* Translated by Andrew Louth, Francis McDonagh, and Brian McNeil. Edited by John Riches. San Francisco: Ignatius, 1984.

──────. *Studies in Theological Style: Lay Styles.* Vol. 3 of *The Glory of the Lord: A Theological Aesthetics.* Translated byAndrew Louth et al. San Francisco: Ignatius, 1986.

──────. *Theology: the New Covenant.* Vol. 7 of *The Glory of the Lord.* Translated by Brian McNeil. San Francisco: Ignatius, 1989.

──────. *Truth of God.* Vol. 2 of *Theo-Logic.* Translated by Adrian J Walker. San Francisco: Ignatius, 2004.

──────. *The Truth of the World.* Vol. 1 of *Theo-Logic.* Translated by Adrian J. Walker. San Francisco: Ignatius, 2000.

──────. *Truth Is Symphonic: Aspects of Christian Pluralism.* Translated by Graham Harrison. San Francisco: Ignatius, 1987.

──────. *The Word Made Flesh.* Vol. 1 of *Explorations in Theology.* Translated by A. V. Littledale and Alexander Dru. San Francisco: Ignatius, 1989.

Bauckham, Richard. *The Testimony of the Beloved Disciple: Narrative, History, and Theology in the Gospel of John.* Grand Rapids: Baker Academic, 2007.

Block, Ed, Jr. ed. *Glory, Grace and Culture: The Work of Hans Urs von Balthasar.* Mahwah, NJ: Paulist, 2005.

Brown Douglas, Kelly. *The Black Christ.* Maryknoll, NY: Orbis, 1994.

Bulgakov, Sergei N. *Apocatastasis and Transfiguration.* Translated by Boris Jakim. New Haven: Variable, 1995.

──────. *Apokalipsis Ioanna.* Paris: YMCA, 1948.

──────. *Avtobiograficheskiia zametki.* Edited by L. A. Zander. Paris: YMCA, 1946.

──────. *Bride of the Lamb.* Translated by Boris Jakim. Grand Rapids: Eerdmans, 2002.

──────. *The Burning Bush: On the Orthodox Veneration of the Mother of God.* Translated by Thomas Allan Smith. Grand Rapids: Eerdmans, 2009.

──────. *Churchly Joy: Orthodox Devotions for the Church Year.* Translated by Boris Jakim. Grand Rapids: Eerdmans, 2008.

──────. *The Comforter.* Translated by Boris Jakim. Grand Rapids, Eerdmans, 2004.

──────. *The Holy Grail and the Eucharist.* Translated and edited by Boris Jakim. Hudson, NY: Lindisfarne, 1997.

──────."Hypostasis and Hypostaticity." Translated by A. B. Gallaher and I. Kutkova. *St Vladimir's Theological Quarterly* 49 (2005) 5–46.

──────. *Lamb of God.* Translated by Boris Jakim. Grand Rapids: Eerdmans, 2008.

──────. *The Orthodox Church.* Translated by Lydia Kesich. Crestwood, NY: St. Vladimir's Seminary Press, 1988.

──────. *Sophia, the Wisdom of God.* Hudson: Lindisfarne, 1993.

Cavanaugh, William. *Torture and Eucharist.* Malden, MA: Blackwell, 1998.

Chauvet, Louis-Marie. *Symbol and Sacrament.* Collegeville, MN: Liturgical, 1995.

Cone, James. *The Cross and the Lynching Tree.* Maryknoll, NY: Orbis, 2011.

──────. "Strange Fruit: The Cross and the Lynching Tree." *Harvard Divinity Bulletin* 35 (2007) 47–55.

Dalzell, Thomas G. *The Dramatic Encounter of Divine and Human Freedom in the Theology of Hans Urs von Balthasar.* Berlin: Peter Lang, 1997.

Douglass, Kelly. *The Black Christ.* Maryknoll, NY: Orbis, 1994.

Emery, Gilles. *The Trinitarian Theology of Saint Thomas Aquinas.* Oxford: Oxford University Press, 2007.

Bibliography

————. "Trinity and Creation." In *The Theology of Thomas Aquinas*, edited by Rik Van Nieuwenhove and Joseph Wawrykow, 58–76. Notre Dame: University of Notre Dame Press, 2005.

Evtuhov, Catherine. *The Cross and the Sickle: Sergei Bulgakov and the Fate of Russian Religious Philosophy*. Ithaca: Cornell University Press, 1997.

Gardner, Lucy, ed. *Balthasar at the End of Modernity*. Edinburgh: T. & T. Clark, 1999.

Gavrilyuk, Paul L. "Kenotic Theology of Sergius Bulgakov." *Scottish Journal of Theology* 58 (2005) 251–69.

————. "Universal Salvation in the Eschatology of Sergius Bulgakov." *Journal of Theological Studies* 57 (2006) 110–32.

Griffiths, Paul J. "Is there a Doctrine of the Descent into Hell?" *Pro Ecclesia* 17 (2008) 257–68.

Hart, David Bentley. *The Beauty of the Infinite: The Aesthetics of Christian Truth*. Grand Rapids: Eerdmans, 2004.

Heidegger, Martin. *Zur Seinsfrage*. Frankfurt: Vittorio Klostermann, 1956,

Hunt, Anne. "Psychological Analogy and Paschal Mystery in Trinitarian Theology." *Theological Studies* 59 (1998) 197–218.

Laurance, John. "Configured into Christ's Body." *Oblation: Catechesis, Liturgy, and the New Evangelization* (blog). 9/13/2011, 10/14/2011. http://blogs.nd.edu/oblation/2011/09/09/configured-into-christs-body-part-i/.

Levering, Matthew. *Scripture and Metaphysics*. Malden, MA: Blackwell, 2004.

López, Antonio. "Eternal Happening: God as an Event of Love." In *Love Alone Is Credible: Hans Urs Von Balthasar as Interpreter of the Catholic Tradition*, edited by David Schindler, 1:75–104. Grand Rapids: Eerdmans, 2008.

Lösel, Steffen. "A Plain Christian Account of Salvation?" *Pro Ecclesia* 13 (2004) 141–71.

Keenan, James. "Impasse and Solidarity in Catholic Theological Ethics." *Catholic Theological Society of America Proceedings* 64 (2009) 47–60.

Kennedy, Stetson. *The Klan Unmasked*. Boca Raton: Florida Atlantic University Press, 1954.

Milbank, John. *The Suspended Middle: Henri de Lubac and the Debate Concerning the Supernatural*. Grand Rapids: Eerdmans, 2005.

Moltmann, Jürgen. *The Crucified God*. Translated by R. A. Wilson and John Bowden. San Francisco: Harper Collins, 1991.

————. *The Trinity and the Kingdom*. New York: HarperCollins, 1993.

Mongrain, Kevin. *The Systematic Thought of Hans Urs Von Balthasar: An Irenaean Retrieval*. New York: Crossroad, 2002.

Moss, David, and Edward T. Oakes, eds. *Cambridge Companion to Hans Urs von Balthasar*. Cambridge: Cambridge University Press, 2004.

Naumov, Kliment. *Bibliographie des oeuvres de Serge Boulgakov*. Paris: Institut d'études slaves, 1984.

Nicholl, Donald. *Triumphs of the Spirit in Russia*. London: Darton, Longman and Todd, 1997.

Nichols, Aiden. *Divine Fruitfulness: A Guide to Balthasar's Theology Beyond the Trilogy*. Washington, DC: Catholic University of America Press, 2007.

————. *No Bloodless Myth*. Washington, DC: T. & T. Clark, 2000.

————. *Wisdom from Above*. Herefordshire: Gracewing, 2005.

Oakes, Edward T. "The Internal Logic of Holy Saturday in the Theology of Hans Urs Von Balthasar." *International Journal of Systematic Theology* 9 (2007) 184–99.

Oakes, Edward T., and Alyssa Lyra Pitstick. "Balthasar, Hell, and Heresy: An Exchange." *First Things* 168 (2007) 25–32.

Bibliography

O'Regan, Cyril. *Gnostic Return in Modernity*. Albany: State University of New York Press, 2001.

———. *Theology and the Spaces of Apocalyptic*. Milwaukee: Marquette University Press, 2009.

Pain, James, and Nicolas Zernov, eds. *A Bulgakov Anthology*. London: SPCK, 1976.

Pitstick, Alyssa. "Development of Doctrine, or Denial? Balthasar's Holy Saturday and Newman's Essay." *International Journal of Systematic Theology* 11 (2009) 129–45.

———. *Light in Darkness: Hans Urs Von Balthasar and the Catholic Doctrine of the Descent into Hell*. Grand Rapids: Eerdmans, 2007.

Plekan, Michael. "Still by Jacob's Well: Sergius Bulgakov's Vision of the Church Revisited." *St Vladimir's Theological Quarterly* 49 (2005) 125–43.

Quash, Ben. *Theology and the Drama of History*. Cambridge: Cambridge University Press, 2008.

Riches, John, ed. *The Analogy of Beauty: The Theology of Hans Urs von Balthasar*. Edinburgh: T. & T. Clark, 1986.

Rziha, John. *Perfecting Human Actions*. Washington, DC: Catholic University of America Press, 2009.

Schindler, D. C. *Hans Urs von Balthasar and the Dramatic Structure of Truth*. New York: Fordham University Press, 2004.

Schindler, David L., ed. *Love Alone Is Credible: Hans Urs Von Balthasar as Interpreter of the Catholic Tradition*. Vol. 1. Grand Rapids: Eerdmans, 2008.

Sciglitano, Anthony C., Jr. "Contesting the World and the Divine: Balthasar's Trinitarian 'Response' to Gianni Vattimo's Secular Christianity." *Modern Theology* 23 (2007) 525–59.

Sergeev, Mikhail. "Divine Wisdom and the Trinity: A 20th Century Controversy in Orthodox Theology." *Greek Orthodox Theological Review* 45 (2000) 573–82.

Siewerth, Gustav. *Metaphysik der Kindheit*. Eisiedeln: Johannesverlag, 1957.

Slesinski, Robert. "Bulgakov on Sophia." *Journal of Eastern Christian Studies* 59 (2007) 131–45.

Swierkosz, Stanislaw P. *L'Église Visible selon Serge Bulgakov*. Rome: Pont. Institutum Studiorum Orientalium, 1980.

Valliere, Paul. *Modern Russian Theology: Bukharev, Soloviev, Bulgakov*. Edinburgh: T. & T. Clark, 2000.

Ward, Benedicta, trans. *The Sayings of the Desert Fathers*. Kalamazoo, MI: Cistercian, 1975.

Weinandy, Thomas. *Does God Change*. Still River, MA: St Bede's, 1985.

Wigley, Stephen. *Balthasar's Trilogy*, New York: T. & T. Clark, 2010.

Williams, Rowan. "Balthasar and the Trinity." In *The Cambridge Companion to Hans Urs von Balthasar*, edited by Edward T. Oakes and David Moss, 37–50. New York: Cambridge University Press, 2004.

———, ed. *Sergii Bulgakov: Toward a Russian Political Theology*. Edinburgh: T. & T. Clark, 1999

Yocum, John. "A Cry of Dereliction? Reconsidering a Recent Theological Commonplace." *International Journal of Systematic Theology* 7 (2005) 72–80.

Zander, L. A. *Bog i mir: Mirosozertsanie ottsa Sergiia Bulgakova*, 2 vols. Paris: YMCA, 1948.

Zernov, N. *The Russian Religious Renaissance of the Twentieth Century*. New York: Harper & Row, 1963.

Index of Names

Index of Names

Thomasius, Gottfried, 14, 41n80, 42n81, 85n5

Valliere, Paul, 37n65
Vladimir, Prince of Kiev, 12

Weinandy, Thomas, 41n80

Wells, Samuel, 111
Weston, Frank, 85n5
Wigley, Stephen, 125n10
Williams, Rowan, 35n62, 37n67

Yocum, John, 89

Made in the USA
Middletown, DE
26 February 2018